WITHDRAWN

LIVES OF AMERICANS

JOHN KENDRICK BANGS
by Francis Hyde Bangs

THE BIG SEA
by Langston Hughes

THE ASTORS
by Harvey O'Connor

OF BRITONS

SIR RICHARD BURTON'S WIFE
by Jean Burton

JOHNSON WITHOUT BOSWELL
edited by Hugh Kingsmill

SHELLEY
by Newman Ivey White

OF FRENCHMEN

PAUL CÉZANNE TOULOUSE-LAUTREC
by Gerstle Mack

OF A GERMAN

THE LIFE OF RICHARD WAGNER
by Ernest Newman

OF AN AUSTRIAN

MOZART
by W. J. Turner

Lanterns on the Levee

NEW YORK: ALFRED · A · KNOPF

1 9 4 1

Manufactured in the United States of America
Published simultaneously in Canada by the Ryerson Press

Published March 10, 1941
Second Printing, March 1941
Third Printing, April 1941
Fourth Printing, May 1941
Fifth Printing, June 1941
Sixth Printing, July 1941
Seventh Printing, September 1941
Eighth Printing, November 1941
Ninth Printing, December 1941
Mar. 1942

FOR

WALKER, ROY, & PHIN

FOR

ADAH, CHARLOTTE, & TOM

Foreword

The desire to reminisce arises not so much I think from the number of years you may happen to have accumulated as from the number of those who meant most to you in life who have gone on the long journey. They were the bulwarks, the bright spires, the strong places. When they have gone, you are a little tired, you rest on your oars, you say to yourself: "There are no witnesses to my fine little fury, my minute heroic efforts. It is better to remember, to be sure of the good that was, rather than of the evil that is, to watch the spread and pattern of the game that is past rather than engage feebly in the present play. It was a stout world thus far, peopled with all manner of gracious and kindly and noble personages—these seem rather a pygmy tribe." After a while, particularly if you have cut no very splendid figure in the show, indulgence in this sort of communing becomes a very vice.

FOREWORD

With some addicts it takes the form of dreaming; silently—the best way, I fear—and these are mostly women; with others, of conversation, and these are mostly old men—very tiresome unless you are one too; but the most abandoned of the whole lot insist they must write it all down, and of them am I. So while the world I know is crashing to bits, and what with the noise and the cryings-out no man could hear a trumpet blast, much less an idle evening reverie, I will indulge a heart beginning to be fretful by repeating to it the stories it knows and loves of my own country and my own people. A pilgrim's script—one man's field-notes of a land not far but quite unknown—valueless except as that man loved the country he passed through and its folk, and except as he willed to tell the truth. How other, alas, than telling it!

CONTENTS

CONTENTS

Lanterns on the Levee

CHAPTER I

The Delta

My country is the Mississippi Delta, the river country. It lies flat, like a badly drawn half oval, with Memphis at its northern and Vicksburg at its southern tip. Its western boundary is the Mississippi River, which coils and returns on itself in great loops and crescents, though from the map you would think it ran in a straight line north and south. Every few years it rises like a monster from its bed and pushes over its banks to vex and sweeten the land it has made. For our soil, very dark brown, creamy and sweet-smelling, without substrata of rock or shale, was built up slowly, century after century, by the sediment gathered by the river in its solemn task of cleansing the continent and deposited in annual layers of silt on what must once have been the vast depression between itself and the hills. This ancient depression, now filled in and level, is what we call the Delta. Some say it was the floor of the sea itself. Now it seems still to be a floor, being smooth from one end to the other, without rise or dip or hill, unless the mysterious scattered monuments of the mound-builders may be called hills. The land does not drain into the river as most riparian lands do, but tilts back from it towards the hills of the south and east. Across this wide flat alluvial stretch—north and south it measures one hundred and ninety-six miles, east and west at the widest point fifty miles—run slowly and circuitously other rivers and creeks, also high-banked, with names pleasant to remember—Rattlesnake Bayou, Quiver River, the Bogue Phalia, the Tallahatchie, the Sunflower—pouring their tawny waters finally into the Yazoo, which in turn loses itself just above Vicksburg in the river. With us when you speak of "the river," though there are many, you mean always the same one, the great river, the shifting unappeasable god of the country, feared and loved, the Mississippi.

In the old days this was a land of unbroken forests. All trees grew there except the pine and its kindred, and, strangely enough, the magnolia. The water-oak, the pecan, the cypress, and the sweet-gum were perhaps the most beautiful and home-loving, but there were ash and elm, walnut and maple, and many others besides. They grew to enormous heights, with vast trunks and limbs, and between them spread a chaos of vines and cane and brush, so that the deer and bear took it for their own and only by the Indians was it penetrable, and by them only on wraiths of trails. Wild flowers were few, the soil being too rich and warm and deep, and those, like the yellow-top of early spring, apt to be rank and weed-like. A still country it must have been then, ankle-deep in water, mostly in shadow, with mere flickers of sunshine, and they motey and yellow and thick like syrup. The wild swans loved it; tides of green parakeets from the south and of gray pigeons from the north melted into its tree-tops and gave them sound; ducks—mallard, canvas-back, teal, and wood-duck—and Canadian geese, their wedges high in the soft air of autumn like winter's first arrows, have still not deserted it.

Such was my country hardly more than a hundred years ago. It was about then that slavery became unprofitable in the older Southern states and slave-holders began to look for cheap fertile lands farther west that could feed the many black mouths dependent on them. So younger sons from Virginia, South Carolina, and Kentucky with their gear, live-stock, and chattels, human and otherwise, started a leisurely migration into the Delta. Forests were cleared, roads constructed (such dusty or muddy roads!), soil shaped into fields, homes built. They settled first on the banks and bends of the river, later on the banks and bends of the smaller streams, for those were high ground over which the then yearly inundations of the river, as yet uncurbed by levees, never quite reached. There is still a great curve of the shoreline called Kentucky Bend, and another, mostly sandbar now, called Carolina.

The roads they built were local affairs, connecting plantation with plantation or with hamlets which grew slowly and without booms into our present small towns. In wet weather, of which we have much, they were bottomless, and old-timers believed they could never be anything else.

The real highway was the river. All life, social and economic, centered there. The river steamers furnished transportation, relaxation, and information to the whole river people. In our town the *Pargo* landed regularly on Sunday, usually between eleven o'clock and noon. Everybody would be at church, but when she blew, the male members of the congregation to a man would rise and, in spite of indignant glares from their wives and giggles from the choir, make their exits, with a severe air of business just remembered. With the *Pargo* came the week's mail and gossip of the river-front from St. Louis to New Orleans and rumors from the very distant outside world. If the occasion was propitious a little round of poker might be started and a few toddies drunk. They were a fine fleet, those old sidewheelers which plied between St. Louis and New Orleans and stopped on signal at the various plantations and river settlements—the *White*, the *Pargo*, the *Natchez*, the *Robert E. Lee*. The last and least of them was the *Belle of the Bends*, which as a small boy I could never see steaming majestically through the sunset to the landing without a fine choky feeling. They had pleasant outside cabins opening on an enormous white dining-saloon, decorated in the most abandoned gingerbread style, which after supper became a ballroom. Almost as comfortable as our ocean liners of today, they were far easier and more sociable; anybody who was anybody knew everybody else, and each trip was rather like a grand house-party, with dancing and gambling and an abundance of Kentucky whisky and French champagne. The ladies (who never partook of these beverages—maybe a sip of champagne) were always going to New Orleans for Mardi Gras or to shop or to hear the opera (well established there before it was begun in New York) or to visit cousins and aunts in the Louisiana and Natchez territory; and as those were days of enormous families, cousins and aunts were plentiful. There never was a Southern family that was a Southern Family some member of which, incredibly beautiful and sparkling, had not opened the ball with Lafayette. For years apparently his sole occupation was opening balls in New Orleans, Charleston, Natchez, and St. Louis. After looking at a hundred or more badly painted portraits of these belles I am a firm believer in this tradition.

If the ladies loved going to New Orleans, the men-folks were never at a loss for reasons to take the same trip. Memphis was hardly more than a country town. The commission merchants (forerunners of the modern bank, co-operative association, Federal Land Bank, insurance company with funds to invest) had their offices in New Orleans and it was they who supplied the planters with the cash for their extensive and costly operations. Here was an ever ready reason to board the boat going south, and one that made unnecessary any reference to the lottery, the races, the masked balls, the fantastic poker games, the hundred and one amiable vices of that most European and sloe-eyed of American cities.

Our Delta culture stemmed from an older one and returned to it for sustenance and renewal, but it lacked much that made the older culture charming and stable. We had few of those roomy old residences, full of fine woodwork and furniture and drapery, which excellent French or English architects built in the Natchez and Charleston neighborhoods and in the Louisiana sugarcane territory. The few we had have caved into the river or burned. But a library was as portable as a slave, and excellent ones abounded—leather-bound sets of the *Spectator*, the *Edinburgh Review*, the works of Mr. Goldsmith and Mr. Pope, *Tom Jones* and *A Sentimental Journey*, translations of Plutarch and Homer, amazing poems about plants and flowers by the grandfather of Darwin, *The Faerie Queene* and Bobbie Burns. (I never came across a copy of Shelley or Keats or Wordsworth in these old collections.) On the bottom shelf would be a fat Bible, the front pages inscribed with long lists of deaths and births in a beautiful flourishing hand. On the top shelf, presumably beyond the reach of the young and impressionable, would be the novels of George Sand and, later, of Ouida. *Paul and Virginia* too was a favorite, but who can now recall that title, though no book ever had more warm and innocuous tears shed over it?

I recall one survivor of that generation, or rather of the one immediately following it. Aunt Fannie, my great-aunt by marriage, was in looks all that the Surry of Eagle's Nest and Marse Chan school of writers would have you believe elderly Southern gentlewomen invariably were. She had exquisite slender white hands, usually folded in idleness on her lap; upon her neat curly white hair, parted in the middle, reposed a tiny white thing of frills and lace which may have been a cap but which looked more like a doily; her face was small and white, with truly a faded-flower look; her dress was black and fitted well and with a sort of chic her still slender figure; she smelled faintly of orris-root, a bit of which she usually chewed with no observable cud-motion. (I don't know why old ladies abandoned orris-root—it's the right smell for them. But, after all, there are no old ladies now.) It was not these things, however, but certain little personal eccentricities of Aunt Fannie's that endeared her to me as a child. She would suddenly drop into a little nap, sitting bolt upright in her chair and with the animated company around her pretending not to notice it. Or, equally inexplicably and with equal disregard of surroundings, she would sob gently and delicately and wipe quite real tears from her eyes with her diminutive orris-scented handkerchief. I attributed this phenomenon to some old and overwhelming sorrow which she carried in her heart and was too proud and ladylike to reveal. Only years and years later I learned that these engaging little habits of hers arose from another little habit: Aunt Fannie took her grain of morphine every day. Being the only wicked thing she ever did, it must have been doubly consoling.

Nevertheless it was this same Aunt Fannie who, a newly arrived bride from Nashville, by raising a moral issue threw the countryside into violent commotion, almost caused a duel, and established a social distinction in our county which has survived more or less to this good day. She gave a house-warming, a large affair, with dancing and champagne and a nougat from New Orleans. In selecting her guests she flatly refused to invite a prominent planter because he openly and notoriously lived with a Negro woman. For some reason the logical duel did not take place; the planter found it easier to move from the community than to live down the stigma or to acquire a paler bolster-companion. Aunt Fannie's husband died, she saw the war and poverty and reconstruction, she raised a daughter and saw her die, she lived on into a new order unsure of itself and without graciousness—if a bit of morphine would blur the present and brighten the past for her, who could have had the heart to deprive her of it?

But, after all, I suppose my paternal grandmother, Mur, was more typical than Aunt Fannie, more illustrative of the class to which she belonged. Left on the plantation during the war, alone with her three babies, while my grandfather, an opponent of secession and a lukewarm slave-owner, was away fighting to destroy the Union and preserve the institution of slavery, she not only raised her little brood single-handed and under the handicap of increasing poverty, but managed the thousand-acre home place. When the effect of the Emancipation Proclamation was realized by the slaves, they became restless, unruly, even dangerous. Her position was one of great difficulty, if not of peril. One evening in the spring of 1864 she learned that the remaining slaves (for many had run away) had met and decided not to plant or work the crop. She immediately called them together and ordered them to meet her in the field the next morning at sun-up. They were there and so was she, sitting in a rocking-chair at the end of the turn-row. (Rocking-chairs have disappeared, a great and symbolic loss.) They met in this manner every morning till July, when the crop was laid by. When the war ended and my grandfather returned penniless, his family managed to live for a year or more on the proceeds from the sale of that cotton crop. At that time my grandmother was twenty-nine, very pretty, with a keen sense of the absurd, and how she could play Strauss waltzes!

Indeed, indeed, the lily-of-the-field life of the Southern gentlewoman existed only in the imagination of Northern critics and Southern sentimentalists, one about as untrustworthy as the other. They had too many duties even in slavery days to be idle. It is true, charm was considered the first and most necessary course in female education, as it is among French women today, and this seems to me sound, because it was a gregarious, sociable, and high-spirited world into which they were born, much addicted to dances and parties of all sorts and visitings and love affairs, and whether that world was delightful or vulgar depended on whether or not the women were ladies. To manage a single household competently is a sizable job. These women on country estates so isolated as to be of necessity self-sustaining and self-governing had the direction of the feeding, clothing, education, health, and morals, not only of their own families, but of the dark feudal community they owned and were responsible for. When there were no bakeries or corner grocery stores or Kress's and Woolworth's, they had to know how to make cloth, bake bread, smoke meat, design quilts, pickle and preserve, nurse and concoct medicines, and supervise the cooking of all and sundry. They held Sunday school for their own and the darkies' children and generally taught white and black alike reading, writing, arithmetic, and the Bible. From them we inherit those golden recipes which give the lie to foreign critics when they say Americans know nothing of gustatory joys, eat to live, and are unaware that good cooking is one of the few things that make life bearable. What of Virginia hams, Maryland terrapin, Charleston roe and hominy, New Orleans gumbo-filé, griades, fourchettes, sea-food—oysters, crabs, shrimp, pompano, red snapper, crawfish, sheepshead—and the hundred exquisite ways of preparing them known to the Creoles, not to the Parisian? What of coffee, dish-water in the North, chicory abroad, but strong and hot and clear and delectable on any Southern table? And the hundred varieties of hot breads? Oh, the poor little boys who never put a lump of butter into steaming batter-bread (spoon-bread is the same thing) or lolled their tongues over pain-perdu! There should be a monument to Southern womanhood, creator of the only American cuisine that makes the world a better place to live in.

Instead, you will find in any Southern town a statue in memory of the Confederate dead, erected by the Daughters of something or other, and made, the townsfolk will respectfully tell you, in Italy. It is always the same: a sort of shaft or truncated obelisk, after the manner of the Washington Monument, on top of which stands a little man with a big hat holding a gun. If you are a Southerner you will not feel inclined to laugh at these efforts, so lacking in either beauty or character, to preserve the memory of their gallant and ill-advised forebears. I think the dash, endurance, and devotion of the Confederate soldier have not been greatly exaggerated in song and story: they do not deserve these chromos in stone. Sentiment driveling into sentimentality, poverty, and, I fear, lack of taste are responsible for them, but they are the only monuments which are dreadful from the point of view of æsthetics, craftsmanship, and conception that escape being ridiculous. They are too pathetic for that. Perhaps a thousand years from now the spade of some archæologist will find only these as relics of and clues to the vanished civilization we call ours. How tragically and comically erroneous his deductions will be!

My memorial to Southern cookery would be more informative. Or one to Southern hospitality, concerning which so many kindly things have been said. And that tradition too must have begun in those earlier times. In such a purely agrarian and thinly populated country there were no hotels or lodging-houses of any kind. The traveler could buy neither bed nor food, but had to hope some resident would give them to him as an act not so much of hospitality as of sheer humanity. A stranger in the Navajo country of Arizona or in Arabia experiences the same difficulty today and has it solved for him in the same way—the natives receive him as their guest. Frequently this must have been trying to the ladies of the household. I have always heard, though I will not vouch for the story, that a stranger dropped in for the night on one of my Louisiana kinsmen and remained a year. The stranger was Audubon, the ornithologist. My French grandmother, whom I called Mère, was not quite so cordial. Neither her plantation home nor her English vocabulary was large. When my grandfather, whom I called Père, unexpectedly appeared one nightfall with a number of friends who had been bear-hunting with him, she first said to him: "Mais, Ernest"—and he quailed, for it was one of her favorite phrases and it could mean all manner of things, but it always *meant*—then she observed to the guests: "Welcome, messieurs, I can eat you but I cannot sleep you." She was a remarkable woman, and very firm.

Well, she has joined the lovely ladies who opened the ball with Lafayette, and the forest country, only half conquered in her day, has become an open expanse of cotton plantations, though woods, unkempt remnants, still cling to their edges and rim the creeks and bayous. Railroads have come, and almost gone, thanks to the shoving and obese trucks and busses. The roads are now of concrete or gravel and there are thousands of miles of ugly wires crossing the landscape bearing messages or light. The river town has a White Way, picture shows, many radios, a Chamber of Commerce, and numerous service clubs. We have gone forward, our progress is ever so evident.

And the river? It is changed and eternally the same. The early settlers soon began to rebuff its yearly caress, that impregnated and vitalized the soil, by building small dikes around their own individual plantations. This was a poor makeshift and in time, not without ruction and bitter debate, was abandoned in favor of levee districts which undertook to levee the river itself at the cost of the benefited landowners within the districts. After reconstruction no more vital problem perplexed Delta statesmen than how to convince the Federal government of the propriety of contributing to the cost of building levees. At first they failed, but later niggardly aid was doled out —a bit some years, others none. Only within the last fifteen years has the government accepted the view urged for half a century by our people that the river's waters are the nation's waters and fighting them is the nation's fight. The United States Engineers under the War Department are now in full charge of levee and revetment work from one end of the river to the other.

But this work has not changed the savage nature and austere beauty of the river itself. Man draws near to it, fights it, uses it, curses it, loves it, but it remains remote, unaffected. Between the fairy willows of the banks or the green slopes of the levees it moves unhurried and unpausing; building islands one year to eat them the next; gnawing the bank on one shore till the levee caves in and another must be built farther back, then veering wantonly and attacking with equal savagery the opposite bank; in spring, high and loud against the tops of the quaking levees; in summer, deep and silent in its own tawny bed; bearing eternally the waste and sewage of the continent to the cleansing wide-glittering Gulf. A gaunt and terrible stream, but more beautiful and dear to its children than Thames or Tiber, than mountain brook or limpid estuary. The gods on their thrones are shaken and changed, but it abides, aloof and unappeasable, with no heart except for its own task, under the unbroken and immense arch of the lighted sky where the sun, too, goes a lonely journey.

As a thing used by men it has changed: the change is not in itself, but in them. No longer the great white boats and their gallant companies ply to and fro on its waters. A certain glamour is gone forever. But the freighters and barge lines of today keep one reminder of the vanished elder packets—their deep-throated, long-drawn-out, giant voices. And still there is no sound in the world so filled with mystery and longing and unease as the sound at night of a river-boat blowing for the landing—one long, two shorts, one long, two shorts. Over the somber levels of the water pours that great voice, so long prolonged it is joined by echoes from the willowed shore, a chorus of ghosts, and, roused from sleep, wide-eyed and still, you are oppressed by vanished glories, the last trump, the calling of the ends of the earth, the current, ceaselessly moving out into the dark, of the eternal dying. Trains rushing at night under the widening pallor of their own smoke, bearing in wild haste their single freightage of wild light, over a receding curve of thunder, have their own glory. But they are gone too quickly, like a meteor, to become part of your deep own self. The sound of the river-boats hangs inside your heart like a star.

CHAPTER II

Delta Folks

I may seem to have implied that all Delta citizens were aristocrats travelling luxuriously up and down the river or sitting on the front gallery, a mint julep in one hand and a palm-leaf fan in the other, protected from mosquitoes by the smudge burning in the front yard. If so, I have misinterpreted my country. The aristocrats were always numerically in the minority; with the years they have not increased. It may be helpful to mention the other and very different children of God who took up their abode beside the waters of the great river.

The Indians left not a trace except the names of rivers, plantations, and towns, the meaning of which we have forgotten along with the pronunciation.

Another element leaving almost as little impress, though still extant, is the "river-rat." He is white, Anglo-Saxon, with twists of speech and grammatical forms current in Queen Anne's day or earlier, and a harsh "r" strange to all Southerners except mountaineers. Where he comes from no one knows or cares. Some find in him the descendant of those pirates who used to infest the river as far up as

Memphis. It seems more likely his forefathers were out-of-door, ne'er-do-well nomads of the pioneer days. His shanty boats, like Huck Finn's father's, may be seen moored in the willows or against the sandbars as far up and down the river as I have ever traveled. He squats on bars and bits of mainland subject to overflow, raises a garden and a patch of corn, steals timber, rafts it, and sells it to the mills, and relies the year round on fishing for a living. He seems to regard the White River as the Navajos regard the Canyon de Chelly—as a sort of sanctuary and homeland, and it supplies the clam shells from which he makes buttons. Illiterate, suspicious, intensely clannish, blond, and usually ugly, river-rats make ideal bootleggers. The brand of corn or white mule they make has received nation-wide acclaim. They lead a life apart, uncouth, unclean, lawless, vaguely alluring. Their contact with the land world around them consists largely in being haled into court, generally for murder. No Negro is ever a river-rat.

Every American community has its leaven of Jews. Ours arrived shortly after the Civil War with packs on their backs, peddlers from Russia, Poland, Germany, a few from Alsace. They sold trinkets to the Negroes and saved. Today they are plantation-owners, bankers, lawyers, doctors, merchants; their children attend the great American universities, win prizes, become connoisseurs in the arts and radicals in politics. I was talking to one, an old-timer, not too successful, in front of his small store a short time ago. He suddenly asked in his thick Russian accent: "Do you know Pushkin? Ah, beautiful, better than Shelley or Byron!" Why shouldn't such a people inherit the earth, not, surely, because of their meekness, but because of a steadier fire, a tension and tenacity that make all other whites seem stodgy and unintellectual.

Other foreigners arrived with their gifts, more or less battered, of other cultures. When the levees were being built with hand-labor and wheelbarrows, the Irish came, many remaining to run excellent saloons or to fill minor political offices. They quickly merged into the life of the community, though their warm-heartedness, love of brawling and excitement, and high-spirited humor were fortunately not lost in the process. From southern Italy and Sicily came fruit-venders who made unobtrusive good citizens, wise in turning a penny and keeping it, taking small part in community life and rarely appearing in the courts. I have noticed that these Latins brought from the Mediterranean thrift and industry, unhurried energy, a sober and simple culture, earthy and warm; but their American offspring seem to regard it as their patriotic duty to unlearn these virtues. Second-generation Italians rival the Anglo-Saxon tough in vulgarity and loudness, their sole saving grace being charm and impulsiveness. Even Asia has contributed to and drawn from the Delta. Small Chinese store-keepers are almost as ubiquitous as in the South Seas. Barred from social intercourse with the whites, they smuggle through wives from China or, more frequently, breed lawfully or otherwise with the Negro. They are not numerous enough to present a problem—except to the small white store-keeper—but in so far as I can judge, they serve no useful purpose in community life: what wisdom they may inherit from Lao-tse and Confucius they fail to impart. Not infrequently they are indicted for crimes of violence occurring among themselves. Representatives of the implicated tongs rush down from Chicago, the Chinese consul rushes up from New Orleans, there are parleys, threats, general excitement. The jury convicts or not. But no one ever supposes the true facts have been developed in court, though all suspect complete knowledge of them reposes in numerous celestial bosoms.

All of these—Jews, Italians, Irish, Chinese, Syrians—contribute to the Delta way of life points of view, rudiments of cultures, traits, more or less assimilable though not yet assimilated. Almost any American community, I suppose, has similar bright strands being woven into its texture. But the basic fiber, the cloth of the Delta population—as of the whole South—is built of three dissimilar threads and only three. First were the old slave-holders, the landed gentry, the governing class; though they have gone, they were not sterile; they have their descendants, whose evaluation of life approximates theirs. Second were the poor whites, who owned no slaves, whose manual labor lost its dignity from being in competition with slave labor, who worked their small unproductive holdings ignored by the gentry, despised by the slaves. Third were the Negroes.

The poor whites of the South: a nice study in heredity and environment. Who can trace their origin, estimate their qualities, do them justice? Not I. Some say their forefathers served terms in English prisons for debt and were released on condition that they migrate from the mother country to the colonies. The story continues that they congregated in Georgia. The story may or may not be true; it is unpopular, needless to say. This much, however, it is safe to assert: they were not blest with worldly goods or mental attainments. The richer coast and tidewater country was not for them; their efforts at tilling the soil had to be among the unfertile hills. Farther and farther west they were pushed by an unequal competition until they lodged in the mountains of North Carolina, Tennessee, and Kentucky and in the clay hills of Alabama and Mississippi. Pure English stock. If it was ever good, the virus of poverty, malnutrition, and interbreeding has done its degenerative work: the present breed is probably the most unprepossessing on the broad face of the ill-populated earth. I know they are responsible for the only American ballads, for camp meetings, for a whole new and excellent school of Southern literature. I can forgive them as the Lord God forgives, but admire them, trust them, love them—never. Intellectually and spiritually they are inferior to the Negro, whom they hate. Suspecting secretly they are inferior to him, they must do something to him to prove to themselves their superiority. At their door must be laid the disgraceful riots and lynchings gloated over and exaggerated by Negrophiles the world over.

The Delta was not settled by these people; its pioneers were slave-owners and slaves. One exception may be noted. Forming a small intermediate white class were the managers and slave-drivers and bosses, men of some ability and force, mostly illiterate. These in time became plantation-owners, often buying up and operating successfully the places lost by their former employers. Here is an ironic and American and encouraging phenomenon. Their children are being what is known as well educated. They will be the aristocrats of tomorrow; they make excellent professional Southerners now.

But the poor whites—"hill-billies," "red-necks," "peckerwoods," they are often derisively called—did not remain outside the Delta. Twenty-five or thirty years ago they began to seep in from the hills of Alabama and Mississippi, probably the more energetic and ambitious of them. The Delta soil seemed good to them; they came as tenants and remained as small farmers. In certain counties they so throve and increased that they now outnumber the Negroes, control the local government, and fix the culture—God save the mark!—of those counties. That fate is probably in store for my own county. I am glad I shall not be present to witness its fulfillment. The river folk do not like white tenants or "red-neck" neighbors. When these shall have supplanted the Negro, ours will be a sadder country, and not a wiser one.

Just now we are happy that the brother in black is still the tiller of our soil, the hewer of our wood, our servants, troubadours, and criminals. His manners offset his inefficiency, his vices have the charm of amiable weaknesses, he is a pain and a grief to live with, a solace and a delight. There are seven or eight of him to every one of us and he is the better breeder. Ours is surely the black belt. It is all very well for Cheyenne or Schenectady or Stockholm or Moscow, where a black-faced visitor is a day's wonder, to exclaim: "There is no race problem! Southerners are barbarians and brutes." There never is a race problem until the two races living in close contact approach numerical equality. The belle of Kamchatka could marry the Crown Prince of Nigeria and the union could be blest past telling, but a hundred years afterwards the Kamchatkans would be unaffected and undarkened by the incident. In our country if such an incident became a custom, the end of the century would behold a Delta population neither white nor black, but hybrid. Many philanthropists, the usual run of sentimentalists, and some scientists are confident this would be well and is in fact inevitable. Assimilation they are sure is the solution, and a desirable one, so long as they do not have to co-operate personally in the experiment. The trouble is that the white Southerner is stubbornly averse to playing the necessary role of party of the second part in the experiment. Whatever his practice may be, he agrees in theory with Anglo-Saxons living among darker races the world over that the hybrid is not a desirable product, that amalgamation is not the answer so far as he can prevent it.

I often conclude that the only Southerners worth talking about are the darkies. But what can a white man, north or south, say of them that will even approximate the truth? The one thing we are certain of is that they are one people, of one blood, with identical background, tradition, environment, alike as peas in a pod—and this is untrue. When the New England and English slave-dealers captured their human booty, they combed a vast section of Africa, populated by tribes unalike in physique, physiognomy, and customs; some were of small stature, stupid; others were superb physical specimens with a certain tribal history and pride; some were blue-black, others brown or reddish brown; some had flat noses and great loose lips, others had features almost as regular and fine as Arabs; some were princes and rulers, others slaves. Now and then the slave-dealers brought along for good measure the Arab tribesmen who had captured and collected the natives for them. All these strains, these differences, may be detected in the Negro population of the South today. These facts are unknown to the Negro and to the generality of whites, both of whom attribute any deviation from the black, spread-nosed, thick-lipped type familiar in caricature to some intermixture of white blood. No race probably ever had less knowledge of its own past, traditions, and antecedents. What African inheritance they still retain lies in the deep wells of their being, subconscious. They know not whence they came nor what manner of life they led there. Their folklore, rich and fascinating, is American, not African. Only in their practices in voodoo, their charms, potions, and incantations, can we catch glimpses of customs practiced by them in their mysterious homeland. This failure on their part to hold and pass on their own history is due, I think, not so much to their failure to master any form of written communication as to their obliterating genius for living in the present. The American Negro is interested neither in the past nor in the future, this side of heaven. He neither remembers nor plans. The white man does little else: to him the present is the one great unreality.

In slavery days the darkies lived in "quarters," a group of cabins not far from the "big house" of the owner. Today each family on a large plantation lives in a two- or three-room house on the fifteen- or twenty-acre tract it is renting and working. Many of them own their own farms, generally forty acres, rarely more than one hundred and sixty. And many, of course, have abandoned farming and moved to town, where they hire out as servants or do manual labor for the railroads, the lumber companies, the government forces on the levee, or grace in idleness the poolrooms and gambling-halls of the colored end of town. None of them feels that work *per se* is good; it is only a means to idleness ("leisure" is the word in white circles). The theory of the white man, no matter what his practice, is the reverse: he feels that work is good, and idleness, being agreeable, must be evil. I leave it to the wise to say which is the more fruitful philosophy, but I know which best develops the capacity to wear idleness like a perfume and an allurement. A white poolroom or soda-water stand is a depressing place where leisure does not seem excellent or ribaldry amusing. But Negro convocations, legal or otherwise, are always enjoyable affairs right down to the first pistol-shot.

So the Delta problem is how all these folks—aristocrats gone to seed, poor whites on the make, Negroes convinced mere living is good, aliens of all sorts that blend or curdle —can dwell together in peace if not in brotherhood and live where, first and last, the soil is the only means of livelihood. Most of our American towns, all of our cities, have their unsolved problem of assimilation. But the South's is infinitely more difficult of solution. The attempt to work out any sort of one, much less a just one, as a daily living problem, diverts the energies and abilities of our best citizenship from more productive fields. A certain patience might well be extended to the South, if not in justice, in courtesy. . . .

But in this respect we of the Delta have been fortunate in our misfortunes. Time out of mind we have been gifted with common disasters, all-inclusive tragedies that have united us or at least made us lean together. The old yellow-fever epidemics were especially helpful. And there's no better cement for a people than moderate poverty. No class or individual with us has ever known riches. Some years the crop and price are good and we take a trip or sport an automobile or buy another plantation; most years the crop fails or the bottom drops out of the market and we put on a new mortgage or increase the old one. Even then no one goes hungry or cold or feels very sorry for himself. If we become too prosperous and entertain the impression we are independent and frightfully efficient (farmers feel that way any good year), the levee breaks and the wise river terrifies his silly children back into humility and that cozy one-family feeling of the inmates of the Ark. Behind us a culture lies dying, before us the forces of the unknown industrial world gather for catastrophe. We have fields to plow and the earth smells good; maybe in time someone will pay us more for our cotton than we spend making it. In the meantime the darkies make up new songs about the boll-weevil and the river, and the sun pours over us his great tide of warmth which is also light.

CHAPTER III

Mur and Nain

In this kind of country and among this sort of people I was born, in 1885. That the month should have been May seems a debatable blessing, for in that season of bloom and untarnished green you are always brimming with delight or despair, groundless in either case, and, worse still, it is then that spirit and body are one and indistinguishable and your thoughts are feelings and the word is made flesh every hour. Besides, it happened to be the morning of Ascension Day, a fact I used to consider significant or symbolic, but of what I could never decide. Yet a pagan month and a Christian day for a start still seem to me a stimulating handicap, with possibilities. Unfortunately my coming impressed no one sufficiently for him to remember the hour, much less the minute, so my friends who ponder horoscopes have never been able to chart me properly between Taurus and Gemini, Venus and Mercury; they only insist the stars were badly tangled at my arrival and no great good can be expected of me, a prophecy I sometimes find comforting in view of the outcome. Anyway, I was born and in May and on Ascension Day, and I have picked up the information that the incident overjoyed no one, because Father and Mother were young and good-looking, poor and well-born, in love with each other and with life, and they would have considered the blessed event more blessed had it been postponed a year or two. No matter how unfavorably I impressed them at the time, they impressed me not at all, and for a much longer period afterwards. I have no single memory of them dating from the first four years of my life. The only persons whose activities were important enough to dent the fairly undentable tablets of my memory were Nain, my colored nurse, and Mur, my grandmother.

Southerners like to make clear, especially to Northerners, that every respectable white baby had a black mammy, who, one is to infer, was fat and elderly and bandannaed. I was a respectable and a white baby, but Nain was sixteen, divinely café-au-lait, and she would have gone into cascades of giggles at the suggestion of a bandanna on her head. I loved her devotedly and never had any other nurse. Everything about her was sweet-smelling, of the right temperature, and dozy. Psychiatrists would agree, I imagine, that I loved her because in her I found the comfort of the womb, from which I had so recently and unexpectedly been ejected and for which I was still homesick. The womb may be comfortable, but I have my doubts, and, without a little first-hand information, I shall continue to believe I loved her for her merry goodness, her child's heart that understood mine, and her laughter that was like a celesta playing triplets. Chiefly I remember her bosom: it was soft and warm, an ideal place to cuddle one's head against. My earliest clear recollection is of a song she would sing me so cuddled—rather, not of the song itself, but of its effect on me. The words and tune have gone, but not what they did to me.

A poor egoistic sort of memory I know, that records nothing of the outer world, but only how certain bits of it pleased or distressed me, yet mine, and no better now than it was then, and no different. Nain would hold me in her arms and sing this song, rocking herself a little. I would try not to cry, but it made me feel so lost and lonely that tears would seep between my lids and at last I would sob until I shook against her breast. "Whut's de madder, Peeps?" she would say. "Whut you cryin' fur?" But I was learning not so much how lonely I could be as how lonely everybody could be, and I could not explain. If she innocently endowed me with a sense of the tears of things, she gave me something hard to live with, but impossible to live, as I would live, without. If her music opened vistas and induced contemplations, unbearably poignant and full of pity, I should perhaps thank her for the Good Friday Spell and the Dance of the Blessed Spirits, for certain Bach chorales and Negro spirituals that, awakening kindred compassions in the core of my being, have guided me more sure-footedly and authoritatively through life than all ten of the Commandments. *Lachrymæ rerum* in a baby's vacant heart? A silly question, but one of the many I do not know the answer to.

Nain possibly comes back to me more as an emanation or aura than as a person. But, no mistake, Mur was a person. She was my first chum. I slept in her room, calcimined a lugubrious blue, whether in a bed of my own or hers I can't recall, and was often awake when she prepared herself for the night. It was a splendid ritual. First she removed her switch, a rather scrawny, gray affair, like a diminutive horse's tail, which, when on duty, enlarged the knot of hair at the nape of her neck. Then she combed it briskly until it fluffed out into a fascinating silver cone before she rested it for the night on the bureau.

Next, and this was awe-inspiring, she removed from her mouth one single tooth attached to an amazing red thing like a live and oddly shaped eave and dropped it into a glass of water. Last she poured something from a brown bottle into another glass of water and drank it. I wondered and wondered why that was necessary, but to my questions she always replied it was Crab Orchard Water. The answer cleared up nothing then or now. Through these mystic rites she was fully clad, only she started out in her black dress and ended up in her white nightgown. I never understood how this transformation was accomplished, though it proceeded under my very eyes, without her being at some stage of it undressed; this was more than modesty, it was legerdemain. When these vivid preliminaries were over, it was time for prayers.

Mur, being an Armstrong by birth, was of Scotch descent and Presbyterian to the marrow. She never outlived the drastic piety of that angular creed, but after she married my grandfather, whom others called the Gray Eagle of the Delta but I called Fafar, she became an Episcopalian, out of deference to his Church of England traditions and leanings. She was as broad-minded as a Presbyterian could be and by temperament neither austere nor intolerant, but I could tell she feared my pretty Papist mother would neglect my spiritual needs. Therefore she taught me the Lord's Prayer to replace Now-I-Lay-Me and every so often read me her two favorite passages from the Bible. I think the Lord's Prayer took all right, but from the start I was immune to the Bible. I did not like those passages of hers and, though one is not supposed to have moral convictions at so tender an age, I did not consider them good morally. One concerned Dives and Lazarus, the other the Prodigal Son. Lazarus had too many sores to be attractive. Abraham must have been horrid with that peculiar roomy bosom of his like a hair-lined cupboard, and it was downright ugly of him not to let Lazarus give a little drop of water to poor old Dives. I could feel Dives' torment and the prickle of Abraham's beard and I was sure Lazarus would have received something nourishing if he'd asked for it instead of for such silly canary-fare as crumbs. I developed a strong distaste for paradise. Nor was the Prodigal Son any better. He could have found a more sanitary place to stay in than the hog-wallow, he just didn't try, and when he came on home he deserved a good whipping instead of a party. The nice boy, who had never run away and got hog-smelly, had a right to be upset.

These thoughts I kept to myself, sitting quietly by Mur, who read the lovely words softly and drew comfort from them and hoped they might teach me goodness. How little our wisest teachers guess what effects their best-intentioned efforts are producing in the minds and imaginations of the bland-eyed neophytes at their knees! Many people these days have Abraham's antipathy for purple raiment and his obsession that a case history of sores is the only admission card to paradise. I cling to my childish preference for hell. With Achilles and Dives and Frederick II for company one could gaze afar off and see Abraham and Mahomet and the Blessed Damozel and be right well content.

Although allergic to Mur's spiritual provender, I found her pantry and general back-gallery doings altogether delectable. Meals in those days managed to be pretty fabulous affairs anyway—always soup, two or three meats, vegetables innumerable, never less than two hot breads—but besides all these Mur habitually had *two* desserts. Imagine ice-cream *and* pudding, ambrosia *and* pie! I don't know whether this glorious termination of dinner was a custom of the times or a personal eccentricity, but I approved of it from the depths of my being. As Christmas time approached, the actual celebration of which left no impression on me whatever, she made elaborate fruit cakes, some blond and some brunet. For that undertaking, which required much thought and measuring, she would spread newspapers before the fire in her room and pile them with pyramids of assorted currants and raisins and nuts. I would lie in bed and watch them in the firelight, quaking deliciously inside and my nose twitching like a rabbit's, though I never actually liked fruit cake.

Dinner parties were rare at our house and I disapproved of them because they meant my enforced withdrawal from the dining-room. But nearly always there were extra and often unexpected guests for meals. Once the ice-cream gave out just before my turn came. This was my first experience of the injustice of things. One is not born a Stoic. I took the event lying down, under the table, loud with woe, and was hustled out, conspicuous in misery. Generally, however, meal time was a nice time and everybody talked a lot. The best thing about it was watching Willis, Mur's very black waiter. When the dining-room was frigid Willis piled the coals high in the fireplace. When he piled them too high it was too hot on Mur's back and she made him stand between her and the fireplace, almost in the fire, an elegant human fire-screen. It was agreeable to watch him break out into a profuse sweat without any loss of dignity—indeed, with increased immobility and self-importance. He must have got dreadfully hot behind. His was a lofty character.

He and I, while not intimate, were on friendly terms and he always let me witness the first stages of turtle soup. To the grown-ups turtle soup was simply the predestined last act of a soft-shell turtle's career and one worth waiting years for. But Willis and I knew the terrific drama preceding it. Someone would bring one of the great monsters to our back steps and leave it there as a gracious and esteemed gift. To Willis fell the hard lot of converting it from an unlikely reptile into a delicacy for Dives and his kind. The turtle gave no co-operation. It resented the situation and withdrew from it by tucking head and flippers into its shell and refusing to emerge. Willis would then give him a jab in the armpit and out the obscene head would dart, the slit eyes pale with hatred, and the horny beaked mouth snapping dangerously at all of us. Nain would scream and snatch me up and scuttle to safety on top of the cistern, while the cook would emit Fo'-Gods, interspersed with strictures on the cannibalism of white folks. Finally that dreadful head would come out long enough for Willis to whack it off with the ax, at which the rest of the turtle would walk off hurriedly, as if the incident were closed. Even this was not the climax of the gory horror—Willis still had to break off the top shell. When this was accomplished, before your startled eyes lay the turtle's insides, unharmed, neatly in place, and still ticking! They did not seem to miss the head, but acted like the works of a watch when you open the back. It was the nakedest thing I ever laid eyes on, and usually while you were watching, fascinated, the whole thing walked off, just that way, and the cook would almost faint. Turtle soup indeed! I don't miss it and I hope not to meet up with it unexpectedly in elegant surroundings.

Mur always dressed in black because my grandfather had not been long dead. It is a pity some of the painted and bedizened old ladies, who have grandchildren but are not grandmothers, cannot know how beautiful and useful and real she was. She taught me to see flowers, and of course anyone who sees them loves them. It would have gone hard with me in certain later hours without that training. She showed me dog-tooth violets outside of Birmingham and so many flowers around Asheville that we invented a game to see which one could spot a new variety first. There must have been many kinfolks and mountains and various happenings around these towns during our visits, but my only memories of them are of wild flowers and Mur. On the other hand, her appreciation of good china, glass, furniture, and draperies was singularly deficient: she aimed only at comfort and had no special genius for that. I remember her horsehair sofas. Her only pictures, besides the oil paintings of prissy-looking great-aunts and such, were an engraving of the Sistine Madonna and another large and quite terrifying one of the death of Queen Elizabeth. After growing up with the latter I understand why one of those fool early Percys was beheaded for attempting to rescue Mary Queen of Scots. In the fine arts Mur's sole flair was for music. Young people loved to dance to her piano-playing and she loved to play for them. Her touch was firm and her sense of rhythm contagious. As I was either moved to tears or bored by anything slower than an allegretto, I recall only her waltzes, marches, and polkas.

Mur's figure was ample and she moved splendidly and serenely like an ocean liner. Back of her silver white pompadour she wore a small widow's bonnet, from which hung a widow's veil to her waist, and there was white ruching at her throat and wrists. Every afternoon she took a nap (which should be compulsory in the interest of sanity), and after her nap she took a walk. I was permitted to be her companion except on those days when her door would be closed and she would walk the floor of her room and Mother would explain: "Mur is thinking about Fafar." On our promenades I sometimes carried her fan as Peter did the nurse's, and we had endless invigorating and informative conversations. There may have been something quaint in our sedate pilgrimages, but no young Mercutio of the countryside ever dared to address her with Mercutio's levity. She suffered fools, but brooked no impertinence; she feared nothing except sin and no one except God. On nights when Father and Mother were out at some party or other and she and I were left alone in the house, which suddenly seemed very big, Mur would stoke up the coal fire and thrust a heavy iron poker deep into its embers where they were turning lavender. The poker point would become red-hot. With that reliable and effective weapon at hand we would settle down to a safe and cheerful evening. Father often teased her by asking what she would do with the poker if a burglar did actually come in. But I knew, and I think he did, that she would have attacked and routed him; he would have been sizzled and spitted like a chicken liver on a brochette. I always hoped just a little bit to witness such a dramatic victory. Instead the poker grew whiter and the flames quieter and bluer and I would move my chair close to hers and she would read aloud to me. What superb things she chose when she was not Bible-minded! Grimm and Hans Andersen, *Huckleberry Finn* and *Uncle Remus, The Rose and the Ring,* and *A Christmas Carol, Pilgrim's Progress* and *Alice in Wonderland.* Mur's reading was not condescending; she loved it as much as I did. She cried at the same places I did, and when she laughed she shook till her glasses fell off. Of course, when we cried—say at the story of the Frog Prince or the Little Boy with Ice in His Heart—we said nothing about it to each other, though Mur sometimes had to stop and blow her nose. Perhaps a diluted course in Lenin and Marx with passages from *Mein Kampf* or a handbook on electricity and aviation would have better prepared a youngster for life as it is. But not, I think, for life as it should be. Old orders change I know, and Mur knew, having herself lived through the death throes of one with all its wreckage of aspirations and possibilities, with bitterness to master and new hope to create. But new orders change too. Only one thing never changes—the human heart. Revolutions and ideologies may lacerate it, even break it, but they cannot change its essence. After Fascism and Communism and Capitalism and Socialism are over and forgotten as completely as slavery and the old South, that same headstrong human heart will be clamoring for the old things it wept for in Eden—love and a chance to be noble, laughter and a chance to adore something, someone, somewhere. Mur and her books did not inform me, they formed me. She should have lived forever to read to one generation after another of little boys, but one night as she was sleeping she died, without premonition or pain, her face no paler than it always was, and a charming smile on her lips. I was a little boy then, but I have never been so close to any living creature since.

CHAPTER IV

Mère and Père

Although Mère and Père, Mother's parents, were born in New Orleans, they were just as French as if they had landed day before yesterday from Lyon or Tours. Mère was plump, squat, and blue-eyed, with a soft face that never learned wrinkles or unlearned its miraculous pink and white. She wore pretty things, light in color, and little bonnets with forget-me-nots and pink rose-buds, and she always managed to look cool, in crises or midsummer. Père would not have had any particular look at all except for his beard, which was so long and silky it could be plaited into one, two, or three plaits and when hooked under and over his ears produced an amazing effect of benign ferocity. The year of fifty-cent cotton Père bought a Delta plantation on Deer Creek and bid adieu to crêpes suzette, absinthe, the old French Opera House, and all his kin except Uncle Alfred, whom no one spoke to or of because he had sold out to Ben Butler. He loaded Mère's nice French furniture, her Pleyel piano, and four little girls, of whom the blondest and prettiest was my mother, on the boat bound for Greenville, and launched forth to make his fortune in the un-French, uncivilized, undeveloped Delta country.

Père was merely bon bourgeois. But through Mère's veins coursed the blood of the Générelly de Rinaldis. Having somehow failed to stumble on this truly magnificent name in song, story, or archive, I recall the tentative inquiry I once made of Mère concerning her forebears. I was told positively, though a bit vaguely, it seemed to me, that the original old Rinaldi from his castle in thirteenth-century Italy had descended on a lovely lady in a neighboring castle and made her, in disregard of her wishes, his consort, and that this exploit satisfied the family's yen for romance and heroism for five or six centuries—in fact, until Mère's grandfather, a dashing and aristocratic youth, was hustled out of revolutionary France by a faithful servant after untold hardships and escapes, and turned up in New Orleans with a few charming water-colors of tulips and roses and a deep sense of wrong. A trifle tenuous, perhaps, as proof of glorious lineage, but Mère was calmly adamant in the conviction that her blood was blue, which gave her the upper hand over Père right from the outset. This was rather sad, because he was a sweet and infinitely polite soul and had been a Captain under Beauregard. Nor did he improve his status with Mère by acquiring this outlandish Delta property. Though she could pioneer, she had neither admiration nor liking for the role—no French woman ever has—and I suspect he rather misrepresented its charm and elegance, being as he was on the poetic and sentimental side. Even naming the place Camelia after her did not pacify her or compensate for its living-quarters, which, far from being a mansion with white columns, were, I must confess, a log cabin, though a commodious one and fairly comfortable for those days. No, Mère never forgave him; you could tell it when she said "Mais, Ernest"; and even when with an "Ach" she tapped me on the head with her thimbled first finger, I suspected the correction was meant for him as much as for myself. Père was not lazy or even fundamentally incompetent, but his competency never got itself focused. He lost the plantation, moved his family to town, started one business venture after another, and failed in all of them. When Father married his daughter she was a very poor girl who made her own clothes—pretty ones I am told—and had never seen more of the outer world than New Orleans and the Sacré Cœur Convent, where Père somehow managed to have her educated. Père was miscast; besides having little girls, his only accomplishment was raising roses. His Maman Cochets and Malmaisons and Maréchal Niels were famous, or should have been in any civilized community. He should have been provided with dominoes, a desiccated crony or two, a siphon, a bottle of Amer Picon, and a corner in a dingy café where some broad-bosomed madame queened it behind an elevated guichet—and of course he should have had seats for the opera twice a week, including Sunday night.

Instead, his life petered out in a drab little country town, very Protestant and very Anglo-Saxon. In such a setting the French family must have seemed an oddity, but it never tried to be less odd or less French. The little girls continued to play croquet on Sunday, to the scandal of everyone, and to enliven shamelessly that dour and boring day by dance tunes on their little French piano, while their betters attended divine services. Their trouble, and their strength, was that they recognized no betters. Not that they minded Anglo-Saxons or took their own religion hard, but they regarded their poverty as an incident and their position as an immutability. Mère would never have sought the advice of a priest, or anyone else, but she could not have imagined herself anything but a Catholic—it was a habit, a good one, she was sure, but not interesting and distinctly not a subject for conversation. Nor would she have called on members of the congregation whom she considered excellent in everything except social standing, or on anyone in this semi-civilized community, first. As the little French girls grew up they were attractive and popular, which made things easier for everybody, yet Mère permitted courting only within the strict French convention. She was a pain to suitors, chaperoning her daughters everywhere and sitting in her corner of the parlor, playing solitaire, when they came courting. She maintained this observation post—half dragon and half Brangäne—even after Mother was engaged to Father, and his only revenge was occasionally to swipe a card from her deck so she couldn't make it. Father was the catch of the town, but Mère had no enthusiasm for the match: she knew he was what Aunt Nana would call "something of a gay blade," and it never crossed her mind that the Percys were any better than the Bourges.

Were they? In the South a question of that kind is apt to fling family skeletons from their closets into the middle of the parlor floor and to set extant sibs and collaterals shrieking like mandrakes. Even today from Virginia to Texas, from Charleston to Natchez, ten thousand crepuscular old maids and widows in ghostly coveys and clusters are solving such unsolvable issues. They are our Southern Norns, keepers of family Bibles, pruners of family trees, whose role is to remember and foretell—to remember glory and to foretell disaster—while in the gaudy day outside the banker's daughter, Brunhilde, elopes with the soda-water jerker. Père had he been less polite, Mère had she been less assured, might have introduced such devastating evidence into the Bourges-Percy controversy as would have titillated Norn circles for months. They must have known the bleak facts of my paternal ancestry, which confidentially were these:

The first Percy in our part of the South, my great-great-grandfather, was Charles. He blew in from the gray or blue sea-ways with a ship of his own, a cargo of slaves, and a Spanish grant to lands in the Buffalo country south of Natchez. Court records show that he was made an Alcalde and called Don Carlos by the Spaniards, and his house was known as Northumberland Place. This was shortly after the Revolution. Where did he come from? How came he by a Spanish grant? What were his antecedents and station? To such questions climbers in the family tree have found no answers: Don Carlos came from nowhere, he issued suddenly from the sea like the Flying Dutchman or Aphrodite—though Mrs. Dana once darkly confided to me that on his westerly flight he had landed at one of the Caribbean Isles and left a record behind him there nothing short of "lamentable, lamentable." Was he a pirate? Or the lost heir of the earls of Northumberland? Or a hero of the Spanish wars? Silence. Mystery.

Don Carlos settled down on his plantation and married him an intelligent French lady from the other side of the river. The Lord blessed them with progeny, and things seemed to be going well and quite respectably when a lady suddenly appeared from England and said to Don Carlos: "I am the long lost wife of your bosom." As if that was not enough, she added: "Behold, your son and heir!" Whereupon she tendered him, not a wee bairn, but a full-grown Captain in the English Navy, also yclept Charles. Certainly a discouraging business all round. It is not recorded that Don Carlos slapped the lady, but of course he was thoroughly provoked and everybody immediately began suing everybody else. Somewhere during the commotion Don Carlos walked down to the creek with a sugar kettle, tied it round his neck, and hopped in. The creek is still there and is called Percy's Creek to this good day. His will left his holdings, not to his English, but to his American family, whether from pique, outrage, or affection I can only surmise. The wives continued their litigation for a while, wrote eloquent letters to the Governor, and acted as outraged gentlewomen usually act. Then everything was hushed up or patched up without a court decision; both families calmly settled down in the same neighborhood and lived happily ever afterwards. Need I say the English lady was not my ancestress? I have a tender feeling for Don Carlos and wish I could ask him confidentially a few leading questions. He was not exactly a credit to anybody, but, as ancestors go, he had his points.

I once drove to Woodville, a little town which has grown up near the old Percy place, to see if I could discover the grave of Don Carlos. I thought his dates might be clarifying, and once in a while an inscription on a headstone is penetrating to the point of cruelty, if you know half the story. Of the usual engaging youth at the filling station I inquired: "Can you tell me where Charles Percy is buried?" "No," he replied, "didn't know he was dead." I elucidated vaguely. He laughed. "Maybe he'll know, he's a Percy," he said, pointing to a pleasant-looking, countryfied man sitting on the ditch bank, spitting tobacco juice. "No," drawled my half cousin, "we never could find where the old bird was buried. I reckon it was on the creek bank, and the creek's changed its course."

Playing Tarzan in the family tree is hazardous business; there are too many rotten branches. Mère and Père would have put such irrelevancies in the class with religion, as distinctly not a subject for conversation. The Percys were nice people; the Bourges were nice people—voilà tout! But I cannot help wondering what were the qualifications that admitted to the post-Civil-War aristocracy. Apparently not pedigree, certainly not wealth. A way of life for several generations? A tradition of living? A style and pattern of thinking and feeling not acquired but inherited? No matter how it came about, the Bourges and Percys were nice people—that is what I breathed in as a child, the certainty I was as good as anyone else, which, because of the depth of the conviction, was unconscious, never talked of, never thought of. Besides Southerners, the only people I have ever met graced with the same informal assurance were Russian aristocrats.

I suspect, however, that no pair ever looked less aristocratic than Père and I, he in his neat but well-worn and out-of-style sack suit, I barefooted and hatless, as we rushed up the levee to see the *Floating Palace* come round the bend. The blast of the calliope way up the river had electrified the countryside. All the Negroes, all the children, and half the adults were swarming to the levee. From the thick of the laughter and shoving and pointing, he and I would watch the magnificent apparition sweep down the center of the stream, black smoke pouring from its funnel and white plumes of steam from the calliope, whose stentorian cacophonies were like the laughter of the gods at some pranks of Hebe's, only off key. Waiting for dark and the show to begin was unbearable. At last the calliope would hit a high note and hold it, until you almost burst, then dash into "Dixie," and we would rush down the levee, squeeze on to the gangplank, buy our tickets, and at last, at last, enter—Elysium. Such a grand, exciting smell of sweating people, everybody eating pink popcorn and drinking pop, such a dazzle of lights, such getting stepped on and knocked over and picked up, and at last the show, the beautiful, incredible show! A little Japanese with jerky angular gyrations climbed a ladder of sharp swords on feet as bare as mine; an adorable lady in pink tights floated through the air with ravishing grace while an elegant gentleman in full evening dress explained she came from the Garden of Eden; a baker's daughter hid seven suitors from her father in his oven and when he returned he built up the fire and they were baked to a crisp; in fact, the baker took them out of the oven for you to see and they were flat and brown, exactly like gingerbread men. This last was surpassingly horrible and gave me nightmares for a solid week, to the confusion of the family, who finally in desperation administered castor oil followed by raspberry jam. But all the rest was divinely beautiful. Show-boat! I never heard of such a name in my time. Everybody knew it was the *Floating Palace* and worthy, a thousand times, of its title.

Mère and Père were at their best, I think, at Roxbury, Aunt Nana's place in Virginia, or possibly I saw them there less interruptedly and less flurried by such incidents as beset those who can't quite make both ends meet. It was an old run-down place, far out in the country, and Mère's corner room was full of sunlight and breeze. On afternoons when it was too hot for me to go on expeditions with the little darkies, the three of us would convene there and Mère would bring out her quilting materials, needle and thread, and that thimble of hers. Aunt Nana might rustle in with glasses of blackberry vinegar, which apparently went out when cocktails came in. It had a kingly color and when chilled with ice, which Uncle George had harvested last winter from the pond and stored in sawdust against such occasions, it tasted like those snow and honey concoctions of the Greeks, just sweet enough and just sour enough and altogether Olympian. Mère's quilts were marvels of skill and took months and months to make. They were born from the tails of neckties and scraps of velvet and silk from petticoats, bustles, and linings. She first sewed the scraps into squares, then she sewed the squares on each side of a panel of watered silk into a quilt shape; next she bordered the whole with a hand's width of velvet, and last she embroidered all of it with wonderful flowers and birds and vines and bows and even little baskets. The result was as personal as that web of Penelope's and as French as the illegitimate daughters of Louis XIV. In the making the vexatious æsthetic problem was to match the colors of the scraps. She tried them out this way and that, sometimes even consulting Père and me on the effect, though this I fancy was mere affability. Pink, of course, matched with blue or lavender or even light green, but never with red. It was unthinkable to set green and blue side by side, or blue and lavender. Red was always difficult, but yellow could be sprinkled nearly haphazard. I would watch with deep interest and so received my first lesson in color-consciousness. Perhaps I should thank her for later hours of delight with Rembrandt and Titian, and blame her perhaps for my being still a little scared and shocked by El Greco.

Meanwhile Père would start humming, and that would be my cue to ask him what opera the tune was from, was it grand or comic, heavy or light, what was the plot, was it as good as *Les Huguenots*? *Les Huguenots* was his classic example of a heavy opera, into which category fell *Aïda, Faust,* and an opera new to New Orleans called *Lohengrin,* which he had been told was *very* heavy. *Les Huguenots* was also grand opera. Grand opera always ended with a death or a suicide, usually two or three of each. Then why was not *Carmen* a grand opera? Well, it was heavy but not grand, because they gave it on Sunday nights in New Orleans, and at the Comique, not the Opéra, in Paris. What! *Carmen* on Sunday nights, like *La Belle Hélène* and *La Fille de Madame Angot* and *Giroflé-Girofla?* Why did they do that? As these distinctions became more tenuous and Pére more hard-pressed, Aunt Nana, who loved peace though she never abandoned an argument, would cough and observe that everybody said the New Orleans Opera House really was more beautiful than the Paris Opéra. Mère would observe: "Évidemment," since the Paris Opéra had no loges découvertes. Père out of the exuberance of his memories would start singing "O mon fils" from *La Juive* and go on louder and louder until he came to shocking grief on the high C of the climax. Mère would look over her glasses and exclaim: "Mais, Ernest," but not in her usual Fricka-to-Wotan manner, indeed so sympathetically that in a distrait moment she would sew crimson next to shrimp pink.

The French do actually love music, but in a maddening way. When a favorite passage is well sung the thing to do is to cheer and cry "Bravo! Bis!"; you do not swoon. Mère would have had no patience with swooning for any cause, or with ecstasy as a result of music any more than as a result of religion. Music was a charming décor, a delightful adjunct to living, in the same category as chic clothes and a considered cuisine. The great French artists felt the same way about it: Clouet, Poussin, Chardin, Renoir never attempted ecstasy. If you wish to express sentiment, that is permissible, in the manner of Greuze and Massenet, but ecstasy, no, ecstasy is too much. Verlaine and Debussy tried it, but they were more neurotic than French, and their success lay not in content but in style, which in its perfection was absolutely French. It is a rare Frenchman who really prefers *Pelléas* to *Héro-*

diade, or Verlaine to de Musset. Mère and Père wouldn't have done so; that I do only proves, I suppose, that moony strain of Don Carlos.

Music would be continued on a less exalted plane by Aunt Nana and me after supper. We would open the parlor, always shuttered and musty and cool by day, light the candles on each side of the black upright piano, and sing duets. "Just a Song at Twilight" and "Love's Old Sweet Song" were our favorites, and we liked a new piece, "After the Ball," which was very sad, almost as sad as the tune Mother used to sing to herself while sewing, "Tit Willow, Tit Willow, Tit Willow." I cannot explain why I so completely misinterpreted Gilbert and Sullivan's intention. I have made such mistakes all my life, and it's too late now to change. It was too late from the beginning. The color of our temperament, our chief concern, is nothing of our making. If we are pink, we can only hope that fate will not set us cheek by jowl with red. If we see the world through mauve glasses, there's no sort of sense in wishing they were white. We may only console ourselves by noting that a certain opalescence, like sun through the misty mornings of London, is not without a loveliness denied the truer and cruder white noons of the desert.

CHAPTER V

Playmates

Any little boy who was not raised with little Negro children might just as well not have been raised at all. My first boon-companion was Skillet, the small dark son of Mère's cook. He was the best crawfisher in the world and I was next. Instead of closed sewers our town had open ditches, which after an overflow swarmed with crawfish, small clear ones, quite shrimp-like, whose unexpected backward agility saved them from any except the most skilful hands, and large red ones, surly and whiskered, with a startling resemblance to the red-nosed old reprobates you saw around the saloons when you were looking for tobacco tags in the sawdust. When these rared back and held their claws wide apart, Skillet said they were saying: "Swear to God, white folks, I ain't got no tail." Theoretically it was for their tails that we hunted them, because when boiled and seasoned and prayed over they made that thick miraculous pink soup you never experience unless you have French blood in the family or unless you dine at Prunier's. Of course anyone could catch crawfish with a string and a lump of bacon, and anyone knows their family life is passed in holes, like snake-holes, from which they must be lured; but who except Skillet had ever observed that a hollow bone lying on the bottom of a ditch is bound to be occupied by one? Maybe he sat there as in a summerhouse thinking or catching a nap or saying to himself: "These boys will never think of this." If you waded up noiselessly and clapped both hands suddenly and simultaneously over both ends of the bone, he was yours and went into the bucket outraged and blowing bubbles, nothing appeased that his high destiny was to contribute his bit to a bisque d'écrevisses.

Skillet's sister Martha was a virago. Like Goneril she never reformed and so kept the plot boiling. She constantly threatened to do away with our crawfish in some low diabolical manner. This led to a painful incident. After an especially successful day we decided to hide from Martha our water-bucket brim-full of the simmering live catch and chose for that purpose an obscure corner behind the bookcase in Mère's parlor. Black fate decreed that on that very night Mère should give what was called a soirée. Now, the parlor was the hallowed place to receive guests, gay and beribboned and with splendid bustles. Fruit punch seemed to make them as lively as cocktails do now (I think Père spiked it). Mrs. Holland sang the Jewel Song from *Faust* and as an encore "Three Little Pigs Went to Market." Everyone said she should have joined the New Orleans Opera instead of marrying Mr. Holland, as obviously she would have had a succès fou in *Mignon* or *L'Africaine,* but Mother insisted she was a natural comédienne and would have been irresistible in *Orphée aux Enfers* or *Les Cloches de Corneville.* Then someone began playing dance music, which, if I recollect accurately, was as enticing and stimulating as the radio, but in a nice way, and without interpolations concerning liver pills and tooth paste. After the dancing, Mother and Mr. Harry Ball were to have sung a duet—they had "parlor voices, but sweet"—and it may have been sung, but I was not destined to hear it. At that moment a ladylike scream stopped the music and threw the gathering into consternation. Mrs. Holland had stepped on a large red crawfish in the attitude of "Swear to God, white folks." It made a crunchy sound. Another was discovered and another; they were all over the place. Mère was indignant, but Mother, though she retired me hastily, and in bad odor, really wanted to laugh. Skillet and I were in disgrace; Martha—need I say?—escaped unscathed.

Crawfishing was not Skillet's only excellence. As a conversationalist he outdistanced any white child in inventiveness, absurdity, and geniality. In Mère's back yard we would sit in a row-boat, a relic of the last overflow, and for hours ply imaginary oars toward an imaginary land that we described and embellished as we approached. These voyages afforded endless opportunity for discussions. One in particular drifts back to me across long years. It was one of those still, hot days when earth things lie tranced at the bottom of a deep sea of summer sun. We were resting on our oars at the moment. Far, far up buzzards circled dreamily, their black wings motionless, tilting, banking, coasting in wide arcs, somnambulistic symbols of the drowse and delight of deep summer. Watching them, Skillet observed in a singsong: "If they was to ever light, the world would burn up." As the birds seemed fixed at their vast altitude, this was a safe prophecy. But I was skeptical, as could have been expected of any horrid little white realist. Skillet, though, was so eloquent in citing reasons and authorities that my disbelief weakened and by degrees I was convinced, for the old excellent reason that I wanted to be. As we watched, the buzzards, careening and narrowing their circles, began to descend. It was exciting to see them drop lower and lower and to think what might happen. At last we could discern their horrible necks and heads. Skillet rose in a kind of ecstasy, thrusting out his arms, flexing his knees, and chanting: "Don't let 'em light, God, don't let 'em light." The flames of a consuming world were practically around us. Only the fire music as it came to Mime about the time Siegfried rushed in with the bear could have expressed our abject and delicious terror. They were hovering over our own back yard and, last touch of horror, there lay one of Mère's chickens dead—indeed, more than dead—their target, stark and untidy on the crust of the earth so unconcerned and so doomed. One of the ghastly creatures suddenly rocked, flapped its wings, and settled down awkwardly on the fence between us and the Fergusons'. "Look, I told you so, the world didn't burn up," I almost sobbed, torn between relief and disappointment. "He lit on a fence. He ain't never teched the ground," whispered Skillet. The buzzard gave an ungainly bound and landed on the too, too solid earth. "Look," I wailed. "He lit on a chip," Skillet observed affably. I was outraged.

Calling to mind with gratitude those to whom we are indebted on our journey is not only a sort of piety, but one of the few pleasures that endure without loss of luster to the end. I like to imagine that Skillet is not in jail or dead, but that he lords it in a Pullman car or pulpit, or perhaps has a farm of his own and many little crawfishers—in fine, that the swooping dark wings continue for him to light on a chip. He is all my memory records of what must have been long months of my childhood; all others it seems were lay figures.

Equally treasurable were Amelia's children on Aunt Nana's farm in Virginia, where I was deposited so many summers. I don't remember the house well except that it was square, airy, and very old, with a corridor behind leading to the kitchen, storerooms, and Amelia's sleeping-quarters; the old furniture and woodwork made no impression whatever. All around were cornfields and dabs of woods, and a few hundred yards in front the small cool river. I must have seen it rain there often, but like a sundial I remember only sunlight, acres and acres of it: sometimes merely pale and fresh and still on the pasture; or heavy like a great depth of blue sea-water on the undulating rows of corn, which, tired of the weight, sagged limply; or in splotches and scarves and sudden widths of glitter on the river; or, best, early in the morning, when it slanted in long gray panels through the orchard and barely silvered the small yellow pears with a sweat of cold dew on them and dew on the grass where they lay. Quantities of little wiggly paths, cow-paths likely, meandered everywhere and nowhere, bordered by straggling colonies of tawny lilies and bushes of pokeberry, indispensable for war-paint on our Indian days. They too were sunny, but managed to make every patch of shade a port of call, and two of them met in the little wood where an old fox-grape vine with the kindliness and humor of old age crooked one arm into a perfect swing. The swing itself would be in shadow, of the breezy arrowy kind, all shreds and patches on you as you swung through it, but you looked out from under the branches across all that shining clearness that lay on the fields and the aspen woodland to the old house far off to the left, and you knew you needed nothing else. When your peace is without grayness, it comes seldom and does not stay long; some are still hunting for it and some are trying to find it again, but know they won't.

At Aunt Nana's there were so many fascinating spots you couldn't make the round of them in a week, and all of them smelled good. The dairy, round, with thick walls and no windows, where the crocks of milk and clabber and cream stood in live spring-water, smelled cold and slightly sour. The corn-bin had a warm yellow smell like a loaf of bread at the moment Amelia opened the oven and pawed it out with the edge of her apron. The barn, from the pile of manure in front (which Père said Uncle George was too lazy to scatter over the fields, and it was beautiful manure) to the stalls, soggy with corn-shucks and urine, had an exciting smell, like autumn, but the smell was definitely good. Of course the kitchen was so full of things to whiff and sniff and inhale with eyes closed that you could stay there all day, only you were always being shooed out, on lucky occasions with the batter-bowl to lick. The best smell, however, was undoubtedly at the mill. That mill was none of your modern contraptions, spotless and intricate and unintelligible. You saw how it worked when it worked, which was occasionally. There was the dam, and the mill-pond above and behind it; there was the huge water-wheel which sloshed and turned when the sluice was opened; there were the great mill-stones, likely the very ones the gods used to use, between which the corn filtered to its golden doom; and there was the miller, a bit sweaty and covered with a lovely creamy dust of meal, especially his eyebrows and mustache. Sometimes I was allowed to ride behind Reuben when he took a sack of corn to be ground. We would wait till the resulting sack of meal was ready to be put over the pommel and jogged home to Amelia, by her to be manipulated into corn-pones of unspeakable crunchiness and savor. The meal would be still damp and warm when turned over to us, and it was hard not to eat it raw, like chickens, so rich and sweet and really fundamental it smelled.

Reuben was too old to be interesting, perhaps eighteen, but Amelia's children—Ligey, Martha, Cora, Friday, and a few more I've forgotten—were exactly the right ages. They seem to have arrived precisely a year apart and all were dark, but some were darker, and no two of them looked alike. I often wondered who and where their father was, and once put the question to Aunt Nana, but she developed one of those little attacks of hurry and said, as well as I could gather, he was a traveling man. However, it must have been a fine father or set of fathers, because they were fine children and as playmates perfection. Small satyrs and fauns could not have been more instructive or resourceful or absurd.

We harried the hillsides for arrow-heads and found many splendid ones—training I found invaluable years later when between showers I hunted sea-shells in Bora-Bora. Sometimes we spent days on end in full flight from a murderous band of gypsies. Cora's cries on one occasion when she was almost captured were so blood-curdling we rushed off down the road and abandoned her to her fate, quite forgetting the plot she furthered with such histrionic fervor. Friday had a genius for discovering hornet-nests. Silvery and rather Burmese in design, one would be hanging on a tree conveniently low, its irascible inmates in a stew and a lather, storming in and out. Led by Friday, we would approach as near as we dared and let fly our barrage against the patiently built castle of the poor earnest insects. But they, unadvised of the other-cheek doctrine we have so long been beseeching one another to follow, would sally forth in the best modern echelon formation, armed to the tip, and we, sounding precipitate and individual retreat, would scatter yowling.

If someone was not badly stung, to be borne lamenting loudly to Amelia's soda and scarifying invective, it was a disappointing adventure.

In our milder moods the river was a favorite haunt. It was the right sort of river. With the dam closed, it could be waded and was all pools and trickles and slimy shelving rocks. Although not scorning such lesser quarry as eels, leeches, water-snakes, and frogs, our constant ambition was to discover a giant sturgeon. This ambition was unlikely but not impossible of fulfillment, because one had found its way into our river as a result of the Johnstown flood and we had seen it with our own eyes hanging from the ceiling of the tool-house, its tail sweeping the floor, glittering in the lamplight, magnificent even in death. We noticed when it was split open that with just a little more room Jonah could have sat inside. We discussed this and kindred issues for days afterwards.

During one of these theological sessions I swallowed a persimmon seed. Doctors had recently discovered appendicitis, attributed it to the swallowing of a seed, and considered it fatal. Solemn with this medical erudition, I explained the grisly situation and announced my approaching demise. All accepted the news with delight and prepared for the end. I lay on the ground and my faithful retainers knelt around me, in the manner of sundry versions of the Assumption of the Virgin. I closed my eyes, and fervent prayers rose loudly. Nothing happened. Nothing ever did happen. Reviving was undignified and bitterly disappointing to all concerned. As a corpse I was a fiasco, but as mourners my colored entourage displayed genius. Racially they are the best diers in the world anyway: they put more force and enthusiasm into the scene, being seriously aware it is the climax of the show, their curtain. If Friday had swallowed my persimmon seed, he would beyond question have died outright and to perfection, although it's a role one can't rehearse.

So many things to do and each summer so short. To chase rats in the barn, a dangerous and slightly sickening enterprise; to teach the kitten to play circus (our cats were Manx, with stubs for tails and bouncing rabbit motions); to climb the roof of the corridor and watch the ducks file out to the pond, cracking dry mirthless jokes to one another and sometimes laying an egg, shamelessly and without stopping, on the bare ground with no thought of a nest; to be allowed to help with the cider press where all the apples with a rotten spot, those claimed and contended for by the yellow-jackets, disappeared into the hopper and gushed out the sides in a seethe of bubbly brown liquor, fit for Ceres; to hunt in the mold of the wood-pile for the turquoise bits that were fox-fire and find instead a land-terrapin closed up safe from the mad world in his neat hinged box, and to devise means to make him come out—so many things to do, and summer so short.

Supervised play and summer camps came after my time. I missed learning the principles of team work and many games which must be helpful if you can think of nothing to do. Instead, Friday's accent, Cora's intonation, and Ligey's grammatical uses contaminated beyond hope of purification the wells of what should have been my pure English undefiled. That was their only evil influence. Of nastiness and bad manners they taught me nothing; older boys of my own color and caste were later to be my instructors in those subjects. From Amelia's children I learned not only gaiety and casualness and inventiveness, but the possibility that mere living may be delightful and that natural things which we ignore unless we call them scenery are pleasant to move among and gracious to recall. Without them it would probably never have occurred to me that to climb an aspen sapling in a gale is one of those ultimate experiences, like experiencing God or love, that you need never try to remember because you can never forget. Aspens grow together in little woods of their own, straight, slender, and white. Even in still weather they twinkle and murmur, but in a high wind you must run out and plunge among them, spattered with sunlight, to the very center. Then select your tree and climb it high enough for it to begin to wobble with your weight. Rest your foot-weight lightly on the frail branches and do most of your clinging with your arms. Now let it lunge, and gulp the wind. It will be all over you, slapping your hair in your eyes, stinging your face with bits of bark and stick, tugging to break your hold, roaring in your open mouth like a monster sea-shell. The trees around you will thrash and seethe, their white undersides lashed about like surf, and sea-music racing through them. You will be beaten and bent and buffeted about and the din will be so terrific your throat will invent a song to add to the welter, pretty barbaric, full of yells and long calls. You will feel what it is to be the Lord God and ride a hurricane; you will know what it is to have leaves sprout from your toes and finger-tips, with satyrs and tigers and hounds in pursuit; you will never need again to drown under the crash of a maned wave in spume and splendor and thunder, with the white stallions of the sea around you, neighing and pawing. That must have been the very wood old Housman had in mind when he sang "We'll to the woods no more." But when he found his way to it he was alone, and it was autumn.

CHAPTER VI

A Side-Show Götterdämmerung

The most moving book ever written, more moving than *Jean-Christophe* or *Death Comes for the Archbishop* or *Anna Karenina,* is *In Silken Chains.* No one ever read it except Aunt Nana and me, and we never finished it. The heroine's beauty—raven hair, magnolia skin, purple eyes—made you feel like the string section of an orchestra, and she was in deep trouble, I don't remember what about, but it was not her fault. Aunt Nana had been reading this gem to me for weeks and we had just reached an unspeakably poignant climax when Father appeared in our midst. "Nana, what in the world do you mean by reading such trash to that child?" Aunt Nana was crushed, I was desolated, he was adamant. We asked weakly what please could we substitute, and unhesitatingly he answered: "*Ivanhoe.*" He did not often lay down the law, but then and there he ruled as authoritatively as Moses that there would be no other novel-reading to poison my mind until I had finished Scott, Bulwer-Lytton, Dickens, and a little Thackeray. This injunction remained in full force until I left for college with a volume of Stanley J. Weyman under one arm and Rider Haggard under the other. In the meantime Aunt Nana and I dutifully settled down to *Ivanhoe*. It produced unpredictable results: Aunt Nana wept herself into an illness over Rebecca, and I, far from being inspired to knightly heroism, grew infatuated with the monastic life, if it could be pursued in a cave opening on a desert.

Father rarely gave advice and never unless he'd taken it himself. He read *Ivanhoe* once a year all his life long, and *The Talisman* almost as frequently. Because of or in spite of Don Carlos he was kin to Hotspur and blood-brother to Richard Cœur de Lion, and he looked the part. No one ever made the mistake of thinking he wasn't dangerous, and to the day of his death he was beautiful, a cross between Phœbus Apollo and the Archangel Michael. It was hard having such a dazzling father; no wonder I longed to be a hermit. He could do everything well except drive a nail or a car: he was the best pistol-shot and the best bird-shot, he made the best speeches, he was the fairest thinker and the wisest, he could laugh like the Elizabethans, he could brood and pity till sweat covered his brow and you could feel him bleed inside. He loved life, and never forgot it was unbearably tragic. His appearances during Virginia summers were brief and legendary—he had to be home, making a living for us.

Uncle George was not deeply concerned with making a living, for in a mild way it made itself from those hundreds of acres in corn and orchard. His real worry was whether or not the fish were biting. After Father's electric advents, Uncle George was restful: he didn't say much or do much or think much, but unquestionably he was a good fisherman. Often when you asked him a question, he grunted for answer and you could take it either way. This usually occurred when we were in the boat on the pond, and the fish weren't biting. He wore a wide limber straw hat, like Matahi's Sunday best in Bora-Bora, and he clenched a stubby pipe between his teeth. He didn't mind just sitting, but after two hours without a nibble, he would take his pipe out, tap it on the side of the boat, and observe: "When the wind's in the east, the fish bite least." To which I would counter: "When the wind's in the west, the fish bite best." Though I knew the answer, I could never resist asking: "When the wind's in the south, what do they do?" "Bite in the mouth," replied Uncle George. "But what does that mean?" "What it says," snapped Uncle George, and though that sounded like sense, it wasn't, and I'd do useful ruminating over how many things sounded like sense and passed for sense which were nowhere near sense. Of course there was no use asking about the north wind: to that I'd never got anything better than a grunt.

If fish could bat their eyes or wall them like El Greco's saints, their death throes would be unbearable to watch and no one would ever have the heart to fish. Even as awkward and impersonal as they are, floundering about on the bottom of a boat, I soon came to the conclusion that fishing was not my sport and hunting was even more lacerating to the spirit. Yet fishermen and hunters are the most pitying, the most gentle and understanding people in the world, and I suspect anyone who isn't one or the other. They are curative to a degree; Uncle George was. You walked along carrying the empty fish-basket and felt easy and liked his grumpiness. Of course he wasn't comparable to Father on the nights he came in from bird-hunting. That never failed to have a home-from-the-wars, home-from-the-seas, ballad brilliance about it. In the first place he looked so heroic and gay, smelling warmish of feathers and corduroy and dogs, and togged out in boots and sweaters and jackets full of pockets, all brown as a cocklebur; and then he never failed to bring in a big bag. He'd tell how each bird was killed and what the dogs did, as he sat before the fire, feeling simply great and drinking slowly a very long toddy, while Mother bustled about the kitchen, making him an oyster soup. To be reared among wise earth-people that way gives you a lifelong distaste for the fidgety folk of cities who palaver and intellectualize and use their features but not their hands and feet.

Long after these things, when Uncle George was broke and had moved down from Virginia to our town, Father managed to find him a poorly paid job as road-inspector. I look at Uncle George's section of that road every now and then; it pulls me together. The concrete north and south of his section is warped and cracked, but his after twenty years stands solid and level. The contractors couldn't buy Uncle George, though he knew ahead of him lay an old age of penury and dependence.

The only thing I held against Uncle George was the stories he'd tell me just about my bedtime when we'd all be sitting in the dark on the front porch. I tried the patience of them all, begging for stories. Père was the most accommodating and the most inept. He would start off in the tempo of the prodded dormouse: "There was once a beautiful little princess and she lived in a wood; she had long gold hair and blue eyes, and wore the most exquisite little dress, all white, with pink and blue ribbons," and then he would give up. I never learned what happened to the little princess: Père was long on feminine pulchritude and short on invention. An unfinished fairy story, like the old South. Uncle George's stories, on the other hand, featured bears or hyenas coming down the chimney, a chimney exactly like ours, and they were blood-curdling. When my last excuse for staying up had been overruled, I'd be sent up the stairs alone to the dark upper story where there wasn't a living thing except probably a bear or a hyena, and I'd be clammy with terror. But no one knew, no one ever did know, not to this good minute. Psychiatrists to the contrary notwithstanding, it was splendid training, most useful in later years.

So I don't bother about Don Carlos's missing link or the Bourges being in trade or about that Italo-French mésalliance of Mère's ancestor or the border cattle-stealing blood of the Armstrongs, who to the scorn of the Whig Percys were Democrats and close friends of Andrew Jackson's, or all the other vague and mixed ghosts back to Adam which went into the creating of my body and temperament. In time we are all good democrats; in the manger we look the same and in the grave. But at this particular time and place, viewed not from a peak in eternity but from the ephemeral now, I rejoice to be of a caste which, though shaken and scattered, refuses to call itself Demos.

In Virginia the big event of the summer was the trip to Fredericksburg. May and Maud, the slickest mules in the county, would be hitched to the carriage that on such occasions replaced the buckboard in which Uncle George and I drove twice a week to Guiney's for the mail. The carriage, of course, dated from before the war and fortunately refused to fall to pieces. It was elegant but shabby, with a sort of prenatal bulge reminiscent of the stage coaches in the Musée Cluny, and there was mold in its color and smell. The winding dirt pike we took passed through a country almost as haunted as Greece: to the right stretched the Wilderness; just over the ridge Stonewall Jackson was shot and was caught dying in the arms of Captain Randolph, whose daughter now earns her living by selling shrubs from her little nursery on the edge of our home town; beyond was Guiney's, where he breathed his last; Spottsylvania Court House was up the right-hand road and we would be going there next week for a barbecue of squirrel—more popular with spiders and ticks than with me; ahead, in their gardens, stood the quiet homes of General Washington's mother and friends. Aunt Nana described it all as we drove along and, although few of the facts lodged with me, I knew it was holy ground and in every field and thicket men had given up the breath they loved for something noble they loved more. It was a countryside of proud ghosts.

Fredericksburg reached, Uncle George would disappear while Aunt Nana and I paid calls. I do not remember the old houses and gardens or the people, but the return trips made a great impression. Uncle George while away from us always picked up a headache. He was not given to headaches and Aunt Nana always inquired, with what seemed to me undue asperity, how he came by this one. Uncle George attributed his condition to peanuts. Aunt Nana replied it seemed strange to her how he always ate peanuts in Fredericksburg when he knew they always gave him a headache. I had never eaten peanuts except at a circus and I would wonder if Uncle George had sneaked off to one without taking me. My inquiries about this were ignored, and even the silence was tart. Finally Uncle George would ask fretfully if a man couldn't eat peanuts *once a year* without being persecuted. I enjoyed the drive home, but no one else did. They seemed dreadfully fuzzed-up over peanuts.

Aunt Nana, descending from her mule-drawn, ancient vehicle in a home-made print dress did not seem shabby or peculiar or anything less than aristocratic to Fredericksburg folk, high or low. Today she couldn't come to town in a T-model Ford, dressed in home-made clothes and unadorned by beauty-shop ministrations and a permanent, without snickers and comments from the ladies of the Saturday Night Bridge Club as well as from the barber's wife. Maybe this is as it should be, but I don't think so. I'm unhappily convinced that our exteriors have increased in importance while our interiors have deteriorated: it is a good paint job, but the lighting and sanitation are execrable. A good world, I acknowledge, an excellent world, but poor in spirit and common as hell. Vulgarity, a contagious disease like the itch, unlike it is not a disease of the surface, but eats to the marrow.

As a class I suppose the Southern aristocrat is extinct, but what that class despised as vulgar and treasured as excellent is still despised and treasured by individuals scattered thickly from one end of the South to the other. Those individuals born into a world of tradesfolk are still aristocrats, with an uncanny ability to recognize their kind. Their distinguishing characteristic probably is that their hearts are set, not on the virtues which make surviving possible, but on those which make it worth while. They could drive tomorrow to the guillotine in Aunt Nana's shabby ante-bellum carriage with so bland and insolent an air that passing Fords would take to the alleys and a Rolls-Royce would stop dead in its tracks, realizing itself parvenu. Having neglected the virtues that have survival value, these charming people are on their way to extinction, while the vulgar are increasing and multiplying and prospering and will continue to do so until their children or their children's children, having attained security, will begin all over again to admire and cherish the forgotten virtues we were not strong enough to maintain. Perhaps in every age an aristocracy is dying and one is being born. In any event aristocratic virtues and standards themselves never die completely and never change at all. General Lee and Senator Lamar would have been at ease, even simpatico, with Pericles and Brutus and Sir Philip Sidney, as Washington was with Lafayette.

This is chilly comfort, however, to the living members of an aristocracy in the act of dying. Under the southern Valhalla the torch has been thrust, already the bastions have fallen. Watching the flames mount, we, scattered remnant of the old dispensation, smile scornfully, but grieve in our hearts. A side-show Götterdämmerung perhaps, yet who shall inherit our earth, the earth we loved? The meek? The Hagens? In either event, we accept, but we do not approve.

My generation, inured to doom, wears extinction with a certain wry bravado, but it is just as well the older ones we loved are gone. They had lived, for the most part, through tragedy into poverty, which can be and usually is accomplished with dignity and a certain fine disdain. But when the last act is vulgarity, it is as hateful and confused a show as *Troilus and Cressida.*

During their last years Mère and Père lived with us most of the time. Père was ill a long while, but no one was very much interested. He had to sit in a dark room days on end, and there were no radios then or phonographs, and no one read to him. He rarely complained and seemed to know that those he loved were vital and busy with their living. I hope he remembered pleasant things most as he sat in the dark and awaited the end.

Nor was Mère spared. I suppose her strength was a temptation to death. No wonder we hate him so unforgivingly: his ways are humiliating and his approaches brutal. His indignities we fear, not him. Mère's heart gave way, she could not breathe, but she could not die. For months she fought. Being propped with pillows eased her a little. Mother was her nurse, for there were no hospitals or trained nurses in our county then, and Mother, because her heart was compassionate and her hands tender and knowing, was an excellent nurse. At last we had to set Mère bolt upright in a straight chair and tie her to its back so she would not topple over when the merciful moments of sleep came. One night she woke suffocating. Mother said: "It will be all right, it will pass. It's a little spell." But Mère gasped: "C'est la mort." Mother leaned to her and whispered: "Tu n'as pas peur?" Mère steadied herself on the arms of her chair and said distinctly and firmly: "Non." So death took her.

CHAPTER VII

A Small Boy's Heroes

Father and General Catchings and Captain McNeilly and Captain Wat Stone and Mr. Everman would forgather every so often on our front gallery. These meetings must habitually have taken place in summer, because I remember Mother would be in white, looking very pretty, and would immediately set about making a mint julep for the gentlemen—no hors d'œuvres, no sandwiches, no cocktails, just a mint julep. After the first long swallow—really a slow and noiseless suck, because the thick crushed ice comes against your teeth and the ice must be kept out and the liquor let in—Cap Mac would say: "Very fine, Camille, you make the best julep in the world." She probably did. Certainly her juleps had nothing in common with those hybrid concoctions one buys in bars the world over under that name. It would have been sacrilege to add lemon, or a slice of orange or of pineapple, or one of those wretched maraschino cherries. First you needed excellent bourbon whisky; rye or Scotch would not do at all. Then you put half an inch of sugar in the bottom of the glass and merely dampened it with water. Next, very quickly—and here was the trick in the procedure—you crushed your ice, actually powdered it, preferably in a towel with a wooden mallet, so quickly that it remained dry, and, slipping two sprigs of fresh mint against the inside of the glass, you crammed the ice in right to the brim, packing it with your hand. Last you filled the glass, which apparently had no room left for anything else, with bourbon, the older the better, and grated a bit of nutmeg on the top. The glass immediately frosted and you settled back in your chair for half an hour of sedate cumulative bliss. Although you stirred the sugar at the bottom, it never all melted, therefore at the end of the half hour there was left a delicious mess of ice and mint and whisky which a small boy was allowed to consume with calm rapture. Probably the anticipation of this phase of a julep was what held me on the outskirts of these meetings rather than the excitement of the discussion, which often I did not understand.

General Catchings was our congressman. He was short, with a fat stomach, a wide face, and heavy fat jowls. Yet he did not resemble Humpty Dumpty or Henry VIII. If I had not seen him I could not have believed that fat men could make tragic figures or that Burbage could have played Hamlet. He had a cold analytical mind of the first water, plus an arrogant integrity. His political weakness was that he could not kiss babies and considered it indecent to rhapsodize over the purity of Southern womanhood. So he was always about not to be re-elected. His English was all sinew and no color, his rare adjectives were like bullets, and he had some strange expressions of his own. He would say to Father: "It is bitter as gar-broth, LeRoy," and I would lose the rest of the discussion wondering what gar-broth might be. I never found out, but in my mind it was associated with those rueful liquors in which the sponge was dipped that they lifted to the lips of Jesus. I realized vaguely that he was always about to be crucified by the people for serving them so devoutly.

Cap Mac, for so we called Captain McNeilly, the editor of the local paper, was bitter too and old and tired and even poorer than the others, who were poor. He read Gibbon and Carlyle and Thucydides and Voltaire till all hours of the night, and his pen was dipped in gall. But he read also the New Testament and the *Sentimental Journey*, and when his heart was moved he could break yours. His paper was his own, hated by many and feared throughout the state, because he had a wrath like the Lord God's and words for the unrighteous in high places that withered and blasted. He loathed corruption and hated public iniquity. The intelligent few worshipped him, the unintelligent many scuttled for cover at the first hiss of his lash. We loved him for his weaknesses as much as for his strength, for his inability to manage his own affairs or his family, for his poor marksmanship when he was constantly being threatened with duels and assassinations, for his failure to appreciate beauty except in women, nature, food, and drink. Father was elated when, showing him a sizable copy of Canova's *Cupid and Psyche*, his sour and single comment was "Kind of raw." The very best brand of Puritan, simple and afraid, and unremittingly a fighter. He is completely forgotten now except by a few hold-overs from his world, soon to join him, and except by those who, delving into the archives of the Mississippi Historical Society, come wiith amazement across his articles on the reconstruction period, so trenchant, so accurate, so cold with fury.

Captain Wat and Mr. Everman were strophe and antistrophe to the tragic matters under way. Captain Wat had been a professor of Greek in Missouri before the war; he was sententious, moralizing, and a trifle eloquent. His bent was philosophizing on a situation instead of solving it. Mother, who was always dropping into and out of the discussions, would invariably grow impatient and exclaim: "Oh, Captain Wat, you never want to take sides. For heaven's sake, stop talking and decide"—which amused him. Mr. Everman agreed with her to the core of his being, because he was red-headed. I loved to watch him. He was incontestably the ugliest man in the world—tall, shambling, with tiny pale eyes, extravagant sandy eyebrows gone to seed, and a masterpiece of a nose that Ghirlandajo would have given his life to paint. He always suggested things vehemently, was always overruled, always accepted the adverse decision, and always concluded with: "Well, LeRoy, what do you say? I'm an old fool." They knew him to be sound of heart and character and it took only a little time to calm him down and start him off right, quivering with ardor and invective, sputtering the fire and smoke of righteousness from corner to corner of the little town, like a disjointed pinwheel.

In these parleys I recall the protagonists far better than the plot. Yet scraps of it come back to me: their hatred of Bryan and free silver; their adoration of Cleveland; their contempt for the nepotism of the then Governor; their determination to elect Captain Hunt sheriff because he was a gentleman and of course honest, courageous, and bankrupt; first, last, and always, their search for means to protect the country from overflow, which involved reelecting General Catchings to Congress and inducing the Governor to appoint able men on the local levee board. These were the men who, before I was a listener, bore the brunt of the Delta's fight against scalawaggery and Negro domination during reconstruction, who stole the ballot-boxes which, honestly counted, would have made every county official a Negro, who had helped shape the Constitution of 1890, which in effect and legally disfranchised the Negro, who still earlier had sent my grandfather to the legislature to help rid the state of "old Ames," the carpetbag Governor.

It is not what they discussed so much as how they discussed it that still makes those meetings so memorable to me—indeed, so epic. They were leaders of the people, not elected or self-elected, but destined, under the compulsion of leadership because of their superior intellect, training, character, and opportunity. And the people were willing to be led by them because of their desperate need of leadership in those tragic times, because they recognized their fitness to lead, tested and proved in the series of revealing crises that only began with the war, and because they came from the class which traditionally had led in the South. Applause or aggrandizement played no part in their calculations. They knew leadership was a burden, they knew there was no such thing in the long run as public gratitude for public service, they also knew that unless the intelligent disinterested few fought for good government, government would be bad.

Even at that time, however, the leadership of the wise and the good never went unchallenged. Rascals and grafters, ambitious men on the make and personal enemies fought them and what they stood for tirelessly and unceasingly. Then too the first trickle of poor whites from the hills into the Delta had already begun. It was often necessary to get in touch with Charlie Scott in Rosedale, Sam Neill in Indianola, the Farishes in Mayersville, and those amazing Kentuckians, Colonel Mat Johnson, Johnson Erwin, and Mr. Merritt Williams, down on the lake. If the matter were of national concern, Father would be delegated to go over to Yazoo for counsel with John Sharp

Williams, who loved him. Though they were decreasingly on the winning side, they were always live forces and rallying-points for righteousness, respected and greatly feared. When they lost, it was a public loss.

One particular local tragedy did much to undermine their prestige and influence. I was too young to understand it all, but I grew up knowing it was a terrible thing.

General Ferguson was one of their intimate friends and advisers and, further, he was the friend of General Wade Hampton, whose friendship was an accolade and a passport. He had been the beau ideal of a soldier, handsome, young, daring, adored by his men, with a record of brilliant military achievement which won him the rank of general at an age when others were lucky to be captains. His home was the center of frivolity and hospitality, famous in the countryside for high spirits and wit. I cannot recollect seeing the General himself when I was a little boy, but I climbed his kitchen roof, taunted to evil by his small daughter, who was a tartar, and I marveled at her older sister, Miss Natalie, galloping by in her long black velvet riding habit, by general consent the most dashing horsewoman in the Delta. In those poverty-stricken years the General was elected by his friends treasurer of the levee board, though he had neither aptitude for nor experience in business or accounting, besides being high-handed and utterly unmethodical. After some years Mr. Everman, secretary of the board and his close friend, checked the books and found him twenty thousand dollars short. It was unthinkable. He had always been a man of unimpeachable rectitude, of untarnished honor. And he had nothing to show for it: he did not gamble, he had no extravagant habits, his possessions were his home and a run-down plantation, both heavily mortgaged. He could give no explanation. Then, while the enemies of the old regime were in full hue and cry, and our people distracted, humiliated, and incredulous, he did the inexplicable, the unpardonable thing—he fled to South America.

It was recent history when I was scraping the bottom of mint-julep glasses, and it still rankled. He lived for years in exile with his family; then, the bitterness having diminished, his property having been seized and sold to pay his deficit, the rank and file having as usual forgotten, he drifted back to his own country and settled down in poverty and obscurity on the coast.

I went to college and law school, the world began to acquire that momentum commonly mistaken for progress, incidents like the disappearance of trust funds occurred daily and caused no special stir, and I don't suppose a dozen people in the town could have told you the Robertshaw house was once the Ferguson house. One cold night during the holidays we were giving a dinner party for some of my Eastern schoolmates—pretty girls and young men, pleased as cockerels. It was still the custom then to entertain at home. We were dressed in our giddiest as a dance was to follow. Mother and Father, at the ends of the table, were as usual in fine form and more fun than any of us. Unexpectedly a knock sounded at the front door. The colored waiter, who was also butler, answered it. We could feel the cold air from the open door and hear the scraps of a conversation that seemed to go on and on. I went out to see what the trouble was. In the light of the doorway against the blustery dark stood a little shabby old man in a gray suit and a bright red tie, his white hair untidy, his white beard untrimmed, with something childlike in his wide, vague, very blue eyes. He said: "Is LeRoy home?" I answered impatiently: "Yes, but—" "Tell LeRoy I must see him now." Father, joining us as he said these words, exclaimed softly: "Why, General Ferguson! Come in. Won't you have some dinner with us?" "Of course, LeRoy," murmured the little old man, and he came into the light still wide-eyed like a ghost, a ghost that is not afraid, but only uncertain, a ghost that can't remember. He sat down with those youngsters in their party clothes just as Banquo's ghost did, but mercifully they knew nothing and rattled on, though I could see Mother wanted to cry. He hardly touched his food and sat quietly, looking but not seeing, trying to remember something. Once he leaned to Father and said softly: "I have come back to go through those records. It was all a mistake. They will show everything was in order." Father said: "Of course, General."

For a month or more he haunted the courthouse and the levee board, pulling out the heavy record books, carrying them unsteadily to a desk, turning their pages backward and forward, and making notes. His presence in the town created little flurry. It had all been too long ago. At last he drifted away. He was mad.

People steal public funds now, but the public is cynical, no one is horrified, and the accused, guilty or innocent, seldom goes mad. Going mad for honor's sake presupposes honor. In our brave new world a man of honor is rather like the Negro—there's no place for him to go.

No one took l'affaire Ferguson more to heart than Mr. Merritt Williams, for he had loved the General and to the end of his days believed in his integrity. When the scandal was at its height, Mr. Merritt, small of stature, but of fabulous strength, was called to New Orleans and boarded the boat at Greenville. At supper he sat across the table from two strangers who began to disparage General Ferguson. Mr. Merritt said: "Gentlemen, I will ask you not to discuss the General." His manner was quiet, almost diffident, and his appearance belied his stoutness. The strangers looked him over and continued the tenor of their conversation. Mr. Merritt said, still more quietly: "Gentlemen, General Ferguson is my friend." The strangers ignored his warning. Mr. Merritt picked up his coffee-cup, a thick old-fashioned weapon weighing about a pound, and hurled it across the table. It hit one of the men squarely between the eyes and laid him low. Before the other could recover from his astonishment, Mr. Merritt was over and across the table and had fallen on him with murderous fists, one on the jaw finally putting him where he belonged. Then Mr. Merritt finished up with the first, who was recovering from the coffee-cup. When it was over, he flicked a crumb from his lapel, strolled forward, sweetly at peace, and watched the moonlight from the bow. The strangers were borne off at the next landing, on stretchers.

I asked Mr. Merritt about it years after when he was well over ninety. He was still diffident and said it was just a little personal matter.

Good men nowadays question what form of government is best and search like Plato for a formula, following which this benighted race of ours may automatically perfect itself. The Delta sages of my youth knew there was no such formula. Being convinced no system of government was good without good men to operate it, they considered it their bounden duty, their prime obligation as members of society, to find such men and elect them to office. Concerning democracy they had no illusions, their fears for it were prophetic; they esteemed it a poor makeshift, but the best devised by man for keeping the peace and at the same time permitting personal liberty. Their point of view, their sense of duty, their relentless striving, while certainly not appreciated or understood by me in my childhood, seeped into me, colored my outlook, prescribed for me loyalties and responsibilities that I may not disclaim—no, not though the sirens call and the flutes sound over the hill. Nor in this respect was my training unusual in the South of my generation. Anybody who was anybody must feel *noblesse oblige,* must concern himself with good government, must fight, however feebly or ineffectually or hopelessly, for the public weal. One of the first things I did after returning home from law school was to stump off to a mass meeting with Mr. Everman at which we read aloud bitter denunciations of a crime of violence. He thought that was the thing a man had to do, even if we were shot for it, as he believed we would be. And so did I. (When I started publishing verse Mr. Everman simply ignored it.)

During my day I have witnessed a disintegration of that moral cohesion of the South which had given it its strength and its sons their singleness of purpose and simplicity. Today there is fretting and fuming on the part of young people over what they should do, how they should act, what is worth while. Standards are in flux: there is no commonly accepted good way of life—and the hospitals can't hold the neurotics, the mental cripples, the moral anemics, the blasted who strove to build a pattern because none existed.

Epstein with his heads neurotic, restless, ugly, is the appropriate portraitist of this generation, but Cap Mac and Father and General Catchings would have been at home on the west portal of Chartres with those strong ancients, severe and formidable and full of grace, who guard the holy entrance.

What was the pattern that gave them strength and direction, that kept them oriented, that permitted them to be at once Puritans and Cavaliers? To recapture the recipe might give sustenance to the undernourished of these times, but I suspect, lacking pepper and tabasco, it would be unpalatable to my contemporaries.

Sipping the dregs of a julep among the patriarchs of Chartres with the Queen of Sheba in her summer dress shedding immortal grace—in what better way could a little boy learn that the austerities of living are not incompatible with the courtesy and sweetness of life? I never heard them over their juleps express a philosophy of life, and if I had it would have been incomprehensible to me, but a philosophy was implicit in all their thoughts and actions. It probably made the Southern pattern. Perhaps it is all contained in a remark of Father's when he was thinking aloud one night and I sat at his feet eavesdropping eagerly:

"I guess a man's job is to make the world a better place to live in, so far as he is able—always remembering the results will be infinitesimal—and to attend to his own soul."

I've found in those words directions enough for any life. Maybe they contain the steady simple wisdom of the South.

CHAPTER VIII

Learning from Teachers

The time came when Mother and Father had to decide on what might be termed my formal education. So far the only efforts of that sort had been Aunt Nana's piano lessons and Mère's instruction in French pronunciation. Neither was too successful. I developed a nice touch, a moderate ability to read notes, and a hatred for Aunt Nana because she would not permit me to step on the loud pedal during scales. But I was a lazy and ungifted musician. My French accent got me to Belgium and France during the war, and delighted no one after I arrived. Heaven help parents worrying over what to do with children a little out of the ordinary! It's a dark problem even with the recent assistance of Doctors Freud and Jung; when Mother and Father faced it they had to decide by ear. I was a sickly youngster who never had illnesses, who hated sports partly because they didn't seem important and mostly because I was poor at them, who knew better what I didn't want than what I did, who was sensitive but hard-headed, docile but given to the balks, day-dreamy but uncommunicative, friendly but not intimate—a frail problem-child, a pain in the neck. To make matters harder, the choice of what to do with me was restricted. I was too young to be sent to boarding school even if Father could have afforded it, there were no local private schools, and Mother had a wise intuition that, though I needed the rough and tumble of a public school, I didn't need as much as I'd get. In desperation they chose the local Roman Catholic convent for little boys and girls run by the Sisters of Mercy and started me off one September morning with a basket of lunch and no advice.

The first thing I learned there was the existence of evil. All the boys were herded together in the same classroom, presided over by Sister Evangelist, a midget of a nun with the valor and will-power of an Amazon, who taught every class, held prayers, occasionally larruped the wayward with the thin cane pointer she always carried, bullied, cajoled, and beguiled us unflaggingly and devotedly. But there was one boy she was afraid of, though I have seen her whirl into him dauntlessly and whip him until he whined. The oldest and biggest boy in the school, he was a monster of evil—cruel, nasty, bullying—with face and body so like Mansfield's Richard III that they published his qualities. All of us knew what he was and feared him. I once saw a rattlesnake in a bare spot of the woods coiled and rattling. That dry incessant hypnotic sound hushed the little sounds of the forest—bird-song, beetle-drone, wing-whir—the little things stood still and held their breath; you could hear the terrified silence. It was that way when this boy standing behind Sister faced us with some obscene pantomime: we were hypnotized with horror and helpless. A sickening lesson but a necessary one for those of us with third-rate bodies who insist on living uncowed in a world of evil. How cope with concrete active evil when your body is weak and the fear in your throat is like cold bile? How breathe the same air with the vicious who are strong? How fashion weapons against such a one and what shall the weapons be? If the gods are good, try charm; if not, try guile; both failing, try flight. Survival virtues, you know. Once there was another defense in vogue—every youth was taught the use of sword or firearms. In the South it was the pistol, as deadly in the hands of the little fellow as of the giant—and the little fellow made the poorer target. Many contend that if you fight with your fists well and honorably and are whipped, your self-respect is saved. Not mine. You meet a brute and a bully—what consolation is there in trying to knock his lights out and having your own dimmed in the effort? But with a pistol, ah! There are too many villains abroad, the well-disposed need breathing-space anyhow. Well, none of us little boys had pistols and our tormentor still lives, a wake of wickedness behind, a long life ahead. Left on his own, death has a poor sense of selection. Anyway, that boy started me thinking about defense weapons and I've thought a lot about them ever since.

Determination ranked high among Sister's virtues, and among other things she determined that mine was a likely soul and she was going to save it. I gave up; there was no use resisting; into her hands I committed my spirit. She would have succeeded in her determination had not I incautiously remarked one day to Mother, who was bending over an ailing Cape jessamine at the moment, that I had decided to become a priest. I had anticipated dismay but not indignation. Mother rose from the flower-bed to her full height, the height, say, of Lady Macbeth or Clytemnestra; too late under the solemn fillet I saw the scorn. But her only observation was that there was no excuse for talking like a fool at my age. I must have been an unbearable little prig. I do hope I've outgrown it. If not, it wasn't Mother's fault. I shouldn't blame Sister Evangelist for my unbridled mystic fervor at this time; evidently my ground was plowed and harrowed waiting for her sowing. I became intolerably religious, going to early mass at the slightest provocation, racking my brain to find something to confess once a month, praying inordinately, and fasting on the sly. It was infinitely trying to the family and so unexpected, so unlike anything in the case-history of any recorded member of the clan, French, English, or Scotch. I just couldn't help it, it was a violent attack, perhaps I've never fully recovered. Indeed, painful as it all was to the family, it was anguish and ecstasy, but mostly anguish, to me. I wanted so intensely to believe, to believe in God and miracles and the sacraments and the Church and everything. Also, I wanted to be completely and utterly a saint; heaven and hell didn't matter, but perfection did. Yet never, never for a moment, was my belief without doubt: the Satan of my disbelief was at my elbow scoffing, insinuating, arguing, day and night. I'm certain Shelley never sank upon the thorns of life and bled nearly so often as I did between ten and sixteen. To be at once intellectually honest and religious is a rack on which many have perished and on which I writhed dumbly, for I knew even then there were certain things which, like overwhelming physical pain, you must fight out alone, at the bottom of your own dark well, beyond ministration of assuagement or word of advice, incommunicado and leper-lonely. If you die it is natural; if you live you have learned pity and the strength of silence.

I didn't die, and, curiously enough, neither did Sister Evangelist. Only last year I saw her, and she must be approximately a hundred. Sister Scholastica, my old music teacher and the only teacher I ever feared because she was absolutely impervious to my charm, telephoned me and announced that I was a godless, ungrateful, heartless monster (she always telephoned that way, never giving her name and knowing I would recognize her voice and style), that Sister Evangelist was on her deathbed in Vicksburg, that she loved me more than any of her thousand pupils, that in my baseness I ignored her and would not even take the trouble to visit her, dying, in fact barely this side of rigor mortis. As usual I took Sister Scholastica's hint and dashed to Vicksburg. At the convent door a scared rabbit of a little nun asked my name and mission, suspiciously admitted me to the cool bare sitting-room, and left me there. There was a long pause during which I assumed they were propping up Sister Evangelist so that she could reach out feebly and blindly to give me her last blessing. It was pretty staggering, therefore, when Sister Evangelist came tripping in, unbent by her hundred years and vivacious as a cricket. She immediately loosed a diatribe of piety and invective, contrasting the promise of my past with the worm-eaten fruit of my present, and all with no more pause, punctuation, or capitalization than the last forty-six pages of *Ulysses*. At the first drop of a comma I got a word in edgewise: "Heavens, Sister! You talk as if God didn't have any sense of humor." She burst into gales of laughter, exclaiming: "Everybody forgets it; even I do sometimes," and the next two hours were chuckling gossip, singularly naïve and gay. The incident helps me to understand better why St. Francis would drop over to visit Santa Clara when he was tired, and to appreciate Fra Angelico's versions of walking all over God's heaven. Those two old ladies with Machiavellian heroism and saintly mendacity had made one last try at saving my soul.

Bless them, I wish they had succeeded!

So probably Mother was right when after two or three years she concluded the convent had done me all possible good but held possibilities of harm. After grievous cogitation she and Father chose as my next teacher Judge Griffin, who lived across the street and had never taught school. To church-goers he was the town atheist, which is only one more proof that the churches wouldn't recognize religion if they met it in the middle of the big road, for he was a saint. His house, where I went for lessons, was a turmoil of grandchildren, dogs, models of inventions, bundles of cotton lint, sacks of cottonseed (he was a great hybridizer), silkworms eating mulberry leaves and spinning cocoons, books on tables, on chairs, in stacks on the floor, and old furniture too big for its quarters, knee to knee everywhere—plus a raccoon. Judge Griffin's father had been the largest cottonland-owner in the world, before the war and the river destroyed his holdings, and he himself had studied at universities east and abroad and had gained knowledge of every world but this one, and much wisdom. Others had become rich from the gadgets he had invented for cotton gins and roller-skates while he became poorer and retired farther from community life into his own family and his own thoughts. With his silver hair and beautiful benign face I had long recognized him as a friend and was enchanted at the prospect of hobnobbing with him as a teacher. I anticipated golden hours and was not disappointed. We browsed and ranged and broke every law of pedagogy. He read me *Paradise Lost* and Cary's translation of the *Divine Comedy* and I perceived grandeur and nobility and heroic struggle, even when I didn't understand. We pondered and discussed the Doré illustrations, which I am told are pretty bad, but which we considered magnificent. He even told me a little about the epic he was writing, *Ruin Robed,* in which Napoleon replaced Lucifer; but I could never induce him to read it to me. And Shakespeare—but there a distressing memory intrudes. We were reading *Othello*—I must have been about ten—and it came over me horribly and deliciously during the first act that Iago's conversation was unadulterated smut. I certainly didn't understand it, but I sensed it, I knew in my soul it was pornography and I enjoyed it exquisitely. ("Je tremble délicieusement," sang Louise.) It was shortlived bliss; torture followed. Conscience pointed out unanswerably not only that my spasm of enjoyment was in itself sinful but that to continue reading such immorality would be willful and therefore mortal sin; furthermore that the excuse I offered of being only a pupil with no control over my teacher's assignment was false, insincere, and cowardly. Torn between what I knew to be my duty and a terrified shyness at mentioning such a thing, especially to my old mentor and friend, I presented myself to the Judge next morning resolute, dry-tongued, and sick through every inch of me. When he picked up his beloved volume of Shakespeare I said thickly but audibly: "I don't think we ought to read any more *Othello.* It's—it's immoral." My venerable master was speechless. He gazed uncertainly and a little mournfully at his chela. At length he said: "Iago does do some ugly talking. Maybe we'd better try *The Merchant of Venice.*" It was one of the two occasions in my life when I showed courage, and in such a poor cause. As usual the reward was incommensurate: *The Merchant of Venice* seemed tame, and still does.

Of Judge's pedagogy I recall little and that not to his credit. Struggling with my handwriting, he suggested that the best-looking hands were those in which the tall letters and the short letters approximated each other in height.

I should like to think that advice was the corrupting influence which, exfoliating in my subconscious, has rendered my script unintelligible to anyone, including myself, but I doubt it. As with all great teachers, his curriculum was an insignificant part of what he communicated. From him you didn't learn a subject, but life. I suspect anyway that the important things we learn we never remember because they become part of us, we absorb them. We don't absorb the multiplication tables (at least not the seventh and eleventh), but those things that are vitamins and calories to the spirit, the spirit seizes on and transmutes into its own strength, wholly and forgetfully. Tolerance and justice, fearlessness and pride, reverence and pity, are learned in a course on long division if the teacher has those qualities, as Judge Griffin had.

What with learning the eternal verities from my old friend and talking poetry instead of doing sums, Mother judged I was growing a trifle remote from ordinary doings. French, practical, opposed to excess even of virtue, she concluded a further change was needed in my scholastic career. So I was transferred to Father Koestenbrock, the parish priest, for mornings of French and Latin, and to Mr. Bass, superintendent of city schools, for afternoons of whatever else immature minds require.

Mr. Bass was red-haired except that he was bald, and he had the sort of pale eyes and vague pinkish features red-heads grow when they decide not to be beautiful. Almost everybody recognizes the temperament common to red-heads—irascibility, generosity, nervous energy, mental quickness, with just a touch of flightiness: Mr. Bass didn't miss a one. I wonder why when the obvious connection between the innards and out'ards of red-heads is generally conceded, it is doubted in people of slant eyes and yellow skins and flatly denied in people of kinky hair and black skins. Someone's always drawing the color line; now they won't let the Negro's interior be as individual as his exterior. I am told there is no relation between what you see of him and what there is of him: the only difference is a sort of hallucination in the eye of the beholder, he's a white man inside. Very like, very like. Mr. Bass, though, was different: his insides matched up perfectly with his outsides. He'd come storming into the classroom with a cocoon when I'd prepared with boundless boredom the lesson on Burke's *Speech on Conciliation,* and the hour would trip by gaily while he explained that the cocoon's poor inmate never got to be a person but was always a transition. Always a becoming, never a being—a sort of Bergson bug. One day he brought in a lunar moth, a fabulous thing of silver-white wings, lyre-shaped, with a breath of apple green over them and frugal markings of rose. Milton for all his headachy classical allusions was abandoned, though the ghost-creature was obviously just blown from the bosom of Demeter's lost daughter. Milton studied and Milton read were quite different, I found. Judge Griffin's was the only method. Poetry should never be taught.

Although a school-teacher from his youth, Mr. Bass, I believe, hated teaching and learning by textbook. He would sit on the edge of his chair as though about to leap up, and flop his knees together very fast as if a grasshopper's sound-box ought to be between them, and you knew he wanted to dart off somewhere and you knew going with him would be much more interesting than staying anywhere. Further, you had a definite hunch where he longed to be going—to his garden. It was the worst-looking garden I ever saw, with no design, no order, really no sense, a hodge-podge of flowers and vegetables. But everything grew there and throve and bloomed as it did nowhere else. He had no preferences: a carrot was as dear as a peony, a black-eyed Susan as a rose; it only mattered that they were living things mysteriously standing in the earth and reaching for the sun. The mystery was everything to him. I never knew a heart so capable of wonder, though of an earthy unmaudlin sort. When soaked with sweat and dabbed with dirt from digging, his ugliness rather resembled Pan's—not the maligned Pan of the nymphs, but that gaunt mysterious god of flocks and herds, of crops and weathers that rustics worshipped. The rustic Pan in him made his garden for use, not looks. Any morning, if you were an early riser, you could catch a glimpse of him hatless, dirty, untidy, a basket bulging with green things under his arm, and on the run. He dropped into people's front yards unbeknownst and planted unpredictable things—iris and tulips of course, but just as likely salvia against a brick wall. Even more secretive were his vegetable errands. Before anyone was out or up, he'd leave heaps of them—tomatoes, corn, okra, and the like—on the back steps of his friends or preferably of the unknown and sensitive poor. Many a family he half supported whose name he never knew.

All of this by some unaccountable transmutation got itself into his teaching. The way he scuttled in and out of the classroom caused a draught, and if you'd seen grass growing from his ears you wouldn't have noticed. Yet he had principles and ideas galore and never hesitated to express them, no matter how hostile the audience. His vehemence was infectious and you knew he was right when you knew he was wrong.

One summer he took me out West—my first real trip. He was an ideal traveling companion. He had the gift of being informal without being intimate, and his eyes and ears were born anew every half hour. We drove in a stagecoach behind ten span of horses from Flagstaff to the Grand Canyon and I almost died happy at the sight of it. It is God's most personal creation; you feel He's just walked off and is expected back any minute. But of course Mr. Bass in his heart of hearts preferred the flower fields and enormous forests of California.

He wasn't Mississippi-born. To be accurate, he was earth-born but he hailed from a farm in Missouri—a farm, not a plantation. His people farmed not to make money but to live well, and they succeeded, not only in that respect but in developing character, individuality, and easy-going self-respect. Many such are scattered over all the states of the South and they constitute its greatest hope. They were here before the Civil War, they will be here when wars have ceased. They, the aristocrats, and the Negroes are the only three classes in the South of which God must be proud. Mr. Bass was plain through and through and rich and unadulterated. Wherever he is sleeping he is thinking how good the earth is and wondering what flowers are just overhead.

Father Koestenbrock and I were rather cronies anyway, he having heard every confession I'd ever made, having given me my first communion and prepared me for confirmation, and, not least, having talked to me about his plans for the new church. He was not a saint and nothing shocked him. I used to peep at him through the confessional grille and he seemed half asleep, only he couldn't have been because he was too big and fat for his side of the confessional and it must have been uncomfortable. He never was interested in my sins and I believe if I had whispered: "I killed Aunt Nana with the butcher knife because she wouldn't let me hold down the loud pedal!" he would have replied: "Say ten decades of your beads, go in peace, and sin no more." Maybe it all came from his being Dutch, a Dutch nobleman. When he said in a special tone "my native city of Haarlem," you smelled great quantities of rich food and the bouquet of four different wines and saw fat strong women in layers of petticoats prodding among piles of red cheeses.

Naturally, he smoked a huge meerschaum pipe which it had taken him twenty years to color a dull Rembrandt gold and which rested on the first pleat of his stomach when he settled back in his chair and said unromantically: "Give the present tense of *amo*." If you didn't, believe me, the very furniture rocked until it looked to be drawn by Van Gogh, and like a car of Juggernaut he lumbered over you and you stayed flattened out until he relented. The thing to do during such a cataclysm was to figure ways of diverting the conversation to Haydn—not always easy. That quieted him and presently he'd be laughing like a Frans Hals, exclaiming: "Ach! Haydn! He knew more than all the rest. Chopin—sick! Beethoven—too religious! Mozart—too elegant! But Haydn—that is music, happy and sober, sane as sunshine!"

With any kind of tact and luck he could then be led to analyze Rubens's *Descent from the Cross* and Raphael's *Christ and Saint Veronica*, engravings of which "from the old country" hung on the walls of his study, or to discourse on Dutch Gothic, the style of architecture he'd chosen for the church he was determined to build. I don't understand how his love of Haydn taught him to sing high mass, but something did, and more understandingly and movingly and musically than ever I heard it sung. The magical melodic line of his Pater Noster with its earnestness and pleading could keep you holy for a week.

But ordinarily in religious matters he was earth-treading like Mère: he was not one to receive the stigmata. Once I thought he failed to see a delicate spiritual point with almost willful obtuseness. I had gone to confession in the afternoon preparatory to Holy Communion at early mass next morning. That night I felt so sanctified that at some mundane intrusion I lost my temper and answered back with more than asperity. It was a bad night I passed, thinking over my sin and debating how I could take communion with it unshriven. Mass had started when I entered the church, so there was no chance for a word with Father beforehand. He knew every member of his little flock and had clearly in mind those who were to take communion that morning. The moment arrived, he stood with the host facing the congregation, and the communicants, in-drawn and bowed, walked up the aisle to the communion rail. I stayed where I was, miserably. Then the unforeseen, the impossible happened. When he had given the host to the last communicant, he looked over the church as if searching for someone, saw me, and, standing before the high altar, in full view of the congregation, motioned me to come to the rail. I went up the aisle alone and conspicuous, knelt at the rail alone and conspicuous, and when he bent over me with the host, whispered: "I can't take communion," turned and walked back to my seat. It took every ounce of courage in my whole being. After mass Father called me to the sacristy and demanded an explanation. I explained. He looked as if he wanted to box my ears and blurted out: "Ach! Don't act like a fool. Kneel. Say an act of contrition," and placed the wafer between my lips. His manner worried me, but it never crossed my mind I wasn't right. It never does.

Père said Father Koestenbrock's French accent was painfully Dutch, which infuriated me as it smacked of disloyalty, though doubtless his French was no better than his English, and I knew it. By temperament I'm afraid I'm partisan and attain impartiality, if ever, only by an effort of will. However Dutch Father's French *r's* and *n's,* his enthusiasm for certain phases of French literature would have done credit to a French curé. He adored Bossuet and Fénelon, and when he started reading aloud the *Oraisons funèbres* or *Télémaque* with spacious eloquence, there was no telling when he'd desist. I would be bowed with boredom, for they seemed to me in spite of the rolling periods about as unctuous and self-satisfied as *Sandford and Merton* (one of Mur's less inspired selections).

Every six months or so I would come for lessons and find him sitting in his bedroom instead of the study, without pipe or glasses, and in his undershirt. He would look at me dully and from a distance and say thickly: "Go away." At home Mother would explain Father was sick again, but she would be visibly upset and a little angry. He would be sick for several weeks. At first I didn't understand, but after a while it came to me one way or another that my teacher was on a drunk. Drunkenness was bad and Father wasn't bad—my first lesson in reconciling the irreconcilable. The immature must be ruthless and intolerant while their own uncertain inner principles and ideals are hardening into the patterns within which they must enact their own future dramas. We must demand of them much, but not tolerance. Father did nothing improper or public, he just stayed drunk in his room, alone, for weeks and weeks. I would have hated another priest for doing the same thing, it would have been immoral and disgraceful. But Father was not immoral, he was good. Suddenly I experienced the beginning of wisdom. Father was lonely, he never would be or could be anything else. Realizing that hurt me a lot. But I thought Father was single and unique in his loneliness: it was only the beginning of wisdom.

As he grew older and tired, he became impatient about

his new church. He ordered the plans, and for a year or more studied and changed and caressed them. His congregation being poor and he a most shy collector of pew-rent, the building fund remained stationary. He talked of visiting his native city of Haarlem, but always found some excuse for not going. At last to everyone's astonishment he announced that the contract for the building of the church had been let. How could it be paid for? The congregation was in a flurry. But he was gay as Papa Haydn and busy, busy from morning to night. The contractor he selected was an elderly German, a proud fine craftsman, with a fiendish temper and an unquenchable thirst. Then began two years of heroic battle: the two old gentlemen fought all over the place, about every item and detail, they throve and battened on the conflict, you could hear them high up in the scaffolding in outbursts of bilingual denunciation that would have done credit to Michelangelo and the Pope. At last the building was completed, the yellow brick walls, the Gothic windows and arches, the rather stumpy steeple of gray slate—a little Dutch Gothic church, well built, homey, in good taste. And the congregation began to inquire about the mortgage. There would be no mortgage. Father had paid for it all himself. His patrimony, hoarded by a prudent Dutch father to protect the old age of his son, had gone into his church, every nickel of it, and he was happy and old and penniless.

The loneliness came back on him, stronger than ever, and there was nothing much to live for. He was an old man and very tired. So he gave up his parish and retired to a home for superannuated priests on the coast, leaving his little church and us. He'd done his best with both. He returned once years afterwards during our Ku Klux fight, and he was glad to be home. He and I talked about things for hours. At last I said:

"This is the only time within a year that two people have talked in this county for as long as we have without mentioning the Ku Klux Klan. What do you think of the Klan, Father?"

"I do not think of it," he replied. "The Church has been here a long time; it will be here a much longer time, after all these klans and foolish things are forgotten. And it is good for the Church. You remember Luther. The Church was rotten in his day, it needed to be attacked. Old Luther made the Church cleanse herself. So now. The Knights of Columbus, worthy souls, became filled with their own importance during the war and did a great deal of foolish bragging. The Klan will bring them to their senses. It is a very good thing for the Church." He rose to go. We knew we should never see each other again. He looked at me, but his voice was matter-of-fact:

"You always had a spiritual nature. As a little boy you were almost a saint. I–I never had a spiritual nature. I only tried my best." I was never so shamed.

Judge Griffin, Mr. Bass, Father Koestenbrock–their names are being forgotten in our little town, the town where they lived. They have gone the way we all take and they left no mark on the world. But before I join them, I bear testimony they left shining marks on one little boy's heart that shine still.

CHAPTER IX

Sewanee

I had been exposed to enough personalities mellow and magnificent to educate a Hottentot and in the process I had somehow received enough formal instruction to condition me for college. Fafar and his brothers had gone to Princeton, Father and his brothers to Sewanee (The University of the South, an Episcopal institution) and to Virginia Law School. Where I should go no one knew, least of all myself, so because it was fairly near and healthy and genteel and inexpensive, Father and Mother drew a long sigh, set me on the train bound for Sewanee, and betook themselves to Europe with Mr. Cook, on their first foreign tour. I was fifteen plus one month, in short trousers, small, weakly, self-reliant, and ignorant as an egg. I had the dimmest notion of how children were born though I knew it required a little co-operation; I had never heard of fraternities, I had never read a football score, I had never known a confidant or been in love. My instructions had been to enter the preparatory school, which was military, but I watched the grammar-school boys in their dusty ill-kept uniforms and I suspected they smelled bad. I developed an antipathy to the military life—which I've never overcome—and so, to the astonishment of the college authorities, I presented myself to them for entrance exams, and passed.

By no means brilliant, I studied hard, often getting up at six, to the scandal of other students, to struggle with Latin and math, and I made excellent grades. I don't know why I studied hard, but I had no shadow of a doubt it was the thing to do. English was my favorite course, whether because of the huge undigested gobs of the best I'd already read or because of Dr. Henneman, it would be hard to guess. He was passionate, black-bearded, bespectacled, with an adoration for *Beowulf*, Chaucer, Shakespeare, a grimace for Dr. Donne and the metaphysical school (oh, woeful unshakable influence), and, much more important, a capacity for furious moral tantrums in which, his beard on end clear out to his ears, he would beat the desk with his fist and roar:

"My God, gentlemen, *do* something!" We earnestly intended to, after such a scene.

And the other great course of those days was Dr. DuBose's Ethics. He was a tiny silver saint who lived elsewhere, being more conversant with the tongues of angels than of men. Sometimes sitting on the edge of his desk in his black gown, talking haltingly of Aristotle, he would suspend, rapt, in some mid air beyond our ken, murmuring: "The starry heavens—" followed by indefinite silence. We, with a glimpse of things, would tiptoe out of the classroom, feeling luminous, and never knowing when he returned to time and space.

It was a small college, in wooded mountains, its students drawn from the impoverished Episcopal gentry of the South, its boarding-houses and dormitories presided over by widows of bishops and Confederate generals. Great

Southern names were thick—Kirby-Smith, Elliott, Quintard, Polk, Gorgas, Shoup, Gailor. The only things it wasn't rich in were worldly goods, sociology, and science. A place to be hopelessly sentimental about and to unfit one for anything except the good life.

Until I came to Sewanee I had been utterly without intimates of my own age. I had liked children whose pleasures were my pleasures, but they had not been persons to me and had left no mark. Here I suddenly found myself a social being, among young creatures of charm and humor, more experienced than I, but friendly and fascinating. I was never generally popular, but I had more than my share of friends. I am never surprised at people liking me, I'm always surprised if they don't. I like them and, if they don't like me, I feel they've made a mistake, they've misunderstood something. There's so much backing and filling about getting acquainted—indirection confuses and sometimes deceives me.

Probably because of my size and age and length of trouser I was plentifully adopted. It is a long time now: some of them have gone the journey, others have fallen by the road and can't go on and are just waiting, and a few have won through to autumn. But then the springtime was on them and they taught and tended me in the greenwoods as the Centaurs did Achilles—I don't know how I ever recovered to draw my own bow. Percy Huger, noble and beautiful like a sleepy St. Bernard; Elliott Cage, full of dance-steps and song-snatches, tender and protective, and sad beneath; Paul Ellerbe, who first read me *Dover Beach,* thereby disclosing the rosy mountain-ranges of the Victorians; Harold Abrams, dark and romantic with his violin, quoting the *Rubáiyát* and discoursing Shaw; Parson Masterson, jostling with religion, unexpected and quaint; Sinkler Manning, a knight who met a knight's death at Montfaucon; Arthur Gray, full of iridescence, discovering new paths and views in the woods and the world; Huger Jervey, brilliant and bumptious then, brilliant and wise now, and so human; and more, many more, all with gifts they shared with me, all wastrel creditors who never collected. Peace to them, and endless gratitude.

I suppose crises occurred, problems pressed, decisions had to be made, those four shining years, but for me only one altered the sunlight. Once a month I would ride ten miles down the wretched mountain road to Winchester, go to confession, hear mass, and take communion. I had been thinking, I had never stopped thinking, I was determined to be honest if it killed me. So I knelt in the little Winchester church examining my conscience and preparing for confession. How it came about did not seem sudden or dramatic or anything but sad. As I started to the confessional I knew there was no use going, no priest could absolve me, no church could direct my life or my judgment, what most believed I could not believe. What belief remained there was no way of gauging yet. I only knew there was an end, I could no longer pretend to myself or cry: "Mea culpa. Help Thou mine unbelief." It was over, and forever. I rode back to the leafy mountain mournful and unregretful, knowing thenceforth I should breathe a starker and a colder air, with no place to go when I was tired. I would be getting home to the mountain, but for some things there was no haven, the friendly Centaurs couldn't help: from now on I would be living with my own self.

There's no way to tell of youth or of Sewanee, which is youth, directly; it must be done obliquely and by parable. I come back to the mountain often and see with a pang, however different it may be to me, it is no different, though Huger and Sinkler and I are forgotten. Then with humility I try to blend and merge the past and the present, to reach the unchanging essence. To my heart the essence, the unbroken melodic theme, sounds something like this:

The college has about three hundred young men or inmates, or students as they are sometimes called, and besides, quite a number of old ladies, who always were old and ladies, and who never die. It's a long way away, even from Chattanooga, in the middle of woods, on top of a bastion of mountains crenelated with blue coves. It is so beautiful that people who have once been there always, one way or another, come back. For such as can detect apple green in an evening sky, it is Arcadia—not the one that never used to be, but the one that many people always live in; only this one can be shared.

In winter there is a powder of snow; the pines sag like ladies in ermine, and the other trees are glassy and given to creaking. Later, arbutus is under the dead leaves where they have drifted, but unless you look for it betimes, you'll find instead puffs of ghost caught under the higher trees, and that's dogwood, and puffs of the saddest color in the world that's tender too, and that's redbud, which some say is pink and some purple and some give up but simply must write a poem about. The rest of the flowers you wouldn't believe in if I told you, so I'll tell you: anemones and hepaticas and blood-root that troop under the cliffs, always together, too ethereal to mix with reds and yellows or even pinks; and violets everywhere, in armies. The gray and purple and blue sort you'll credit, but not the tiny yellow ones with the bronze throats, nor the jack-rabbit ones with royal purple ears and faces of pale lavender that stare without a bit of violet modesty. If you've seen azalea—and miscalled it wild honeysuckle, probably—you still don't know what it is unless you've seen it here, with its incredible range of color from white through shell pink to deep coral (and now and then a tuft of orange that doesn't match anything else in the whole woods), and its perfume actually dangerous, so pagan it is. After it you'd better hunt for a calacanthus with brown petals (what else likes its petal brown?) and a little melancholy in its scent, to sober you. We call our bluets "innocence," for that's what they are. They troop near the iris, which when coarsened by gardens some call fleur-de-lis, and others, who care nothing about names, flags. Our orchids we try to make respectable by christening them "lady-slippers," but they still look as if they had been designed by D. H. Lawrence—only they're rose- and canary-colored.

After Orion has set—in other words, when the most fragile and delicate and wistful things have abandoned loveliness for fructifying—the laurel, rank and magnificent for all its tender pink, starts hanging bouquets as big as hydrangeas on its innumerable bushes. But on moonlight nights there's no use trying to say it isn't a glory and a madness! And so the summer starts—summer, when we're not seraph-eyed enough to see flowers even if there were any. In the fall, when our souls return, a little worse off, a little snivelly, there are foggy wisps of asters whose quality only a spider would hint at aloud, and in the streams where the iris forgathered there are parnassia, the snowdrop's only kin. Mountain-folk alone have seen their virginal processions, ankle-deep in water, among scarlet leaves, each holding a round green shield and carrying at the end of a spear, no thicker than a broomstraw, a single pale green star. Last, chilly and inaccessible and sorrowful, in the damp of the deep woods, come the gentians, sea-blue and hushed.

Now all these delights the Arcadians not infrequently neglect. You might stroll across the campus and quadrangles of a sunny afternoon and guess from the emptiness and warm quiet there that they had gone out among the trees, lying perhaps in shadow, idly, like fauns, and whistling at the sky. Some may be so unoccupied, though not faun-like to themselves. But more I fear will be amiably and discreetly behind closed doors on the third floor, playing not flutes or lyres or even saxophones, but poker. Still others will be bowed over a table, vexed to the soul with the return of Xenophon or the fall, too long delayed, of a certain empire. A few will be off in the valley bargaining for a beverage called mountain-dew with a splendid virile old vixen who in that way has always earned a pleasant livelihood. Later they will have consumed their purchase to the last sprightly drop and will be bawling out deplorable ballads and pounding tables and putting crockery to uncouth noisy uses in the neighborhood of one or another of the old ladies, who will appear scandalized as expected, but who in the privacy of her own chamber will laugh soundlessly till her glasses fall off on her bosom and have to be wiped with a handkerchief smelling of orris-root.

Yet I would not have you think that the Arcadians are all or always ribald. Even those with a bacchic turn are full of grace and on occasion given to marvels. I myself have witnessed one of them in the ghastly dawn, slippered and unpantalooned, his chaplet a wet towel, sitting in the corner of his room, his feet against the wall, quite alone, reading in a loud boomy voice more beautiful than chimes *Kubla Khan* and the *Ode to a Nightingale.* One afternoon of thick yellow sunshine I was audience to another who stood on an abandoned windlass with tulip trees and a blue vista for backdrop reciting pentameters, which though you may never have heard, we thought too rich and cadenced for the race of men ever to forget. I can remember them even now for you:

I dreamed last night of a dome of beaten gold
To be a counter-glory to the Sun.
There shall the eagle blindly dash himself,
There the first beam shall strike, and there the Moon
Shall aim all night her argent archery;
And it shall be the tryst of sundered stars,
The haunt of dead and dreaming Solomon;
Shall send a light upon the lost in hell,
And flashings upon faces without hope—
And I will think in gold and dream in silver,
Imagine in marble and in bronze conceive,
Till it shall dazzle pilgrim nations
And stammering tribes from undiscovered lands,
Allure the living God out of the bliss,
And all the streaming seraphim from heaven.

Perhaps a poet whose dear words have died should be content if once, no matter how briefly, they have made two lads in a greenwood more shimmery and plumed.

Nights, spring nights in special, temper and tune the Arcadian soul to very gracious tintinnabulations. Three Arcadians on one occasion, I recall, sat through the setting of one constellation after another on a cliff in the tender moonlight with a breathing sea of gray and silver tree-tops beneath them and discussed the possibility and probability of God. One, upholding the affirmative, announced that he needed no proof of divinity beyond the amethyst smudge on the horns of the moon. This was countered by the fact that this purple lay not in the moon itself but in the observer's eyes. The deist, troubled, at last concluded anyway he'd rather be a god looking out than look out at a god. Only this was all said with humor and a glistening eagerness—a sort of speech I could once fall into, but long ago.

Myself one of these mountain dwellers for four years, I

have observed them, off and on, for thirty more. It is to be marveled at that they never change. They may not be quite the same faces or the precise bodies you met a few years back, but the alterations are irrelevant—a brown eye instead of a blue one, a nose set a little more to the left. The lining is the same. Neither from experience nor observation can I quite say what they learn in their Arcadia, though they gad about freely with books and pads. Indeed, many of them attempt to assume a studious air by wearing black Oxford gowns. In this they are not wholly successful, for, no matter how new, the gowns always manage to be torn and insist on hanging from the supple shoulders with something of a dionysiac abandon. Further, even the most bookish are given to pursuing their studies out under the trees. To lie under a tree on your back, overhead a blue and green and gold pattern meddled with by the idlest of breezes, is not—despite the admirable example of Mr. Newton—conducive to the acquisition of knowledge. Flat on your stomach and propped on both elbows, you will inevitably keel and end by doting on the tint of the far shadows, or, worse, by slipping into those delightful oscillations of consciousness known as cat-naps. I cannot therefore commend them for erudition. So it is all the more surprising that in after years the world esteems many of them learned or powerful or godly, and that not infrequently they have been the chosen servitors of the destinies. Yet what they do or know is always less than what they are. Once one of them appeared on the first page of the newspapers because he had climbed with amazing pluck and calculated foolhardiness a hitherto unconquered mountain peak, an Indian boy his only companion. But what we who loved him like best to recall about that exploit is an inch cube of a book he carried along with him and read through—for the hundredth time, likely—before the climb was completed. It was *Hamlet*. Another is immortal for cleansing the world of yellow fever, but the ignorant half-breeds among whom he worked remember him now only for his gentleness, his directness without bluntness, his courtesy which robbed obedience of all humiliation. Still others I understand have amassed fortunes and—to use a word much reverenced by my temporal co-tenants—succeeded. That success I suspect was in spite of their sojourn in our greenwoods. The Arcadians learn here—and that is why I am having such difficulty telling you these things—the imponderables. Ears slightly more pointed and tawny-furred, a bit of leafiness somewhere in the eyes, a manner vaguely Apriline—such attributes though unmistakable are not to be described. When the Arcadians are fools, as they sometimes are, you do not deplore their stupidity, and when they are brilliant you do not resent their intellectuality. The reason is, their manners—the kind not learned or instilled but happening, the core being sweet—are far realer than their other qualities. Socrates and Jesus and St. Francis and Sir Philip Sidney and Lovelace and Stevenson had charm; the Arcadians are of that lineage.

What Pan and Dionysos and the old ladies dower them with is supplemented by an influence which must appear to the uninitiated incompatible. By the aid of a large bell jangled over their sleeping heads from the hands of a perambulating Negro, the Arcadians at seven each morning are driven, not without maledictions, to divine service. A minute before the chapel bell stops ringing, if you happen to be passing, you may imagine the building to be on fire, for young men are dashing to it from every corner of the campus, many struggling with a collar or tie or tightening a belt in their urgent flight. But at the opening of the first hymn you'll find them inside, seated in rows, as quiet as love-birds on a perch. More quiet, in fact: as the service progresses you might well mistake their vacuity for devotion unless you happen to notice the more nocturnal souls here and there who, sagging decorously, have let the warm sleep in.

Nevertheless, the Arcadians add to their list of benefactors those elderly gentlemen about King James who mistranslated certain Hebrew chronicles and poems into the most magnificent music the human tongue has ever syllabled. In their litanies should be named no less those others (or were they the same?) who wrote the Book of Common Prayer. Each morning these young men hear floating across their semi-consciousness the sea-surge of their own language at its most exalted—clean and thunderous and salty. Some of the wash of that stormy splendor lodges in their gay shallows, inevitably and eternally. Who could hear each morning that phrase "the beauty of holiness" without being beguiled into starrier austerities? If someone daily wished that the peace of God and the fellowship of the Holy Ghost might be with you always, could it help sobering and comforting you, even if God to you were only a gray-bearded old gentleman and the Holy Ghost a dove? Suppose you had never rambled from the divine path farther than the wild-rose hedge along its border, still would not the tide of pity for the illness of things rise in your heart at hearing: "We have wandered and strayed from Thy ways like lost sheep"? Lusty Juventus hereabouts may reflect and forget that there was a modern spiciness in the domestic difficulties of David, but it treasures unforgettably: "The heavens declare the glory of God, and the firmament sheweth His handiwork," and "He maketh me to lie down in green pastures, He leadeth me beside the still waters." Such glistening litter is responsible, perhaps, for the tremulous awe and reverence you find in the recesses of the Arcadian soul—at least you can find them if you are wary and part very gently the sun-spotted greenery of Pan.

Girders and foundations are fine things; and necessary, no doubt. It is stated on authority that the creaking old world would fly into bits without them. But after all what I like best is a tower window. This hankering is an endless source of trouble to me and I like to think to myself, in defense, that it comes from having lived too long among mountain-folk. For they seem always to be leaning from the top of their tower, busy with idle things; watching the leaves shake in the sunlight, the clouds tumble their soundless bales of purple down the long slopes, the seasons eternally up to tricks of beauty, laughing at things that only distance and height reveal humor in, and talking, talking, talking—the enchanting unstained silver of their voices spilling over the bright branches down into the still and happy coves. Sometimes you of the valley may not recognize them, though without introduction they are known of each other. But if some evening a personable youth happens in on your hospitality, greets you with the not irreverent informality reserved for uncles, puts the dowager Empress of Mozambique, your houseguest, at her ease, flirts with your daughter, says grace before the evening meal with unsmiling piety, consumes every variety of food and drink set before him (specializing on hot biscuits) with unabashed gusto, leaves a wake of laughter whenever he dips into the conversation, pays special and apparently delighted attention to the grandmother on his left, enchants the serving maid with two bits and a smile, offers everyone a cigarette, affable under the general disapproval, sings without art a song without merit, sits at last on the doorstep in the moonlight, utterly content, with the dreamy air of the young

Hermes (which only means the sense of impending adventure is about his hair like green leaves), and then if that night you dream of a branch of crab-apple blossoms dashed with rain—pursue that youth and entreat him kindly. He hails from Arcady.

CHAPTER X

A Year Abroad

Arcadia no more. But what next? Father thought I'd overstudied and I was undoubtedly puny, so a year's respite from schooling seemed advisable. But how employ it? Had there been dude ranches in those days I don't doubt I should have landed on the back of a broncho and swung a lariat with the worst of them, but thank God they were still in the womb of time along with movies. From first childhood I had saved every penny of birthday and Christmas money for a trip abroad. It was my obsession, my one mundane objective—and I had amassed five hundred dollars. Here was my great opportunity; so, Mother and Father dubiously consenting, I seized it.

They traveled to Paris with me and uneasily sought respectable quarters I could afford. Our choice wasn't a triumph. It was a third-floor room in what was coyly termed a hotel, on the rue de Vaugirard, opposite the Senate. French rooms can smell damper and look dowdier in a pretentious way than any in the world. (In comparison the cabins on my plantation seem air-conditioned, riant, and functional.) Mine contained a thick bed curtained in morose red with coarse linen sheets eternally damp; the sparse furniture, though stuffed and overstuffed, was neither sittable nor lyable, and a quiet moist dinginess exuded, from the walls like mold or gangrene. It was fit habitat for a rubber plant, and its tutelary deity was Marie, the homeliest femme de chambre in Paris and scatter-brained to boot. I added hopefully a small upright piano and bought boulets for the tiny fireplace, but that room never attained cosiness or even comfort. Its sole recommendation was the rental, which came to exactly eight dollars a month, not including Marie's tip.

So far as I could detect, I had only two co-lodgers: a desperately poor medical student, a Pole, and a blowzy girl whom I sometimes passed on the dark stinking stairway as she started on her professional rounds. The Pole and I finally spoke, but as I didn't recognize his "Varsovie" as among my geographical familiars nor he my "Paderewski" as an entity of Polish affiliation, we didn't progress far. Nevertheless once a month we found our way together to the Concerts Rouges, each paying his own admission and fifty centimes for a vile concoction with a cherry in it. Looking back I know he was a courageous noble creature and we could have meant much to each other. He and Marie taught me a great and needed lesson in compassion. I had the American contempt for whores, but they never referred to the blowzy young girl as anything except "la pauvre" and were sorry for her when business was bad. My only real intimate was the charming old lady who collected fifty centimes at the cabinet d'aisance opposite the Luxembourg. We met every lucky morning and exchanged pleasantries, she dignified and very sage, because, I suppose, of her unimpeded opportunities for observation.

Even at this age I had great affection for the world and did not want to miss any of its beauties. This obligated me to appreciate whatever men of taste and heart found lovely, which in turn drove me to study, to school my eyes and ears, to train the sensitive and unruly bondsman in my body. I attended free lectures at the Sorbonne along with Russians and Poles who could find no other place to keep warm in this piercing French winter, and I hoarded every cent for theaters, concerts, and operas. To please Father, I joined—and this still doesn't sound true—a fencing school. The results were meager. I developed my single visible muscle on the inside of my right leg, for which I have never since found any use, and one of my fellow students opened my eyes to the possibility of conjugal infelicity by referring to his wife as "un sac." I practiced hours on my tinkly piano, the only hard practicing I ever did, and it seems sad my assiduity was expended on Mendelssohn's *Songs without Words.* Every Sunday afternoon found me at the Concerts Colonne or Lamoureux sitting on the floor of the top balcony amid bespectacled music students out of the Ark with scores in their laps. At the Comique the fabulous Mary Garden was singing Mélisande and Louise, and at the Opéra Bréval was looking exactly like Brunhilde. Bernhardt was still doing Tosca and Phèdre, the Odéon as usual was putting on *L'Arlésienne,* and Bartet and Sorel were declaiming shapely lifeless hexameters at the Comédie. Réjane's homeliness and style were exquisite though her plays on the eternal French theme were a trifle disturbing to my American Puritanism. I adored all French actresses and considered all French actors conceited and artificial.

My best hours, though, were the many I spent in the Luxembourg Gardens. Having paid two sous to the wretched perambulatory old shrew for a comfortless iron chair, I would drag it against one of the big boxes holding a pomegranate bush, tilt back, and read aloud, for the good it would do my accent, *La Cousine Bette* and *Salammbô*. You may have read Proust and Villon, Racine and Rabelais, you may have lived a year in Tours, you may have drunk Vouvray and eaten escargots and *tripes à la mode de Caen*, you may have scrutinized Mont Saint-Michel, the Eiffel Tower, and the Musée Cluny, you may have visited the tomb of Napoleon, you may have slept with ten cocottes and got lost in the Métro, but you still haven't halfway understood France and the French unless you have loitered hours and hours in the Luxembourg Gardens in autumn.

I was talking to a Japanese gentleman once after I'd come from weeks of prayerful solitude at Nikko, steeped still in the dream of its vast cryptomerias, its gold and scarlet temples, its terraces rising higher and higher to unexpected *torii* and tombs, its fantastic bell-towers and stone lanterns, its pools and rivulets, its guardian beasts and writhing gods, its limpid gloom and exalted airiness, and I questioned him concerning the miracle of its creation. He answered:

"What is most abhorrent to the Japanese soul is obvious plan. The expected is uninteresting. Plan, of course, there must be, so subtle it is concealed, so imaginative it appears unplanned. Axes and balances, geometrical design, formal arrangement—anyone can learn these; they must be avoided if your creation is to appear not man's but the excellent whimsy of the gods. Nothing is so tedious, so obvious, so boring to the Japanese soul as the garden of Versailles. It is a problem in mathematics. Nikko is as inconceivable as a sunset or a moth's wing."

The Luxembourg is mathematical, it is not a whimsy of

the gods; gods I suppose wouldn't walk in it, but men—men with the pathos of autumn in their souls, disillusioned of high endeavor, patient and thankful for the late sunshine and quiet little things, men can walk there in peace, a peace full of sadness and without regret. It was made by men, for men, on man's scale: it is full of comfort and tenderness. Its chestnuts have a somber gold and their leaves fall slowly, in zigzags, filling the fountain of the Medici and glancing from the shoulders of the children as they whip their tops and roll their hoops. The old men in their corner behind the Palace play croquet passionately, but the leaves drift through their fiery outbursts and clutter the course to the next wicket. They sprinkle with cicada rustlings the amazing tennis courts between their rows, where the players never play but always are hunting the ball, there being no backstops. They lay a tarnished curtain between Polichinelle and Pierrot bickering stridently in the little marionette theater and their wonder-eyed birdlike audience in twittering rows. They even blow into the central fountain flanked by its prim beds of asters and dahlias and mingle their sunset barques with the small boys' sail-boats that eternally head for the drip of the upper basin and turn over, necessitating rescue squads from the ranks of passing elders. But it is all a dream, a tender gracious unreality, like Watteau's *L'Embarquement pour Cythère*: the children's cries and laughter are muted; the slow-passing lovers cling wordlessly together; and each bench has its single occupant looking out over the autumn, over the gold trees in their sculptured masses and the pale bubble of the Panthéon, over the curving balustrades and the queens of France in their still white rows, and seeing maybe nothing, or maybe the enchanted world that does not last and time that does not pause. They ask little, for they know it is little they will receive for all their asking, but that little is so dear, as it always is to the autumn-hearted who know life is pitiful and infinitely sweet.

No one ever missed so much during his first year abroad as I. I was desperately shy: my French was halting and ungrammatical; buying tickets, engaging rooms, asking directions, ordering meals were delicate tortures; and to make it worse I was constantly going places and doing things because I was afraid to. Except for the merciful and occasional appearances of Huger Jervey, Arthur Gray, and Huger Elliott, I saw and spoke to no one, I was completely unconscious of human beings. I lived with John Addington Symonds, Ruskin, Cellini, and Shelley. Yet despite all this, or because of it, I betook myself, trembling and hopeful, to almost every nook and corner of France and Italy, even landing before the winter was over in Egypt.

I haunted art galleries and churches like a New England spinster and must have passed months in the Louvre, the longest, tallest, widest, worst-hung, most exhausting, irritating, and magnificent gallery in the world. There wasn't a room of it I wasn't familiar with, and by the aid of a compass I even found the Houdons (west by north) and the Michelangelos (north by northeast). I specialized in madonnas, holy families, and allegorical pieces, and was cold to portraits unless they were by the early Florentine sculptors and to everything Dutch except Rembrandt. Murillo was the only Spanish painter and Ingres the only French. Manet was shocking and Monet impossible.

Because I was less sensitive to sculpture than to painting, I tried harder to appreciate it and spent hours with the Greeks. My admiration was for the conventional masterpieces—the *Venus de Milo,* the *Niobe,* the Naples *Psyche,* the *Victory* of Samothrace, the Pompeian bronzes —and I missed completely the *Birth of Venus,* the *Sleeping Fury* and the *Charioteer* of Delphi. I was always happening on a Hermaphrodite, in some discreet alcove, and I would examine the sleazy mock-modest little monster with horror and fascination. I could never imagine how it could have been created by the Greeks, usually so healthy and frank. I stumbled on the answer years later. When the Greeks practiced bisexuality honestly and simply without thought or condemnation they did not create these slick symbols of love divided in its objectives. It was a later, more sophisticated, more prurient age, the age of the nasty *Crouching Venus* of Syracuse, that, titillating and ahing, symbolized what they understood and were ashamed of by these sentimental decadent man-woman creatures, false art and false biology.

It's a grievous and a long way you travel to reach serenity and the acceptance of facts without hurt or shock. By that time you are too old to practice your wisdom and to young ears your advice might as well be uttered in Icelandic. Ripeness is all, said the wise one, and I suppose that's all there is to it. But one isn't ripe at nineteen. I was gourd-green, fearful, treading ledges without a Virgil.

While I was missing so much, I collected some imperishable memories: Luxor in moonlight; Notre-Dame in any light; the hill-towns of Italy, particularly Perugia; my first nightingale at Nîmes; my first Greek temple at Pæstum; the brumal gold interior of St. Mark's before it was cleaned; Shelley's grave with camellias blooming against the wall of the Protestant Cemetery and violets in purple shallows over the graves; the tall Egyptian women at dusk bearing on their heads to the Nile their water-jugs, the night air stirring the veils half from their faces and flattening their single garments in ripples against their straight proud bodies.

But it was lonesome going. I missed Mother and Father and the Centaurs, yet I wasn't suffering regular homesickness or ordinary loneliness. At sight or sound of something unbearably beautiful I wanted desperately to share it, I wanted with me everyone I'd ever cared for—and someone else besides. I was sick for a home I had never seen and lonely for a hand I had never touched. So for a year I ate and walked and lived and slept with loneliness, until she was so familiar I came not to hate her but to know whatever happened in however many after years she alone would be faithful to me and, departing a little way for some brief beatific interlude, would always return. And that perhaps is the only important thing I learned that year. What must be learned at last had as well be learned early.

CHAPTER XI

At the Harvard Law School

This year of travel after college was supposed to have afforded me a breathing-spell during which I could judiciously select my future means of livelihood. I agreed uneagerly with Father that a man should earn his keep, and Father was willing to give me an education in any profession I might choose or to set me up in business. No young man could have asked more; it was a magnificent opportunity. I found myself not only bewildered but uninterested. In my day people didn't flatfootedly choose to be teachers or scholars, scientists or preachers, much less hermits or saints. I had no penchant for any business, no talent for any art. Weighing my abilities, I had to confess they were of no commercial value and, to be honest, were, so far as I could judge, non-existent. The necessity of earning a living plus a desire to live plus the failure to discover in myself any quality convertible into cash—here was a combination sufficient to fling one tail-spinning into the deepest inferiority complex. All along of course I had a sneaking persistent desire to write, but I realized I had nothing to write about, being ignorant of man and of his home, this dark sphere, and even of that palpitating speck, myself.

So I did not choose the law, it chose me. Father was a successful lawyer, as were his brothers, as had been his father. With his growing reputation and practice and because he loved me he would be glad to take me into his office. I was not more unfit for the law than for anything else I could think of. Ignobly and without decision I asked Father to send me to the Harvard Law School. After all these years I look back on that request as craven and unimaginative. But I don't regret it and if I had it to go through with over again I should be equally nonplussed and not more courageous. On leaving college if we had some inkling of our own aptitudes we could plan our lives more usefully and more happily. For the unfortunate without aptitudes of course there's no hope of direction except from wind and tide. Conceding myself to have been an extreme case of jelly-fish, yet I notice today that college graduates continue to be distressfully disoriented and, remembering, I grieve for their waste and pain. Yet down wrong turnings too there's plentiful adventure.

Harvard's law school was my own choice, not Father's, for he leaned to Virginia, where he and his brothers had sat worshipfully at the feet of old Minor. The reason for my selection had little enough to do with law. I wanted to be near Boston with its music and theaters, which I would miss the rest of my life in my future Southern home, and I wanted to meet the damyankees.

Carl Sandburg observed casually in the preface to his life of Lincoln that one of my grandfathers fought in the Union Army. I rejoice in his error because except for it my name would never have found its way into the pages of his magnificent study. I probably told my poet friend that Fafar made speeches against secession, that he was a Whig and something less than an admirer of Jefferson Davis and that his two older brothers had felt so bitterly the unwisdom of secession that they refused to enlist in the Confederate Army. Fafar, though, enlisted; in fact, he raised a company which he captained and at the time of the surrender he was a Colonel on Bowen's staff. But he never spoke of the war, it hurt too much, and besides, silence was General Lee's example. So they never talked of the war at home and I never heard Yankees referred to as damyankees. My feeling toward them was one of curiosity, not hostility. Yet when I lit in their midst I did feel a drop in the temperature. It wasn't Sewanee or the Delta.

I have enjoyed spells of more intense happiness but never three years of as uninterrupted happiness as I did at the Harvard Law School. I was aware it was my last fling at life unweighted by responsibility and that awareness tautened my every sense to miss no vibration. By good chance I roomed at Winthrop Hall, which stands in a green space back of the Longfellow House and which was then the popular dormitory for law students from Yale. With my usual desire to like and be liked, I was a little dazed at first by the atmosphere of reserve, by the angular restrained manners. Grace wasn't abounding, but I came to find that character and intelligence were. I sensed that I was under inspection and on probation until I proved myself "the right sort," which it seemed to me anyone should have known me to be from the start, and besides I couldn't imagine what harm anyone would have come by had I turned out to be the wrong sort. Southerners are far easier to meet and never so intimate after meeting.

I found myself in a strange land but a pleasant one. It's

easy to remember why it was pleasant, but not easy to explain or analyze why it was strange. It lacked something of giddiness and absurdity. The ability to be a trifle daft, which I had considered native to young people, was unhappily absent. A certain rigidity hinted of pomposity or dullness ahead, as well as of strength. Even now, if I think of the Brattle Hall dances, I feel the way a banana plant looks after a frost. New England's self-consciousness was without artlessness and its show of superiority betrayed unsureness. People tried to impress one another, and real folks make no such effort.

On my first vacation South Mrs. Lovell, whom I loved most of all the old Sewanee ladies after Mrs. Preston, asked me a startling question: "Will, up North there did you meet anyone who was"—she paused—"a gentleman?" My emphatic and amused "Yes" didn't convince her. "I mean among the Northerners." No amount of affirmatives could have convinced her. She counseled quietly: "I'm certain you will find you are mistaken." Being a daughter of General Quitman, famous in the Mexican War, and having been born and bred in one of the great homes of Natchez perhaps accounted for her provincialism, but she was a good hater anyhow and she had seen reconstruction. I am not a good hater. I detect likenesses more readily than differences and the former strike me as the more important and the more interesting. That one of my fellow creatures happens to be a German or a Hottentot or even a Northerner seems less exciting to me than that he is a human being, engagingly and pitifully like me. Mrs. Lovell was wrong, no doubt of that whatsoever, but, all the same, Harvard was un-Southern in feel, though I can't recall instances of difference to prove it. Yet these inconsequentials stick in my mind as if they meant something.

For the first month or two a chap named Freddie sat next to me in class and we usually exchanged casual remarks. He seemed nice and I knew nothing about him except that he was a real Hahvard, by which we outlanders meant a graduate of Harvard College with a broad *a.* I learned later that Freddie had been something of a person in college and came from an old and rich Boston family. One day as I was walking to the Square Freddie came toward me from it. It was our first meeting outside of classroom. He glanced up and recognized me. As I started to speak he looked me through and cut me dead. It was the first time I had ever been cut. I have never been more surprised or more angry. Inquiring later the reason for this gratuitous rudeness, I was told a Harvard man's prominence was gauged by the number of men he could afford to cut. Things may have changed there since my day. I hope so. With us a cut is used as a moral weapon, except by social climbers. It was our third year before Freddie and I met again as members of one of those silly exclusive clubs which young people, at best hopeless snobs, persist in forming, and on that occasion, I must confess, he was more affable than I. I think he really was a nice and intelligent young American. He just hadn't been brought up right. Gus Westfeldt, my roommate from New Orleans, had a similar experience, but his reaction was more instantaneous and effective than mine. He delivered the *Mayflower* princeling a sock on the jaw and a bit of advice which I recall but can't repeat. I guess they thought Southerners were queer too.

My next lesson in differences was more amusing. Harley Stowell and I had been invited to dine with a middle-aged professor and his wife at their home. Except for the usual bolt-upright atmosphere it was a tasteful house and everything except me ran smoothly and decorously. An immense bird-cage full of canaries filled the end of the dining-room to my right behind our host. On each plate sat a snowy napkin innocently folded and refolded into a sort of battleship. I must have been feeling unpardonably vivacious, for in undoing my napkin I gave it an airy little flirt to the right, and to my horror out of it soared a small brown roll shaped like a torpedo which described a slow parabola and lit with a wiry bang on top of the bird-cage. No one could pretend it hadn't happened. A bandersnatch or a whooping crane flying across the room could not have had higher visibility. The impact with the bird-cage sounded like a Stravinsky chord on an untuned harp, and all the canaries burst into a pæan of dismay or applause. I couldn't decide whether I wanted to die or giggle. But my hosts never batted an eye. They were wonderful; their nerves must have been shattered, but, without allusion to projectiles, we proceeded with the soup course. To ignore completely such a calamity takes praiseworthy poise, but I'd have felt more reorganized if they all had gone Japanese and bombarded the bird-cage with their rolls or, better still, if everyone had burst out laughing and cheered: "Good shot" or "It's a birdie" or "The last time Senator Omygosh did that he hit two canaries and killed the auk." Someone would surely have been that silly and that merciful a thousand miles south of the Charles.

My last example of difference isn't worth recording except for its mention of some wholly charming New Englanders. Bobbie Schurman had a genius for discovering beautiful girls whom Aunt Nana would have described as "comme il faut." One fine fall day he lured the Crocker girls down from Fitchburg for an afternoon concert of the Boston Symphony. They had as much chic and loveliness and animation as any Southern belle, but that afternoon they felt positively dashing because they were going unchaperoned to the symphony with two young men. I fancied their flurry on this score was one of those mysterious aberrations of feminine coquetry, but realized the error of my diagnosis when I suggested after the concert that we go for tea to the most proper of Boston hotels (and I imagine that meant the most proper hotel in the world). They were scandalized by the suggestion. It wasn't proper, it wasn't ladylike, it just wasn't done. We argued and pleaded so chivalrously and dolefully that finally, unable to resist the sheer bravado of the proposal, they actually drank tea and nibbled toast with us in a huge oak-paneled dining-room heavily populated with dowagers. It was far less intimate than the Boston Common, and the girls felt like soubrettes. Fascinated, I mused that no Southern girl would have given our proposal a thought, unless it had not been made.

After tea we accompanied the girls up to Fitchburg, where Bobbie and I were to be their guests over the week-end. We quaked a little about our reception after such devilish gallantries and with cause, for all of us were sternly scolded. Not between Tierra del Fuego and the Arctic Circle could a more gracious and delightful household have been found than that of the Crockers in Fitchburg in those days. It was everything a home full of young people should be. Yet even there I experienced a contretemps which I hope was typical of nothing. One of President Theodore Roosevelt's sons was also a house-guest. Although I suspected he might be fairly dour and lofty, after dinner I rambled over to him and began talking of an incident which had occurred to his father and mine on a bear-hunt they had recently taken together. As I began to talk, his expression took on the glassy hauteur of the Ritz head waiter when he wordlessly reminds a couple from Hushpuckna where they came from and where they should go. Snubbed. I left the story unfinished. But this time I wasn't surprised or angered. Surely he belied his breeding. I was in the midst of proof that bad manners were not inculcated in these parts or indigenous. Before the Civil War a good many of the Southern leaders were guilty of this same sort of stupidity. Not satisfied with knowing they were as good as anyone else, they came to believe they were better than anyone else. Always a fatal delusion. They should have remembered hubris from their Greek. Except for them the Civil War could possibly have been avoided, as could, except for their like, many a modern conflict between capital and labor and between nation and nation. Manners are essential and are essentially morals.

Beyond peradventure there were differences, but so oblique and unessential that after a few months I was not conscious of them. My intimates, except Gus, were all Northerners and, curiously enough, all from New York State. Mentally they were more disciplined and morally more innocent than the Southern boys. Everyone studied seriously and dissipation of any sort was almost unknown. A Saturday night Boston binge was an event, and drinking in the dormitory was restricted to our annual beer night. Our chief dissipation was conversation. Every night at eleven, after study was over, a coffee percolator would be started in someone's room and weary students would drop in. It was a superior brand of talk we indulged in, covering a wide range of subjects, with a minimum of inhibition and a maximum of gusto. Occasionally sparrows on the roof or that wretched woodpecker on the tin gutter would halt our sessions with news of the sunrise. I wonder if this most civilized form of entertainment is fated for extinction by man's most effective mental opiate, the radio? Instead of hot orchestras, impromptu interludes often interrupted our symposiums. It would cross someone's mind that I had been less than appreciative of Bobbie Schurman's Christmas gift, a copy of *Uncle Tom's Cabin*. The rebel would be pinned to the floor and sat on by rowdy well-wishers while others would read aloud Mrs. Stowe's more sadistic and blood-boiling passages, with Simon Legree gestures. Or Stanleigh Friedman, fresh-laureled as composer of "March, March on Down the Field," would start playing the score of *Tristan und Isolde* and in his mounting passion would burst into astonishing song as he reached the "Liebestod." They were splendid evenings.

By day of course sterner doings were afoot. We were attempting to learn the law and we took it hard. The first year our confusion mounted to despair. One night Jakie Smith rushed into my room with the sudden illumination: "I know what it is! The law is common sense plus clear English!" I've never heard a better definition of what the law should be and isn't. In comparison "Pop" Gray's dictum: "The aim of the law is settlement, not justice," seems weary and defeatist. The virtue of the Socratic method of the Harvard Law School is not that from it you learn what the law is, but that by it you learn how to think. Whatever ability I may have to reason in a straight line from premise to conclusion derives from the discipline of those three years and especially from Professor Williston and his horse Dobbin. I lost hours of sleep, pounds of flesh, buckets of cold sweat over Dobbin, the hero of every supposititious contract, the villain of every supposititious sale. From Professor Williston I also learned that one can be proved a fool so quietly and inexorably that the fool will harbor neither anger nor resentment. But this technique I have never been able to master. Cold logic I admire, but have no talent for. My sort works only above boiling-point.

Whatever I learned in class was absorbed and left no conscious memories. I recall less of that phase of my life in Cambridge than of any other. The grace of New England elms, whiffs of New England lilacs, spring which came in May and for its tardiness came with intolerable rapture, the long winters with crystal storms and interminable widths of snow never the same color, the sound of the puckered thaw like crabs feeding, walks around frozen ponds on snow-shoes or through sparsely green woods, in either case well-companioned, often by Elsie Singmaster or Bob Black, the red winter sunsets which turned the bare branches to amethyst and crimson—such items I recall far more vividly than torts or the statute of uses. And then the Boston Symphony on Saturday nights and the week in spring when the Metropolitan came! To have the great masterpieces of music, matchlessly performed, poured into your fresh ears with Harold Bruff or George Roberts or Harley Stowell in the seat next to you —well, one could ask nothing more of life—that was ecstasy. We cherished Gadski, though she looked like a horse, and when she lay down by Tristan's body she couldn't rise by her own power. We beamed on Schumann-Heink as she stood on the deck of Tristan's boat gazing seaward and trying to look tragic but failing because of her funny nose and her arms too short to meet across the bolster of her bosom. But when her voice poured from the tower across the moonlight we shuddered, knowing that never in life would we again hear any slow river of sound as beautiful. We adored Farrar with that ineffable springtime voice of hers, and for us there could never be another real Mimi or Nedda or Butterfly or Elizabeth. When Papa Hertz's black beard stood on end and he began bouncing at a climax we were blissfully happy. And, besides, there were Caruso and Sembrich, Louise Homer and Scotti, and, most glorious of all, the divine Fremstad with her head high, her shoulders back, her goddess figure, as though she had just stepped from the porch of the Erechtheum. We were critical and ignorant, but our reactions were ardent and genuine and we held no truck with those clichés which lend a spurious air of knowledge and appreciation to musical conversation. When Karl Muck, whom we considered Wagner's son and the most electric and impeccable of conductors, played Mahler or Bruckner or Sibelius we felt personally affronted, and, unbelievable as it seems now, we were apt to be heavy-lidded through Bach and Brahms. There was so much that we had not yet experienced and that lay ahead, particularly fiery furnaces and anvils of pain. But every concert was an adventure and usually we'd be plumed and dripping fire as we made for the Brattle Street trolley through the winter murk.

Boston meant nothing to me. Cambridge meant nothing to me. The ghosts of Emerson and Thoreau did not haunt my ways nor the tall shadows of William James and Santayana cross my paths. The strong tart flavor of New England was not savored by my palate. I missed much, as usual, but much more I did not miss. I had day-dreamed too long, and though dreamers are needed by this world of ours, day-dreamers are not, nor sleep-walkers. The law was a dash of cold water, a first film of nacre for a very shell-less oyster. However uncertainly and shyly, I could proceed into the frightening concourse of men at least awake and not wholly unarmed. I had gathered a kitful of new memories, Elysian sounds and sights, for the rigorous journey, and in the enemy country

I had taken hostages against the long cold, new friends to whom I could shout when the going was rough and on whom I could brood when, silence answering, I knew for them the going had been too rough. Harold Bruff and George Roberts were worth three years of any man's life.

CHAPTER XII

The Return of the Native

Probably there is no nostalgia so long-lived and hopeless as that of the college graduate returning to his native town. He is a stranger though he is home. He is sick for a communal life that was and can never be again, a life merry with youth and unshadowed by responsibilities. He is hungry for the easy intimacies which competitive anxious living does not provide. He is unproved when proof is demanded on every side. In this alien environment, the only one he may now call his own, he is unknown, even to himself.

My case was no different from most, I suppose, and I hated it: eight years of training for life, and here I was in the midst of it—and my very soul whimpered. I had been pushed into the arena and didn't even know the animals' names. Besides, I labored under individual disabilities: I had been to Europe; I had been to Harvard; my accent, though not Northern, was—well, tainted; I had had it easy; I probably considered myself *it*. For crowning handicap, I was blessed with no endearing vices: drunkenness made me sick, gambling bored me, rutting per se, unadorned, I considered overrated and degrading. In charitable mood one might call me an idealist, but, more normally, a sissy.

It must have been difficult for Father too. Enjoying good liquor, loving to gamble, his hardy vices merely under control, he sympathized quizzically and said nothing. But his heart must often have called piteously for the little brother I had lost, all boy, all sturdy, obstreperous charm. Fortunately I wasn't meek and I wasn't afraid. When put upon, I discovered that a truculent tongue did more to save than a battalion of virtues. But it wasn't fun. I had attacks of nausea, but not of tears.

Yet these handicaps on my debut were a minor worry. My real concern was what the show was all about and what role I should or could play in it, queries which, since the curtain was up and I on the stage, seemed fairly belated.

For eight years—in fact, for twenty-three—a great number of people had been pouring out money, skill, time, devotion, prayers to create something out of me that wouldn't look as if the Lord had slapped it together absent-mindedly. Not Alexander the Great nor Catherine II had been tended by a more noble corps of teachers. It humbles me to call their roster, but calling it is no penance: Nain and Mur, Mère and Père, Sister Evangelist and Judge Griffin, Father Koestenbrock and Mr. Bass, Dr. Henneman and Professor Williston, the Roman Catholic Church and Browning, the sea and the sun, Beethoven and Wagner, Michelangelo and Andrea del Sarto, loneliness and friendship, Sinkler and Harold, Mother and Father. They made a longer procession than the Magi and the shepherds combined, and the gifts they brought were more precious. Obviously I was cast to justify the ways of man to God, as it were. But how? What does one do with a life, or at any rate intend to do? It was time to inventory my ambitions and, having selected one as paramount, to pursue it whole-heartedly. For months (maybe for years, maybe until now) I hunted about for a good ambition. Money? No, positively—not because my financial future was assured or my financial present anything more than adequate to supply my simple needs, but it wasn't interesting and it wasn't worthy. Nothing to debate here. Fame as a lawyer? I had been a B man at the law school, which is eminently respectable but not brilliant as Harold and George had been. I suspected that if I should give everything I had to the law I might realize such an ambition, but I had no notion of doing any such thing. I wanted to do whatever piece of work fell to my care as well as I could, but beyond that I wasn't concerned over what opinion my brethren of the bar held of me. Power? I knew nothing about it and it certainly wasn't my métier. Civic usefulness? Perhaps; that was getting warmer, but I had no desire to hold office and I knew no way of dedicating one's unendowed life to usefulness. Other things, I did not know what, except that they were things inside, seemed realities, while money, fame, power, civic virtue seemed things which required an audience to become real. So with my ruminations I reached nowhere, a lonesome sort of spot. Now that the show is nearly over, I'm only just beginning to see what one may truthfully call the good life, but of the plot I still know so little that I can't swear whether it's been tragedy or comedy, though I have an inkling. Perhaps, after all, stumbling through life by ear, though slower, makes more exciting traveling, and if you have a good ear you're just as apt to arrive as if you'd dipped about in the wake of one of those twitchy compasses.

I didn't exactly plunge into life, rather I tipped in, trepidly. In spite of doubts and misgivings, there was living to be done and I set about it. Our town wasn't a thing of beauty in those days. The residences looked like illegitimate children of a French wedding cake. Besides all the icing they usually sported a turret or cupola to which Sister Ann couldn't have climbed if she *knew* somebody was coming, for it never had stairs. The brick stores, most of them still in situ, as we lawyers say, managed to look stark without looking simple. Curbs, gutters, and open ditches, while satisfactory to such stalwart conservatives as crawfish and mosquitoes, still abided hopefully the coming of the W.P.A. Sidewalks were often the two-board sort that grow splinters for barefoot boys, and the roads, summer or winter, were hazards. There were lovely trees and crape myrtles but where they grew was their business. There were flowers, but no gardens. Just a usual Southern town of that period, and its name was Greenville. There must be something in that name attractive to towns because every state in the Union has one. It's a name without charm for me. I prefer Alligator or Rolling Fork or Nitta Yuma or Rosedale, our neighbors—at least they have individuality, of one sort or another. But, aside from all that, in 1909 I retook Greenville for my home (and kept it) and could boast that I was a full-fledged practicing attorney-at-law.

While not what you might call indispensable in the office, I looked up authorities for Father with great interest and once or twice stumbled on an original legal theory, the discovery of which pleased him even more than myself. I was terrified at the thought of arguing a case, particularly before a jury, but somehow I steeled myself to do it and with some passion, though never brilliantly and never to this day without a spasm of nerves before and after. But the law was the least of my troubles. Making a rut, for comfort, was a grimmer endeavor, one that required years of effort—probably it is one of those lifetime jobs, and just when you are beginning to feel snug you are routed out permanently.

In those days the center of social life for the young people was the Elysian Club. The oldsters played poker at the Mississippi Club and the middling mature indulged their usual bacchanalian bent, unassisted by pards and mænads, at the Elks'. No doubt about it, our town was plumb social. Although it cherished a "reading-room" and a poolroom, our club's raison d'être was its dance floor. It was a fine floor, but it was housed in a room replete with unsynchronized angles and curves which it must have taken the local builder months to conceive and no time to execute. Beyond question it was the ugliest room in the world, but thoroughly entrancing when Handy appeared and the dancing started. Delta girls are born dancing and never stop, which is as it should be, for surely it is the finest form of human amusement except tennis and talking. The club's dances were famous from Hushpuckna to Yazoo City, and they were the right sort of affairs, with rows of broad-bosomed lares and penates against the wall and so many good-looking animated girls drawling darkest Southernese and doing intricate steps by instinct or inspiration that no one could think of going home before daylight. Drinking was not permitted in the clubhouse and there were no parked cars for intermissions. An intoxicated youth was a crying scandal and an intoxicated female would certainly have caused hara-kiri or apoplexy among the penates. There are dances now in the Delta, a never ending round, but I am told they are more stimulated and less stimulating.

Now and then Father and Mother appeared at our functions and remained an hour or two because they loved young people. Father himself would occasionally indulge in a whirl on the dance floor, but, being practically tone-deaf, he was an awful dancer and knew it, though fairly unabashed and invariably amused. Mother never understood or forgave in me a certain lack of enthusiasm for things social. People, whole throngs of them, delighted her, and her delight was infectious. Everyone became a little more charming than he was meant by God to be when she was around. I liked people, too, but individually and separately, not in throngs. I soon learned, when surrounded, not to go bounding off like a flushed fawn, but crowds were not then and are not now my natural habitat, and even individuals, no matter how fascinating, I find more exhausting than hard work or boredom. Mother regarded my antisocial tendencies as pure mulishness, but Father, although disappointed no doubt, never showed it except by a far-away expression and a little smile.

I often took to the levee in sheer lonesomeness and confusion of soul. Our woods are not made for walking because the vines and bushes are too rampant and the rattlesnakes too much at home. But the high levee is perfect for a stroll, which you can extend, if so minded, a hundred miles in either direction. Across the river you see Arkansas, a state almost as unfamiliar to us as Montana, but we know it has one great virtue—it grows willows and cottonwoods right down to the water line. In spring they are done by Puvis de Chavannes in pastel green, in summer they are banked in impenetrable tiers of lushness, in fall they have a week of pale flying gold, and in winter they are at their best with their wands rose- and copper-colored and their aisles full of blue smoke. There wasn't a time of year I didn't walk there and watch them across the vari-colored river, which, though it seems home, seems too the most remote and secret stretch of all God's universe. It is most itself and to my liking when with the first crystal rush of winter the ducks and geese and water-turkeys, in wedges, follow its pale protecting sandbars south. At first I walked there alone, but later I discovered three familiar spirits who also enjoyed walking and talking. Will Francis and Lyne Starling and George Roth certainly tided me over a bad passage and are with me still.

It was on these levee walks that I began to think of poetry and to jot down lines. At Sewanee I had tried my hand at lyrics and unfortunately, as I was editor of the college magazine, some of them found their way, anonymously, into print. I reread them a few years ago and I cannot imagine an experience more embarrassing. In Paris I had written a feeble sonnet on Chatterton and at Harvard I improved slightly with two winter songs, one of which, to my amazement and delight, *McClure's* published, still anonymously. All these were secret indulgences and only Miss Carrie knew of them.

This is not an account of my poetry nor of me as a poet. But since much of my life has gone into the making of verse which I hope is poetry, I may as well state now and as briefly as I can how and why I wrote.

What I wrote seemed to me more essentially myself than anything I did or said. It often gushed up almost involuntarily like automatic writing, and the difficulty lay in keeping the hot gush continuous and unselfconscious while at the same time directing it with cold intellect into form. I could never write in cold blood. The results were intensely personal, whatever their other defects. But by some quirk I was always aware in the act of putting words to paper that what I was feeling and thinking had been felt and thought by thousands in every generation. Only that conviction would have permitted me to publish without feeling guilty of indecent exposure.

I judge there's nothing at all unusual about such mental processes, or about these:

When you feel something intensely, you want to write it down—if anguish, to stanch the bleeding; if delight, to prolong the moment. When after years of pondering you feel you have discovered a new truth or an old one which suddenly for you has the excitement of a new one, you write a longish poem. To keep it free from irrelevant photographic details you set it in some long-ago time, one, of course, you love and perhaps once lived in.

That is how I wrote and why I wrote. As to technique I tried to make it sound as beautiful and as fitting as I could. Old patterns helped, but if rhyme seemed out of place, the choruses of *Samson Agonistes*, some of Matthew Arnold's unrhymed cadences, and Shakespeare's later run-on pentameters suggested freer and less accepted modes of communication. As far as I can make out, the towering bulk of English poetry influenced me tremendously, but not any one poet, though I hope I learned as much as I think I owe to Browning's monologues and to Gilbert Murray's translations of Euripides.

Thinking of these lonely trial years would be impossible for me without thinking of Caroline Stern. Everybody in town called her Miss Carrie. The first time I saw her I was far gladder than she realized. One of the convent boys, a fattish one who loomed huge to my apprehensive vision, had announced to me as we dawdled on the corner that I would have to fight him then and there. As in so many conflicts, the casus belli was obscure and immediately forgotten. I accepted the challenge with the least possible enthusiasm and began taking off my coat very deliberately, to give the Lord time to take a hand.

At this moment Miss Carrie appeared, surveyed the scene, and paused. The conflict petered out before a blow was struck. Evidently my guardian angel had taken the form of Miss Carrie. It was an unusual guise. She was as tiny as Sister Evangelist, but birdlike. She must have weighed eighty pounds. She had a sensitive face, pale, with a large Jewish nose and enormous brown eyes, lustrous and kind. Her hair, which curled pleasantly, was just darker than wasp red. But I found later there was nothing else waspish about her, though she was a gallant fighter. She never thought anything was worth fighting for except moral issues, and it sickened her when an individual or a nation refused to fight for them. On this occasion she stopped and viewed our bellicose stance, meaning no doubt to whirl in if developments required. Then as always she looked tidy but a tiny bit disheveled, as if a not very rough breeze had just deposited her unexpectedly. She had the air of a volunteer as we gardeners use the term, and that air always kept Mother from appreciating her, because Mother by instinct and training was chic.

Miss Carrie—she must have been in her twenties then, though of course she seemed to me far gone in overblown maturity—had mistaken my unwilling preparations for battle for simon-pure heroism and, since she admired nothing more than knightly prowess, I found myself a few days later a visitor in her little house. It was a bare little place with an improvised look and hardly enough furniture for convenience. Her dwarf of a father, an Alsatian Jew, lived with her, a querulous old fellow who had failed as a country merchant and, now idle, lived by her scanty earnings as a teacher. She tended and scolded him as if he were a child. Her passionate adoration had been for her mother, whose death a few years before had left her the bread-winner and spiritually in solitary confinement. It would have been mortally lonely for her had she not known Judge Griffin, who gave her the nourishment she needed, his deep patriarchal love.

Miss Carrie's passion for painting was beyond bounds, consuming. While still in her teens, by impossible denials and scrapings, she had managed to save enough money to study in New York for a year. I think she must have lived in a state of ecstasy that whole year—she needed to, for I am sure she went hungry half the time. She would tell me about the classes, about copying the head of Bastien-Lepage's *Joan of Arc*, about her friend Annie Goldthwaite, who became famous, about all the young doings of the League. She loved to remember it and longed to go back. But hardly had she returned home to her school work than she developed lead poisoning. Her doctor forbade her to paint again. Against orders she was trying it when I met her. While sketching me, she would say with shy pride: "At the League they said I had a real sense of color. Someone once mistook one of my oils for a Henner," and she laughed softly at the delightful recollection. But in a year or two the blood-poison returned and she had to give up painting again, this time forever. It was her whole life and that meant she had lost her life and must find another. If this had been different and that had not happened, she might have become a great painter. Instead she became a great soul.

She was a teacher born. Mr. Bass recognized her gift and soon had her teaching anything, everything—painting, history, English, whatever classes happened to be without a teacher at the moment. She was always exhausted, generally undernourished, and always eager. The children adored her. She read me my first poetry (Milton and Shakespeare didn't count, they were just Milton and Shakespeare) and I resisted it mightily. This resistant attitude of mine lasted for years—in fact, until I read *Dover Beach* at Sewanee. Perhaps it was due to Father's having read me when I was a little fellow Tennyson's *I'm to be Queen of the May, Mother,* which I had found so unbearably pathetic I had burst into tears. Or perhaps I did actually detest poetry's inversions and circumlocutions as much as I thought I did. But poetry fascinated me, like a fearful sin, and Miss Carrie kept on reading it to me. Mother disapproved of these goings-on and observed, accurately enough, that there was no telling what kind of impractical notions Carrie was putting into my head, and my visits to her must stop. Father wondered if they did any harm anyway. But I announced I was going to see her when I wanted to. Mother closed the discussion, not weakly but impotently, by remarking that for an obedient child I was the most hard-headed she had ever encountered.

I kept on seeing Miss Carrie until I could see her no more. Many of the young people, mostly her former students, felt similarly drawn to her, and those who had moved from town were eager to visit her on their return trips. We came to her as to a clean upland spot smelling of pine. There was a childish gaiety about her, and her great wisdom was completely innocent. Apparently she made no effort to be right, she just was right. She gave you the fine feeling you were shielding her when in fact you were drawing from her your strength.

While I was at college she joined the Episcopal Church. That must have been a cruel decision for her to feel she must make, for it meant, and she knew it meant, breaking with her own people and with the faith of her fathers. The Jews at home never forgave her for it. After a few years she stopped attending church, and that too must have meant a grievous struggle. So she went her way alone and built her own lonely altar. She must have been a very Jacob for wrestling with God, but when I knew her best, after her youth, she didn't wrestle any more, she merely walked with Him and leaned on Him when she was tired. It's a good thing He was there because she was often tired and she had no one else to lean on.

Beginning with my return home from Harvard, every scrap I ever wrote I showed Miss Carrie or mailed to her, coming by her house Sundays for her criticism. Though a partial critic in my case, she was a sensitive and a fearless one. We fought over words and cadences and sometimes I was worsted. She knew far better than I when I was growing didactic, and vehemently opposed the tendency. One week I sent her three or four short pieces and when I arrived I was pleased and astonished to hear her say ardently: "At last you have written a perfect poem!" I didn't know to which one she was referring, but it was *Overtones,* the one poem of mine which critics and anthologists, almost without dissent, have liked. At the very time she was giving me so much, she was making a selection of her own poems and saving every nickel to have them published. For years she had been writing poetry and a good many of her lyrics had appeared in the more distinguished magazines. At last she named her collection and found a publisher, one of those who advertise little and charge much. Denied an outlet in painting, she had turned to poetry, and now her very own book—*At the Edge of the World,* by Caroline Stern—in a pretty yellow binding was to appear in the kindly world. She was so excited and hopeful, she often wore a cherry-red ribbon at her throat, but though it was not her color, none of us would tell her so because that ribbon made her feel reckless and mischievous. Although there was plenty of Joan of Arc and St. Theresa in her, she was fundamentally a little girl. Her book appeared, and that was all. The critics ignored it, there were no sales, after a year the publisher wrote no copies were available. It did not deserve such treatment. Though she had more fancy than imagination, more feeling than art, and though she was not endowed with the sense of the magic word, they were good poems, charming, and so like her. She was hurt inside, but she did not complain and she never grew accusatory or bitter. When she read favorable reviews of my volume, a little later, she thrilled, and when the reviews were unfriendly she was furious. All the while she continued to teach with undiminished enthusiasm hundreds of children and to give cheer or comfort to her numerous young friends in their happiness or troubles.

After her father's death she had built herself a small home with two extra rooms which she rented as an apartment. Between paying by the month for it and paying for the publication of her poems she had little enough left to fill her birdlike needs. When I think of the stark little living-room where I found so much peace and encouragement and of the scanty meals she referred to vaguely and when I remember I never gave her a present worth having or thought of helping out in any one of a hundred possible ways, I am appalled at the self-centered egotism of youth and its incapacity for real understanding or pity.

Once in a while you would find she had visited the doctor or was not feeling so well, but none of us was disturbed or really interested—people were always getting sick and Miss Carrie was naturally frail. She was alone most of the time and bought a Ouija board for company. It did astounding things for her—wrote hours on end faster than anyone except her could read, leaped into the air, went into frenzies, or moodily refused to budge. It amused us enormously. But I found after a while it wasn't so amusing to her. Her mother would speak to her, and God, and Matthew Arnold would send me long messages. She was puzzled and incredulous, but Ouija became almost alive, almost a person to her. She had no one else to live with except God, and He isn't enough by Himself. One night when Ouija had announced God was speaking and she was listening intently to the strange poetic moralizing, the wretched three-legged thing suddenly bounded into the air and spelled out violently: "Carrie, you are a damn fool. This isn't God. Good night," and could not be coaxed into further comment. The incident distressed her more than she would confess.

Once as I was leaving she told me quietly she was going to the hospital next day—an operation, she didn't know what for; she'd be out in two weeks. She was out in a few days, although they had operated. Then she began to waste away before our eyes. Soon she was taken to the hospital again, and this time for good. Although she didn't complain she asked everyone what was the matter with her. At last they took Ouija away from her. One afternoon when I came in she smiled and said: "I know the truth now. I asked the nurse and as she was leaving without answering I picked up a pencil and said: 'Ouija, tell me,' and it wrote: 'Cancer.'" The last time I saw her she had drawn a heavy white veil across her face and her body weighed no more than a bird's.

Miss Carrie was not "my favorite Jew." I have had dozens of favorites. To no people am I under deeper spiritual obligation. But I am not unaware of the qualities in them (absent in her) which have recurrently irritated or enraged other people since the Babylonian captivity. Touch a hair of a Jewish head and I am ready to fight, but I have experienced moments of exasperation when I could willingly have led a pogrom. No, Miss Carrie was not my favorite Jew. She was my favorite friend. She never failed me, but looking back I am not certain I did not fail her despicably—I suspect I was patronizing. She was so different, so unworldly, so fundamentally innocent, and her friendship was so unwithheld and shameless. I don't often trouble to be ashamed, but if I was patronizing, Miss Carrie and her God would have to forgive me. I never could.

Miss Carrie had failed in everything—in painting, in poetry, in making money, in winning love, in dying easy. Yet she was one of the few successes I ever knew. I think I learned more from her of what the good life is and of how it may be lived than from almost anyone else.

CHAPTER XIII

The Bottom Rail on Top

Hardly had I fallen into my stride—not a very springy one—when I was called to Sewanee because of Dr. Henneman's death and asked by the desperate Vice-Chancellor to help my Alma Mater through the ensuing crisis. Arriving on the mountain I was presented with the English department, all five classes, everything from *Beowulf* to American literature (which meant the New England school with Lanier and James Lane Allen thrown in for lagniappe), and no assistants. I couldn't spell or punctuate or paragraph or construct a sentence that didn't wobble like a caterpillar. But I got by—partly by not pretending to possess these necessary qualifications and mostly by being gifted with a handwriting nobody could read even when exposed on a blackboard. The students liked me, and I found I had some of that peculiar gift, a talent for teaching, which consists, I suspect, largely in communicable ardor and which in any event does not derive from erudition. Nevertheless, my ignorance of English literature was a real handicap, because, after all, that was what I was supposed to be teaching. When we came to Marlowe I talked about Giorgione and the Venetians, and when we came to prose I gave up and talked about morals and Southern deficiencies. At that, some of those boys, hardly younger than myself, grew to love Browning and Shakespeare. I worked all hours to keep one hop ahead of the classes and, whatever they may not have learned, I learned a lot, particularly about human nature. I also discovered I couldn't teach and write poetry at the same time—they tapped the same reservoir. So after my six months were up, refusing an offer of the chair of English, I returned home, and Mother and Father were glad to have me back.

As a youngster I had not loved Father deeply, though I had admired him boundlessly. He was stern, though he never corrected me, and shy, and high-spirited at all the points where I was flat. During my religious period I resented his unchurchliness. I must have been a hard child to get close to. But now that I had learned a little sense, though not much, he was my chief delight. Of all my experiences our daily walks together to and from the office are those I would least want to forget, and they continued through the years, until I had to do my walking alone. He emitted sunshine and strength. We talked of everything—of the condition of the crops (it was always too wet or too dry), of the market, which, to my disapproval, he loved to play, of the Mississippi judiciary and its decline, of the parlous state of American politics, of friends and enemies, of everything. Once—this was in the early days—I asked him if he'd heard that one of our young married friends had brought on a miscarriage. He looked vague. I launched into a moral diatribe and averred that such conduct merited social ostracism. He still looked vague. It dawned on me that he knew all about it and was not aghast. I sensed we were diverging in judgment on a matter I considered important: I was confused and distressed. He knew I would learn in time and he knew that a narrow idealism at the start is bracing and formative. But he said nothing—advice was for those not strong enough to make their own decisions or to apply the decisions others make for them, advice was waste of time.

As summer approached we would always concoct delirious plans for trips to strange ports. Travel and the thought of travel fascinated him as much as they did me and he thoroughly approved my reckless determination to spend every cent I earned on going places. We barred Australia, Siberia, South Africa, and Iceland, but every other nook of the globe allured us, especially those full of the ghosts of countless generations, holy with their dust and tears.

When he would stop suddenly with his hands in his pockets and exclaim: "Consound Cam's kittycats!" I would know what had happened: Mother had filched more than her quota from his trousers pockets as he slept. It was a custom, one indulged in by her with skill and elaborate secrecy and consented to by him with considerable amusement. She could and did check unreservedly on his account, but the booty from these forays was her very own and she never reported the uses to which it was put. She would decide some poor girl needed a new evening gown, or the washerwoman needed a ton of coal and a gold tooth, or Mrs. X's roof was leaking, or Mrs. A should go to Memphis for the opera, and she supplied their needs by this violent brigandage. He never upbraided her, but only tried to resolve after some especially outrageous depredation to carry less cash on his person. He could never remember his resolution, and Mother never repented or reformed.

After a while I discovered to my amazement that Father

did not like to work. He was a tireless worker and had a large demanding practice, but he worked only because he had a family to support and wanted the pleasant things of life for himself and them. He would have preferred to play golf with that extravagant high-betting foursome of his, or to hunt lions in Africa or tigers in India or moose in Alaska, or merely to lie on the deck of a sunny steamer with a hundred detective novels, *Ivanhoe,* and *The Light of Asia.*

He was hunting birds in Arkansas when Senator McLaurin of Mississippi died. It was a death that did not stir my pulse or suggest to me consequences that might have any personal bearing on me or mine. It was a turning-point in my life.

The most prominent politician in Mississippi at that time was James K. Vardaman, a kindly, vain demagogue unable to think, and given to emotions he considered noble. He was a handsome, flamboyant figure of a man, immaculately overdressed, wearing his black hair long to the shoulders, and crowned with a wide cowboy's hat. He looked like a top-notch medicine man. He had made a good governor of Mississippi and he craved public office because the spot-light was his passion and because, eternally in need of money, he abhorred work. At the slightest opportunity he would quote Bobby Burns fervently and with appreciation, but his oratory was bastard emotionalism and raven-tressed rant. For political platform he advertised his love of the common people and advocated the repeal of the Fifteenth and the modification of the Fourteenth Amendments to the Federal Constitution. He did love the common man after a fashion, as well he might, but although he hated the "nigger," as he called the Negro, he had never studied the effects of the abolition of the Fifteenth Amendment and he had never considered by what verbiage the Fourteenth Amendment could be modified. He stood for the poor white against the "nigger"—those were his qualifications as a statesman. He was very popular in Mississippi; they called him the Great White Chief.

Father rather liked Vardaman—he was such a splendid ham actor, his inability to reason was so contagious, it was so impossible to determine where his idealism ended and his demagoguery began. Besides he had charm and a gift for the vivid reckless phrase. A likable man, as a pool-room wit is likable, but surely not one to set in the councils of the nation. Father considered his Negro-baiting mischievous and his proposed changes in the Constitution impractical and undesirable. He was not a moral idiot of genius like Huey Long; he was merely an exhibitionist playing with fire. So Vardaman announced his candidacy for the United States Senate while Father was hunting quail in Arkansas.

Father wanted to be a force for good government, but he did not want to hold office. He did not want to be senator from Mississippi, but he wanted to keep Vardaman from being. Vardaman stood for all he considered vulgar and dangerous. Most people we knew felt the same way about him. The vacancy created by Senator McLaurin's death was to be filled, not by popular vote, but by the Mississippi legislature. Everyone conceded that on the first ballot of that body Vardaman would receive a plurality, but it was hoped that if several anti-Vardaman candidates ran, between them they could muster a majority and hold it until they could agree on the strongest of their number as the anti-Vardaman candidate for the final ballot. With this strategy in mind and confident that no Delta man and no gentleman could possibly be elected, Father consented to be one of five prominent citizens to enter the race against Vardaman. The strategy decided on succeeded, but only after an increasingly bitter battle in the legislature which lasted for fifty-seven interminable nerve-racking days. When the last ballot was cast, only five votes prevented Vardaman from representing Mississippi in the Senate. The anti-Vardaman forces won and the state was torn to shreds.

I don't suppose a state legislature is ever an impressive body of men. Mississippi's at that session was not: its members were not venal, but most of them were timid and third-rate. I moved to Jackson, the state capital, for the eight weeks of the fight in order to be with Father and to help as best I could, and Father's two brothers, Uncle Walker from Birmingham and Uncle Willie from Memphis, both brilliant and both popular, joined us. Father couldn't get chummy with people and, though his friends worshipped him and would have died for him, they did not call him LeRoy. As the struggle in the legislature progressed he became beyond question the dominant figure of the anti-Vardaman forces, although on the first ballot he had received only thirteen votes. His trouble was that he was a natural leader of men. Unwillingly the other four candidates conceded his pre-eminence and fitness and on the fifty-seventh ballot withdrew in his favor. So, at the last, it was Father against Vardaman. On the night of Washington's birthday 1910, a night of frenzied excitement, by a vote of eighty-seven to eighty-two, Father was elected United States Senator from Mississippi.

Nothing is so sad as defeat, except victory. There was the wildest enthusiasm among our people. Arriving home by train the next night, we were greeted by crying crowds, bands, and a torchlight procession. They had even found a little cannon for the levee, about like the one Fabre and his grandchildren used to test the hearing of cicadas. Our townsfolk were as deaf with joy as his cicadas. But Father was worn out and oppressed by the responsibilities ahead. Mother and I, though happy in a way, were dazed. And I was haunted by that desperate figure of Vardaman rushing up and down the rostrum after the last ballot screaming: "Black as the night that covers me."

The years Father served in the Senate were not dramatic or crucial years in the history of our country, but they were the end of a period in which great men represented our people. Father admired Mr. Root and Joe Bailey, disliked Lodge, loved John Sharp Williams, and was drawn to that Western group, so able and so feared by the Republicans, Dolliver, LaFollette, Borah, Cummings, and Norris. He fought the Civil War pensions racket, opposed our breach of faith with Great Britain in the Panama tolls case, helped with levee legislation, concerning which he knew more than any other man in Congress, and contributed materially to an excellent survey of our immigration laws. President Taft trusted and liked him in spite of Father's friendship with the ex-President; and Secretary of War Dickinson was his old and good friend. Had he been returned to the Senate he would have served our people helpfully and with distinction during the great period of the war.

But he was not returned by the people of Mississippi. Hardly had he taken his seat in Washington when he became engrossed in his race before the people for re-election, probably the most vicious and sordid campaign experienced by Mississippi since reconstruction days. While the overt issue in Father's race with Vardaman before the legislature had been Vardaman's stand on the Negro question, the undeclared issue had been the unanswerable charge against Father that he was a prosperous plantation-owner, a corporation lawyer, and unmistakably a gentleman. In his race before the people the Negro issue was to disappear with the emergence from under cover of the increasingly popular social issue and with the unexpected appearance of a new issue.

About two months after Father's election one of Vardaman's supporters in the legislature appeared before a grand jury and announced that one of Father's supporters had bribed him to vote for Father, that he had accepted the bribe money in bills, that he had taken them home and kept them in his safe, that he was now returning them intact to the grand jury. He added that he had broken his promise to vote for Father and instead had voted for Vardaman. We were stunned. Although we knew the shady reputation of the accuser we were not sure his story was false because the alleged bribe-giver was no intimate of ours but only an enemy of Vardaman. We were sick to the soul. But it occurred to the district attorney to examine the bills left with the grand jury. It was found to our own astonishment and relief that many of them had been issued after the date on which the self-accused bribe-taker said he had received them; indeed, after the date of the election. His story was a palpable and proved lie. But it was a lie with a thousand lives. The liar became the hero of the hour and his lie Vardaman's campaign ammunition. Vardaman's stand on the Negro question, Father's stand on current legislation in the Senate, simply held no interest for the sovereign voters of Mississippi. They were eager to learn if Father was a member of any church, if he hunted on Sunday, if his house was painted, if he had Negro servants, if Mother was a Catholic. They printed such questions and presented them to him when he spoke. He answered them truthfully, and unsatisfactorily. All over the state roved the self-accused bribe-taker vomiting his own infamy and cheered to the echo. The Hearst papers took up the hue and cry; George Creel published a foul attack in the *Cosmopolitan;* the professional lovers of carrion snickered and pointed. A man of honor was hounded by men without honor—not unusual perhaps, but the man was my Father.

The man responsible for tearing Father's reputation to tatters and saddening three lives was a pert little monster, glib and shameless, with that sort of cunning common to criminals which passes for intelligence. The people loved him. They loved him not because they were deceived in him, but because they understood him thoroughly; they said of him proudly, "He's a slick little bastard." He was one of them and he had risen from obscurity to the fame of glittering infamy—it was as if they themselves had crashed the headlines. Vardaman's glamour waned and this man rode to power.

Such was the noisome situation in which Father found himself mired and out of which he must fight his way with only integrity, courage, and intelligence for his weapons. A different assortment was needed—those count only in a world of honor. But the world in which he used them was not a world of honor; it was a new-born, golden age of demagoguery, the age of rabble-rousers and fire-eaters, of Jeff Davis and Tillman and Bleese and Heflin, of proletarian representatives of the proletariat. Vardaman was not the first nor Huey Long the last. I accompanied Father and his dear friend and campaign manager, Will Crump, from one end of the state to the other, at the first to try my hand at being agreeable to the voters and at the last to guarantee that Father received sherry and raw eggs and a little rest every day, for he was fagged and weak and, though not a big man, he had lost thirty pounds.

I recall a speaking at Black Hawk in a clearing of the woods with a few hundred persons present in spite of the drizzle. I had learned that the crowd planned to rotten-egg Father. I had found the hampers of eggs and stood by them with a pistol in my pocket which I intended to use. I looked over the ill-dressed, surly audience, unintelligent and slinking, and heard him appeal to them for fair treatment of the Negro and explain to them the tariff and the Panama tolls situation. I studied them as they milled about. They were the sort of people that lynch Negroes, that mistake hoodlumism for wit, and cunning for intelligence, that attend revivals and fight and fornicate in the bushes afterwards. They were undiluted Anglo-Saxons. They were the sovereign voter. It was so horrible it seemed unreal. But they didn't throw any eggs. They didn't refrain from fear of me, but Father was not the sort of person you threw eggs at—his eyes held a fearful warning. I have seen him cow better men than that gang of poor degenerates.

The worst day of all, as I remember it, was at Lauderdale Springs. A few of us had gone over from home to hear the speech, armed and sick at heart. Uncle Walker came to my room after midnight to say that one of our group would have to kill the bribe-taker in the morning as he was to attend our meeting and was scheduled to denounce Father. At six we met in the cold dreary dining-room for breakfast, Uncle Walker, his seventeen-year-old son, LeRoy, and I sitting at a table to ourselves. I had target-practiced most of the night in front of the mirror, so as not to forget to release the safety. A few yards from us at a table alone sat our intended victim.

Uncle Walker had a voice like Polyphemus', but he couldn't hit a balloon. Suddenly he leaned across the table, pointed to the man, and boomed out the epithet which makes an American fight if he's a man. The object of his outburst did not fall for the ruse, he made no motion to his hip or elsewhere, he kept on eating oatmeal.

At last we arrived at Lauderdale Springs, where a thousand or more people were seething about in front of a vacant hotel from the porch of which Father was to speak. Father's few local supporters drew him aside and told him the situation was grave. They insisted that on no account should he mention Vardaman or his henchmen in his speech, but that he must confine his remarks to non-controversial topics like the tariff. Otherwise there would be bloodshed. With that admonition they took the morning train back to Meridian. Father and Uncle Walker sat together an hour, painfully weighing this advice. They concluded it was too late in life to start being intimidated and this was not the occasion to talk tariff.

When Father rose to speak he was greeted with a roar of boos, catcalls, hisses, and cries of "Vardaman! Vardaman!" It was impossible to hear a word he might say. The din was insane and intolerable, and it showed no sign of diminishing. Obviously the crowd was determined to make it impossible for him to speak at all. The self-accused bribe-taker sat smiling on the porch at his immediate left. Father faced that obscene pandemonium, paused for the courtesy of silence, and, when he did not receive it, his eyes narrowed. Then burning-cold insults poured from his lips, he jeered them as cowards afraid to listen, and dared them to keep on. He cowed them by sheer will-power and lashed them into silence by leaping invective. At last the whole crowd was shamed into silence except one heavy man who sat in the middle toward the front and kept on howling insanely: "Vardaman! Vardaman!" I was glad to observe Billy Hardie immediately behind him with his pistol across his lap. Suddenly out of the crowd leapt a wiry stranger who jumped to the porch and, holding to a post, leaned out over the audience. He pointed into the face of the big man screaming "Vardaman" and called: "I know who you are and you know who I am. Shut up—or I'll come down after you." His eyes blazed like gray fire. The man shut up. He was wise. We found afterwards our unknown ally was Hunter Sharp, the best pistol-shot in Mississippi, noted for his daring and the number of his victims. Quiet restored, Father launched into the most scathing denunciation I have ever heard from human lips. It was the only speech of the kind he made during the campaign. He exposed Vardaman in all his weakness and the methods used by his henchmen with his consent. At the climax he turned to the man sitting next to him and, white with avenging anger, blasted him with his own infamy. The bear-baiting cowardly crowd, wild with excitement, cheered and cheered and cheered.

A few weeks before election day, coming back together from a hard week, Father asked me: "What do you think of it?" and I had to answer: "Not a chance." He smiled a little and said: "Right." The night the polls were closed and all Mississippi was counting ballots, Father, Mother, and I felt so relieved to be at last from under the long humiliating strain that we went to bed early and slept soundly. Father was not only defeated, but overwhelmingly. Thus at twenty-seven I became inured to defeat: I have never since expected victory.

Father did not like to lose at poker or golf or politics; in fact, he couldn't be called a good loser, if by that is meant one who loses without visible irascibility. But in this, the great defeat of his life, he was tranquil and found smiles and little spurts of merriment for his broken-hearted supporters. The only effect on him I could detect was an inner sadness, beyond reach, the kind of look I suppose Lazarus never outgrew after he had once died. A letter from him written about this time to one of his supporters is typical:

Greenville, Miss.,
November 19th, 1912.

Mr. W. W. Cain,
West, Miss.
My dear Mr. Cain:

Your letter is like "the voice of one crying in the wilderness." I have always thought that it is worth while to have made the fight and lost for the sake of the friends I have made, and your letter convinces me of the correctness of that view. I do not expect to shirk any duty that comes my way, but I am not seeking or desiring any political preferment. There is no office of honor that does not carry with it corresponding duties, responsibilities and work. I have no hunger for the honors and less for the work.

If I can keep this small corner of the United States in which I reside, comparatively clean and decent in politics and fit for a man to live in, and in such condition that he may not be ashamed to pass it on to his children, I will have accomplished all that I hope to do.

A good deal has been written about "shooting at the stars." I have never thought much of that kind of marksmanship. It may be characterized by imagination, it is lacking in common sense. I rather think it is best to draw a bead on something that you have a chance to hit. To keep any part of Mississippi clean and decent in these days, is a job that no man may deem too small. I certainly appreciate your kind expressions. With best wishes, I am,

Cordially yours,

LeRoy Percy

An old man wet with tobacco juice and furtive-eyed summed up the result: "Wal, the bottom rail's on top and it's gwiner stay thar." He wasn't much as a human being, but as a diagnostician and prophet he was first-rate. It was my first sight of the rise of the masses, but not my last. Now we have Russia and Germany, we have the insolence of organized labor and the insolence of capital, examples both of the insolence of the parvenu; we have the rise of the masses from Mississippi east, and back again west to Mississippi. The herd is on the march, and when it stampedes, there's blood galore and beauty is china under its hoofs. As for Mississippi, I don't mean to imply she has reached the nadir toward which she is heading. We still have Will Whittington in the lower and Pat Harrison in the upper house of Congress and that's creditable for any state. When Father was defeated good men all over the South were heart-broken, but today Mississippi is like the rest of the South, and the South is like the rest of the nation: the election of demagogues horrifies nobody. The intelligent are cynically amused, the hoi-polloi are so accustomed to victory they no longer swagger. The voters choose their representatives in public life, not for their wisdom or courage, but for the promises they make. Vardaman was a great forerunner of a breed of politicians not more able but less colorful than himself.

Perhaps it is a strengthening experience to see evil triumphant, valor and goodness in the dust. But whatever the value of the experience, it is one that comes sooner or later to anyone who dares face facts. Mine came sooner because of Father's defeat. Since then I haven't expected that what should be would be and I haven't believed that virtue guaranteed any reward except itself. The good die when they should live, the evil live when they should die; heroes perish and cowards escape; noble efforts do not succeed because they are noble, and wickedness is not consumed in its own nature. Looking at truth is not at first a heartening experience—it becomes so, if at all, only with time, with infinite patience, and with the luck of a little personal happiness. When I first saw defeat as the result of a man's best efforts, I didn't like the sight, and it struck me that someone had bungled and perhaps it wasn't man.

After the election not only Father but Mother needed desperately some interlude of peace. I hardly know what Father would have done in Washington without Mother. She laughed at his shyness, made him meet people and go to parties. More important, he thought aloud to her every problem he pondered, and her unfailing sanity clarified his thinking and freshened his spirits. During the long anguish of the campaign, she set her heart not on winning but on sustaining him and on keeping home pleasant and full of life. So we all needed a trip and chose the one Father and I had most wanted to take for years. We sailed for Greece.

Our approach was roundabout and leisurely. From Italy we dawdled down the beautiful Dalmatian coast, along Montenegro and Albania (ravaged that summer by cholera), turned the Leucadian promontory, passed Ithaca, and finally, with considerable peace of soul, pulled into the harbor of Patras and touched the soil, the hot, sandy, unkempt, sacred soil of Greece. We reached Athens after dark. In bed that night I figured I couldn't possibly wait until after breakfast to see the Acropolis, and besides it would be great fun to put one over on Father and tell him all about Athena's Hill over coffee and rolls. At six o'clock, with Baedeker under my arm, I rushed, as fast as my feet and my ignorance of the way allowed, to the Acropolis. No one was ascending the broad flight of steps to the Propylæa, but as I stood in its shade trying to catch my breath after the climb, I heard a great hubbub within the enclosure. I stepped in, facing the Parthenon. Voluble workmen in a group at the foot of a ladder were gesticulating and protesting. Father had beaten me to it. He was sitting on the pediment of the Parthenon where the Parcæ had sat and looking across Mars Hill to the blue sea and the mountains beyond. The curative morning was flooding over him, and he laughed when he saw me.

CHAPTER XIV

1914-1916

Ishmael lived one hundred and thirty-seven years. During that time he must have laughed and joked and loved; he must have looked at the sky and sat beneath the cool palm trees; he must have been glad—but he was a wanderer and a stranger all his days.

The North destroyed my South; Germany destroyed my world. In the dog-days of 1914 the mad dog of the world broke loose. After 1918 the world forgot that hydrophobia is curable only by death and it is paying for the oversight now. Again the mad dog is loose. His victims clutter the roadside, but still my own people, with the mentality of priests and tradesmen, prefer to pass by on the other side. In 1914 I didn't like the other side and I didn't want to pass by. All of me that said this is right and that is wrong said France and England must not be destroyed; Germany must not dominate: my mind did not judge, my being affirmed. Nevertheless I did pass on the other side. I was a tourist in a tourist's world, with no premonitions. An entrancing world it was, where prices were low and passports unheard of, where scenes fit for postcards were round every corner and treasures of art at every turn.

I was spending the midsummer of 1914 in Sicily and because of the heat I had the whole island to myself. As I had always been tormented by acrophobia I decided it would show a deplorable lack of nerve if I failed to climb Mount Ætna for the sunrise (double-starred by Baedeker). It was a long, tiresome ascent, beginning in a carriage, continuing by donkey, and ending afoot with a scramble through the ashes of the cone. By dark the donkey-boys (aged sixty) had become howling drunk and were bawling out bawdry while they hung for support to the tails of the donkeys. There was bright moonlight and a bitter wind. My guide, who stank unforgettably of civet and garlic, was chattering with cold and I had shrunk to half my size. At the observatory, where we were to have three hours' sleep before the ascent to the crater, if we could ignore fleas and bed-bugs, I asked him disagreeably, as I was trying to make myself comfortable in the hay in the corner, if Ætna donkey-boys always got drunk. He said no, but they were scared this time because ours was the first ascent anybody had made since the last eruption. He added that the last person he had guided to the top was an Austrian Grand Duke. I was not interested in Austrian grand dukes and wished he would shut up. He continued that in yesterday's paper he noticed the Grand Duke had just been assassinated at Sarajevo; one duke more or less—what time did we start up the crater for the sunrise? After the sunrise would be Taormina and Assisi and Paris. What a fascinating world!

Even in Paris I felt not the least tremor of doom. I paid my respects to Notre-Dame, looked in on the Salon Carré for old times' sake, paused in the gold gloom of Saint-Germain-des-Prés before the Mater Afflictorum with her cluster of candles and her small coterie of petitioners. That night I joined Frank Hoyt Gailor for sole cardinal, a bottle of Graves, and raspberries with sour cream. It was so pleasant a world we decided to watch it drift by from one of its most agreeable spots—a chair behind a table on the Grands Boulevards. We taxied to our favorite corner. The chairs were gone! There were no chairs or tables on any Paris sidewalk! We knew the world had come to an end. Within three days we had been involved in street-rioting, Mme Caillaux had been acquitted of murder, Jaurès had been assassinated, and war was declared. My world fell to pieces before I felt it tremble. I was to be a bit of an Ishmael the rest of my days, but I didn't know it then.

Safely back home, I wondered why I had left France. I was miserable. Men were fighting for what I believed in and I was not fighting with them; men were suffering horribly for my ideals and I was safe at home applauding and sympathizing. I tried the usual opiate—travel—and my private opiate—writing poetry. But I was shot through with discontent and probably with self-disappointment. I could have enlisted in Canada—why didn't I? There were excuses enough, I suppose, and I adopted them as reasons. Physically I was not made for a soldier, nor spiritually, for that matter. I was an only son; men around me were not enlisting; et cetera, et cetera aplenty. But from this vantage point of age and safety I think, granting everything, that for me, feeling as I did, not to have enlisted was inconsistent and shabby.

My cousin, Janet Dana, who had led as sheltered a life in New York as I had in Greenville and who alone of all my intimates felt as passionately about the war as I, entered training as a nurse and in due course reached a hospital in France. This was the last straw. Yet I temporized and equivocated. By accident I came across an advertisement in the *Outlook* asking for volunteers to join the Commission for Relief in Belgium under Mr. Herbert Hoover. I boarded a train for New York, applied to join the Commission for service in Belgium, and was accepted. My qualifications were that I spoke French quickly and inaccurately and that during the Mississippi floods of 1912 and 1913 I had headed the relief work in my section of the Delta. I hardly surmised what the work of the Commission covered or what service I could be to it. Americans under Hoover were feeding the starving Belgians—this much I was certain of and it seemed enough. Of course I hoped it would be a trifle heroic.

I remember nothing whatever of the partings at home or of how I got from Greenville to London. But I remember well the opal mornings of London and the cold velvet-black nights with the single corner lights blue and hooded, and I remember what seemed to me the youth of all the world in uniform, walking the streets, crowding the tearooms and pubs, on leave from France, from Gallipoli, from Palestine, gay and aureoled with daring. I was more eager than ever to get going, to be working at something related to the war, even though it were safe and minor. After waiting three weeks for a permit and a boat to cross the North Sea, at that time a perilous crossing, I finally received my orders, caught the deserted mail-boat at Harwich, a boat from *Outward Bound*, and by morning was safely ashore at Rotterdam. Then a week's dreary delay in slush and rain while spies ransacked my hotel room, and at last I was hustled across the border into the forlorn and snowy flatness of Belgium.

During the first days of the war Mr. Hoover, a rich mining engineer unknown to the American public, had had the imagination and energy to gather together what young Americans were within reach and to form them into a committee to feed the civilian population of Belgium and of the enemy-occupied area of northern France. At no time were there with him within the German lines more than forty-two Americans. They were novices, volunteers, and they did a surpassingly fine and ingenious job, by ear. Mr. Hoover collected money where he could find it, procured the necessary permissions and promises of co-operation from the Germans, and was himself the buying agent for wheat, corn, and meat the world over, from the Argentine and Australia to Canada. Germans, Belgians, French, English, and Americans trusted him, not only for his integrity but for his organizing genius and for his passionate non-partisanship. When his work was finally established in Belgium, he left Brussels for London and single-handed, against bitter opposition, persuaded Lloyd George and Lord Eustis Percy to finance his operations and to continue them under his direction for the duration of the war.

When I arrived in Brussels, the romantic pioneer period of the Commission's work had ended and Mr. Hoover's young Americans occupied positions of prestige and authority, while an enormous Belgian committee administered the details and performed the wearisome chores. The Belgians could have done the work equally well without us, but we were needed to maintain civilian morale, to act as liaison with the Germans, and to guarantee that the food distributed went into Allied and not into German mouths. There was nothing dangerous or onerous or exciting about our tasks, though in the sectors where we were required to live with and be directed by German officers, whom we called our "nurses," they sometimes tested our tact and temper. The simple truth is we were the spoiled darlings of Belgian society, entertained, furnished with servants, and provided with handsome residences richly furnished in the worst Victorian. For us, if it was war, it was war de luxe. It should have been a delightful experience—everyone, except an occasional German officer, was more than kind, my fellow Americans were fine intelligent chaps (particularly that red-headed, husky-laughtered running-mate of mine, Pink Simpson), and there was no lack of excellent food, excellent wine, and red-cheeked healthy Belgian girls who liked to laugh and to show you their albums of family photographs after dinner. It should have been great fun—but as far as I was concerned it wasn't.

No, in spite of the pleasant luxury, I didn't enjoy my life as member of the Commission. There was plenty of surface gaiety, but there were too many glimpses beneath. Across the golf-links and the moated parks of our friends' estates where we strolled week-ends, during lulls in the winter's bluster, drifted, like rumblings of far-off summer thunder, the sound of artillery fire from the front, and the ease and the laughter would seem inane, and I would wonder how many were mangled by that burst.

I don't suppose the dull ache which made the pedal-point of my waking hours was solely my unfulfilled desire to be a soldier in the trenches. Probably I had never been at peace. Probably I had always wanted to escape a life that had seemed to me filled with nothing and less noble than a human life need be. Probably, although I had no liking for hardships, a soldier's hardships and his likely end seemed to me a better poem than I could ever hope to write. And yet it is true that in a quiet, drugged fashion I was tormented by the thought that others were suffering for what was right and I was not suffering.

Furthermore, in Belgium we could never quite forget we were prisoners, well treated, indeed pampered trusties, yet prisoners.

I remember one winter twilight walking down a broad Brussels boulevard. The lights were just on, ice glinted from the trees, snow was deep and dry on the ground, pedestrians were hurrying home for supper through the crunchy silence. Plodding along, I became conscious of someone whistling a tune and suddenly the name of the tune came back to me—the *Marseillaise*! That martial air was forbidden by the Germans; to sing, play, or whistle it meant imprisonment. I looked around for the dare-devil whistler and saw instead the other passers-by becoming aware of what was happening. Everyone stopped or looked over his shoulder or into the eyes of those near him; everyone straightened up, quickened his step, and smiled. One after another we located the brash offender and were filled with warmth and excitement. It was a hulking young driver of a van pulled by two magnificent Percherons. Slouched over the reins, devil-may-care, in his workman's corduroys and broad red sash, without lifting his eyes or looking to right or left, he whistled piercingly and accurately from end to end the forbidden thrilling music.

But there was no such recompense when I watched the Germans herd together the unemployed civilians (called "chômeurs" at the time) and send them as slaves into Germany to work in the munition factories. German "atrocities" in Belgium were widely advertised and for the most part non-existent, but the wholesale enslavement of the able-bodied males of a helpless little country received slight publicity and only passing condemnation. Yet it was an example of wicked stupidity that Germans alone could have been capable of. The Belgians—of whom I was not an unqualified admirer—reacted to the indignity with a heroism beyond all praise. Most of them refused doggedly to work in the munition plants, and the Germans with their usual ruthless logic attempted to force them to do so by starvation. The Belgians were starved, actually and literally, but they were not starved into making munitions. When they had become physical wrecks, the Germans, finding them useless, returned them to Belgium. I saw trainloads of them arriving in the Antwerp station. They were creatures imagined by El Greco—skeletons, with blue flesh clinging to their bones, too weak to stand alone, too ill to be hungry any longer. This was only a miniature venture into slavery, a preliminary to the epic conquest and enslavement of whole peoples in 1940, but it seemed hideous and unprecedented to us in 1917.

When, therefore, in the early spring news reached us that our country was about to enter the war and had broken off relations with Germany, there was only shouting in my heart. Indeed, all of us walked on air and found it difficult to hide from our Belgian friends, terrified at the prospect of our withdrawal, our pride and enthusiasm. I at once applied for permission to return home. The Commission did not relish my request and pointed out the indispensable humane service we were rendering. I listened but did not hear. I insisted on the safe conduct out which had been promised me when I came in. Six other kindred spirits joined in my revolt: we were intractable and eloquent rebels. So the anxious Commission requested of the Germans a safe conduct for us through Germany into Switzerland. It was intimated that we would be required to take an immunity bath of several months in some German concentration camp so that any knowledge we might have of troop movements would by the time of our release be too stale to help the Allies. But we were undismayed. The whole Commission became interested in us as a test case. Finally the permits were granted and all arrangements completed for us to board a train to the Swiss border under the protection of a German officer, our last "nurse." With mingled emotions of sorrow and gladness we spent the last day telling our pitiful Belgian friends good-by; then the seven of us met for our last Belgian dinner at the Palace Hotel, across the street from the railroad station.

We took a table in the brilliant crowded dining-room, feeling, after our feverish day, flat and full of foreboding. We were leaving these wretched civilians to the mercy of the German army; they were afraid and we were afraid for them. We realized that each of us had reached his individual crossroads where the sign-posts showing the mileage and the destination had been blown down; and we were troubled by the possibility, now to be tested, of internment in Germany. We took a cocktail, ordered our meal and a bottle of wine. We were very sad. As it was not customary for us Americans to frequent the Palace, it being the favorite resort of German officers, our presence was noticed and commented on by the other diners, and we soon realized we were creating something of a sensation. A stray attaché joined us and asked us to drink with him one last solemn toast in champagne. We accepted. A Portuguese gentleman rushed over and greeted us as long-lost allies; another bottle was opened. Two young German officers who had been "nurses" of ours in northern France drew their seats up to our table and began fraternal lamentations. "Alas," said the little one we all liked though he was a confirmed embusqué, "to think that in a few months we shall be at the front line together, you on one side, we on the other, trying to kill each other!

Waiter, a bottle of champagne." We all wept and our spirits rose. Others joined us, vague individuals. It became a celebration. Everybody felt better and better. We all loved one another and said so and pledged our devotion in glass after glass of magnificent champagne.

At last someone thought to look squarely and honestly into the face of a watch and discovered we had ten minutes in which to collect ourselves, pay the check, get across the street to the station and into the train. There was a stampede. In the mêlée Arthur Maurice lost his hat and overcoat. But we made it across the icy street more or less upright, and debouched into the waiting-room of the station in superb spirits, giddy with love and optimism, teeming with becks and calls and wreathèd smiles. It was something of a set-back therefore to find the whole staff of the C.R.B. and half the Brussels population jamming the waiting-room, in tears, anxiously and solemnly waiting to bid us adieu. They had brought hampers of food, cases of wine, and bouquets of flowers, and only our tardiness had kept the weeping burgomaster from delivering an oraison funèbre of incomparable poignancy. Our German nurse had been frantically looking for us for an hour. He collected our remnants, and as the train pulled out we were boosted into it through the windows amid the sobs and cheers of our sorrowing friends. We landed in different compartments and it took hours to collect us. Our poor nurse was a nervous wreck. United at last, we settled down to headaches.

The next few days would have been dismal enough even had we been feeling first-rate. Rain, rain, rain—heavy, unceasing, cold—in Cologne, up the Rhine, into Switzerland. The landscape was a blur, the faces along the way gray and mirthless. Of course there were no sleeping-accommodations on our train and we dozed as we could, our nurse being unfailingly thoughtful and courteous. About the second night, while the others were sleeping, we stopped at some city, soaked and dimly lighted. It was about two in the morning, a miserable hour at best. I heard German voices outside our coach and the phrase by which they called us: "die amerikanische Hilfskommission." My heart sank, for I felt certain we were at last to be hauled from the train and headed for a concentration camp. I wakened our nurse. Outside, in the torrent, stood an old gentleman in a superb uniform of scarlet and gold with a few attendants. He was the burgomaster of the city and said he had come to the train to meet us in order to present the respects of himself and his city to the gallant and ardent young Americans who under untold difficulties had fed the population of unfortunate Belgium. The gallant and ardent were rumpled, unshaven, and half-asleep, but touched to the quick, and they truly regretted their inability to respond in words equally courteous and kindly. I should like to know the name of that old gentleman's city—I am sure it was not Prussian.

I cannot describe the feeling of breathing the free Swiss air, of touching the soil of a republic, without seeming exaggerated and sentimental. For months we had not dared speak of subjects nearest our hearts, we knew we were being watched and ears were everywhere. We were not anxious to say things, but we were choked by the things we were forbidden to say. Americans at home cannot possibly know what that feeling is, and so they cannot possibly appreciate the freedom so abundantly theirs. The right to call the President of the United States a dog-faced son of a sea-cook or something fancier, though you believe him the Messiah, is a right worth dying for. Liberty unthreatened is always liberty about to be lost. In

Switzerland we avidly read the newspapers so long denied us and talked at large and wondered about our own country, what it would do, for none of us doubted what it should do. At last our band of seven, papers in order, permits granted, boarded the night train for France—for Paris! Our elation was almost unbearable.

About five in the morning we piled out at a way station to hunt for hot chocolate. As we were drinking, newsboys came rushing up, crying at the top of their lungs: "la guerre," "les Etats-Unis," "la victoire," "le Président Veelson." Hurriedly we bought the morning paper. America had declared war on Germany! We could hardly see to read the President's incredibly moving and just words. We were spectators no longer, we were part of the tragedy.

Paris was brilliant with sunshine, our flag, so poignantly beautiful in foreign lands, was flying from every window, bunting and streamers festooned the streets, bands were playing. It was the glory of war and we were glorious, then if never again. We couldn't take time to wash or shave or stay indoors, and all Paris knew we were Americans. We trailed from bar to bar, the toast of strangers, passers-by, Frenchmen, Englishmen, soldiers, civilians. It was all vague and beautiful, it was fun turned ecstasy, drunkenness after Bacchus' own heart.

When we finally made it back to our hotel in the afternoon, a magnificent gentleman in a Prince Albert with the red button of the Legion of Honor on his lapel was awaiting us. We were bidden to attend as guests of the French Senate the speech of Premier Ribot welcoming our country into the war. We were dashed by the grandeur of the situation and by the unworthiness of our general appearance and condition. But stranger things had happened (though not to us), so we climbed into the sleek waiting automobiles and were borne in state to the Palais du Sénat. We looked like hobos, and our liquor was wearing off. We sat in our box and surveyed the French Senate with as much aplomb as we could muster. My recollection of Monsieur Ribot's address is singularly dim, but at its close a startling incident occurred. The senators from occupied northern France, whose guests we really were, in their overflowing enthusiasm for us, for America, for the Allies, for everything, turned to our box from their places on the floor of the Chamber and burst into cheers of "Vive l'Amérique!" "Vivent les Alliés!" finally producing a huge American flag and waving it violently at us. The rest of the senators, assuming of course that if we were not President Wilson in person, we were at least the American Ambassador and his suite, rose and joined in the uproar. We limply got to our feet and acknowledged the overwhelming though mistaken ovation. Across from us, neglected and unobserved, stood at the front of his box the real American Ambassador, hunting an opportunity to bow. When those Frenchmen discovered their mistake—O mon Dieu! it was moving in the extreme. And we teetered out, wrecked with laughter, and heading for a hot bath via the American bar.

CHAPTER XV

The Peewee Squad

Although I made the trip from Paris to Greenville in record time, the fever of war had beaten me home. The Delta was in the first throes of heroics. Women were knitting and beginning to take one lump of sugar instead of two, men within the draft age were discussing which branch of the service they had best enter, men above the draft age were heading innumerable patriotic committees and making speeches. People found themselves all of a sudden with an objective in common, with a big aim they could share, and they liked it immensely. You could sense the pleasurable stir of nobility and the bustle of idealism. Life that had seemed a habit and not a particularly good one had become overnight purposeful adventure, brisk with fine things to do and finer though more tragic things to anticipate. The Delta had reached the stage of exaltation. I loved it unreservedly. But Mother and Father looked as if they had just taken communion: there was a stillness in them which covered, I suspected, a great sadness.

I wanted to join the army, the infantry, at once. But,

being a year over draft age, my only chance was to enter an officers' training camp, and the first one had already started. A second, however, would open in two months. All the young men I knew had entered or been rejected by the first camp, or were trying for the second.

The most miserable people in the home town were the boys who had been rejected. Among them were two of my best friends, Tommy Shields and Widdie Griffin. Tommy's disqualification arose from a badly infected sinus which he must cure before he could be accepted in any branch of the service. It took him six months of operations and torture to effect that cure, but he stuck it out and he served. More than six months, maybe more than a lifetime, would be needed for Widdie to recover from his experience at camp. He had always been one of my favorite people, he was one of Judge Griffin's grandchildren, and we had played Buffalo Bill and Indians together. He was a woods creature, all eyes and ears, with a leprechaun shyness and whimsicality. When a baby, he had been dropped by his nurse and in consequence his shoulders were stooped, but he had no scar or break, he could accomplish miracles with a gun or a fishing rod, he excelled at track and baseball, and he had won the state championship for trap-shooting. He didn't like war or politics, but he was a gentleman, he was in love with danger, and he had infinite grit. So among the first to present themselves at Fort Logan H. Root for admission to the first officers' training camp was Widdie. One of the preliminary requirements was a physical examination, during the course of which Widdie found himself, along with some hundred other youngsters, all stark naked, filing before the desk of an examining officer, a Major in the medical corps. The Major had a voice of brass. When Widdie approached him he rasped out: "What to hell are you doing here? Fall out of that line, you're nothing but a damn hunchback." When Widdie returned home he told nobody what had happened. He went about as quiet as a ghost and his eyes looked as if he had been crucified.

With a stay in Belgium to my credit during which I had doubtless seen real German soldiers and heaps of German atrocities, I was inevitably expected to be a rabble-rouser at all patriotic convocations within the radius of two hundred miles. My first month home was a crowded itinerary of speeches. With emotions all over America waiting to be fired, the smallest spark in any speaker fell on audiences all tinder. I tried my best because I believed in what I was saying and audiences were distressingly responsive, but I have reason to suspect my speeches were pretty bad. I don't remember a single word of any one of them. Yet I must qualify that statement: one speech I remember very clearly. I received an unexpected invitation to address the officers' training camp at Fort Logan H. Root. For once I accepted with eagerness an invitation to speak. The meeting was held out of doors. The whole camp—about twenty-five hundred men—was present, the student officers sitting on a fan-shaped slope of grass, and between them and me a huddle of officers. About ten feet in front of me sat the Major who had examined Widdie. I started off with the usual items—the Belgian civilians and their troubles, the German army and its occasional insolence, the deportation of the chômeurs and their tragic saga. This live young bunch was so hungry for authentic news from abroad they followed me with real interest. Then I began to discuss German and French officers I had met and the difference between them, due to the different theories of discipline in which they had been schooled. I described the German officer's attitude toward his subordinates as arrogant and harsh, his will imposed by fear, if necessary by cruelty, and I contrasted that with the attitude of the French officer, who was a father to his men, guiding and protecting and controlling them as if they were his children. Surely the German system was inimical to all we cherished. Surely with Americans the French system could be made to work. But in which school were American officers, these very student officers before me, being trained? I had learned of recent happenings which had made me wonder and doubt and fear. I began citing concrete instances, and the crowd stiffened with excitement. I have no orator's eloquence, but sometimes when I am shaken with feeling, that feeling in spite of the words communicates itself to my listeners. On this occasion I was shaken with indignation and the desire to avenge Widdie. I began slowly to tell the story of Widdie's examination by the Major sitting in front of me, omitting nothing except his name and Widdie's. By the sudden stir and whispering of the crowd I saw they were familiar with the incident and knew my target. Then I told what I thought of the Major whose manners and brutality had been typical of the worst tradition of the German army and I closed by appealing to them not to follow his example.

When I had finished, no officers lingered to congratulate me, but the students were beside themselves with excitement and, if I remember accurately, the Oklahoma contingent had me on their shoulders and were yelling like coyotes.

My speech-making came to a sudden end when I discovered thirty days before the opening of the second camp that I was twenty pounds underweight. No amount of ardor and patriotism would be accepted as a substitute for those missing pounds. I immediately took to bed. Daily I managed to get into me and keep down four tablespoonfuls of tanlac, six raw eggs, a quart of cream, and the three usual hefty meals. On the fateful day I was to be weighed I supplemented the ration with four bananas and a quart of water. I tipped the scales at 135, a net gain of 23 pounds in thirty days. I was as proud as if I had captured a machine-gun nest. When I brought the good news to Mother, she looked incredulous; then she looked like Mère when she would tap me with her thimble, and suddenly she left the room. I was at last about to begin to be a soldier.

The second officers' training camp for our part of the South was held at Leon Springs, Texas. It bulged with five thousand anxious, husky young Southerners who believed that if they failed to become officers the war would be lost and they might just as well have been born out of wedlock in New England. A vast army was being created out of nothing in no time, it would be sent overseas, and men of the training camps were to be its officers. I don't suppose any of us ever felt, before or since, so necessary to God and man. To save the world we were called on to learn in three months what it takes West Point four years to inculcate. If any of us failed, he would have usurped the place of some other chap who could have made the grade, he would have wasted his government's time and money, he would have disgraced his family, and he would have failed in the supreme test of his whole life.

Of the dozen home-town boys in camp, five of us landed in the peewee squad of Company D. Every company has two ends, a big end composed of six-footers, flashy and incompetent, who lead when the company is marching and are the joy and pets of the instructors, and a little end composed of pale runts whom the big end calls peewees and the instructors ignore. In the little end reside the brains of the company. We watched with growing contempt the ineptitude and bland blockheadedness of the big end and tightened our belts. When anyone fainted as we were lined up to pass a doctor with a hypodermic needle, he was always one drawn by Michelangelo. When after paratyphoid shots on Saturday afternoon someone collapsed in the barber shop or the hotel lobby, crashing loudly like a tree, you didn't need to look around, it was one of those superb military figures, all brawn and no guts. Who got themselves lost on night maneuvers and fell over parapets in the trenches? Big 'uns. Who, when asked an intelligent question in class, looked like God's afterthought? The question answers itself.

The five peewees from home were Allen Crittenden, Emmet Harty, Sam Weil, Ferman Millette, and myself. We just soldiered. In uniforms too big for us, we had no air martial or otherwise; indeed, to the naked eye we were undeniably insignificant. The physical work in camp was too much for us and we had the Pauline propensity for dying daily. Someone—a whole crowd of unfortunate someones—was going to be sent home ("broken" was the term used) and we knew it would be us. We banded together in an offensive and defensive alliance, and the woes of one were the woes of all. Although no one noticed us, we found some consolation in analyzing our superiority to the big stiffs. They had always been able to rely on their bodies, hence they had never been forced to develop their self-control and their will-power. When their bodies failed them, they had nothing else to fall back on and they merely passed out. The peewees of the world, never having been able to rely on their bodies, had always had to develop their strength in their souls. From the beginning most situations had been impossible for them, so they had been forced to spin from their intestines grit and endurance. Peewees stuck till they broke.

There was a dash of truth in our cheering theory. Most of the men I saw screaming and gibbering in battle or weeping at the whine of a shell or sniveling in the dark were big blonds who didn't know they had a nerve in their bodies.

Our bunch bunked side by side at one end of the barracks, we coached each other in book work, we whispered correct commands to whichever one of us had the misfortune to be corporal, we hazarded disgrace by helping one another reassemble in order the contents of our packs, when, spread on the ground at inspection, they seemed maliciously bent on disintegration—in brief, we stood by in every emergency, and there was one an hour. No soldier can soldier alone. The tasks assigned are too numerous and too intricate for one man, peewee or big stiff. A buddy is as necessary as a rifle. Of our quintet I was the greatest recipient of aid and solicitude because I was more incompetent and they more kind. Any afternoon by the time of the four-o'clock rest period I was strewn on my bunk, three-fourths corpse and too far gone to pray for resurrection or dissolution. I would hear Emmet's deep serious voice above me: "Percy, can you make it?" As I never knew the answer I never gave it. "I'll step over to the canteen and get you a cup of cold milk"—and he half dead himself!

Weeks passed and none of us had been sent home. We began to be hopeful. We even began to like our instructors. But I continued to hate Captain Harris. Having been until recently a top sergeant of the regular army he was uneducated and brusque. Every morning he inspected our barracks to see that we had made up our bunks and had policed around and under them. I labored piously at this chambermaid's job. One morning as he passed slowly between the double row of bunks with that quiet X-ray gaze of his, he stopped in front of mine and inquired: "What's that under your bed?" I unbent from attention to a humiliating angle and spied with despair one single tiny white feather which undoubtedly had just blown there from beneath Emmet's bunk. It was poised like a fairy caravel, but to me it looked as big as a battleship. "A feather," I murmured weakly. "Looks to me like dirt and I don't want to find it there tomorrow." He moved down the line. I was apoplectic and longed for the eye of a basilisk. Besides, I heard suppressed snickers from the other peewees, who were supposed to be at attention.

A week or two later as we lay on our bellies in the broiling Texas sun after a long day of hell, I again and unfortunately attracted Captain Harris's attention. We were doing an exercise invented, I take it, by the Inquisition and known as "push and pull." You thrust the rifle from your shoulder to your full arm's length, then snap it back, and thrust it out again and back again, and on and on and on. After about the tenth thrust I found there wasn't another thrust left in me: I couldn't push and I couldn't pull. I lay on my stomach—and I giggled. At any rate it was better than crying and I didn't care if Emmet did kick me. At that moment Captain Harris's voice, registering zero, poured over me: "Mr. Percy, this ain't no kindergarten." It certainly wasn't. Oh, how I hated that man!

After such a reverse it was a genuine pleasure to hear Sam Weil denounce the stupidity of the army, the inefficiency of the instructors, the general injustice of life. He was highly articulate, had no illusions, and not only looked facts in the face but smote them between the eyes. After taps, when the rest of us were bordering on collapse, he would rouse to loud and colorful conversation.

indiscreet, corrosive, and passionately just. The next day he would answer questions as accurately as a Red Seal record and he always made a hundred on quizzes. Scholastically the acknowledged superior of any other man in the company, the peewees were proud of him. But he had the defect of his qualities. The commanding officer picked the hottest day of the year to order us for the first time to put on full packs. Each weighed seventy pounds. By late afternoon, when we had marched countless miles, done push and pull, attacked dummies with bayonets, crawled and charged, we knew they weighed a hundred. We were limp, our tempers frayed, our morale gone, with it our strength, and it was time to start to camp if we could make it back without being carried. This was the moment our bumptious tactical officer selected to call us to attention and make a speech. He announced that we would double-time into camp! It would be hard, he conceded, but it would separate the men from the boys, and anyone who couldn't take it would return to his civilian habitat tomorrow morning. Choking with thirst, reeking with sweat, furious and exhausted, we started double-timing, those packs like stone mummies between our shoulders. The little end of the company happened to be in front. After a few minutes I got the blind staggers, which is as hard on the man each side of you as on yourself. We were in a column of fours and Sam was of the first four. Suddenly he fell, lay flat on his face like a sprawled-out starfish, and split the double-timing cursing column from end to end. He had fainted. But we peewees were outraged. We knew he hadn't fainted, he had only decided it was one stupidity too much.

Sam's departure was our first casualty. It was almost like a real death. Our fear of suffering his fate grew into an obsession.

Millette had been no favorite of ours at home nor we of his. But army life is peculiarly revealing because it affords no privacy. You can't eat and sleep, march and undergo hardships and humiliations with a man twenty-four hours on end, day after day, without becoming his dear friend or his bitter enemy. You have seen him all over, nakedly, the way God and Velásquez see men, and he must be little better than a jelly-fish if he inspires any less neutral emotion than loving or loathing. It wasn't long before we were finding Millette a very fine peewee. He was better company than any of us, he had wit and an exuberant sense of fun, and he could do more extraordinarily and unexpectedly kind things than you had any right to expect from a lifelong friend. Such things he did only because someone needed them done. He had given up an excellent job to enter camp and we felt confident he would pull through; in fact, we were more certain of him than of any of the rest of us.

Our prognostications would have been justified had it not been for that battalion drill. Our inexperience made of it a terrifying ordeal. The officers themselves were excited over it (I suspect some higher-ups were lurking about the outskirts). By some misfortune Crit, Emmet, and I were separated from Millette and placed in the second squad from the rear, while he drew a corporal's position in the rear squad. We assembled on an unfamiliar wide parade ground under a summer sky. The stir and commotion were hard on the nerves even of peewees. Watching so many soldiers drilling at once with new commands being bawled at us and new officers in charge got us weak-kneed, lathery, and a trifle addled. We wheeled and marched, circled and sidewised, we became giddier and giddier. At last a strange voice bellowed the command by which companies fall into a battalion front, each quad in staggered formation marching up separately and oming to a halt on the company front at the corporal's ommand: "Squad—halt!" Our squad had made it to its lace without mishap, had halted, and was standing at ttention. Behind us we could hear Millette's squad narching up to take its place on our left. It's a beautiful ormation and we were doing it well. Everybody was vatching with pride and enthusiasm. Millette's squad vas the last to move into place. Except for it the whole attalion was standing at attention. Suddenly we heard is voice, clarion-clear, like a major's or maybe a general's, vith a triumphant ring in it. But, unseated I suppose by he splendor of it all, his ringing command was "Battalion—alt!" instead of "Squad—halt!" His three bunkies standng at attention and listening breathlessly almost dropped n their tracks. But his squad, instructed to disregard mistaken commands, kept marching. The parade ground was stricken with horror. Every eye was on that squad. It kept on marching. Again Millette's gallant voice rang out: "Company—halt!" The squad kept marching; it marched now like Beatrice Lillie, *vi et armis,* clear through an unyielding detachment planted in front of it. Corporal Millette gave no further command. His vocabulary had excommunicated the word "Squad" and without it that wretched unit of his gadded on like Dukas's broomstick. The last we saw of them they were disappearing into the woods. Homeric laughter shook the parade ground. It would have been funnier if it hadn't been so sad.

So that left Crit and Emmet and me. We didn't feel like three musketeers. In spite of all our intelligence we felt so, so like peewees. It must have been about this time that the epidemic of Liberty Loan drives swept the country. Our camp planned a huge "pep" meeting designed to sell bonds to us student officers. I was invited (a polite army term for "commanded") to make a speech as representative of the students. Mother visited us a few days before the event and, on seeing me, burst into tears, explaining that I looked like a "picked chicken." But the speech went off well—better, if I may judge by the applause, than any other I have ever made. I was vastly assisted by the preceding speakers, old army officers who were not only platitudinous, but neither earnest nor sincere. Bonds were bought in quantity and consequently my fellow students were convinced I deserved and would receive a captaincy at least and—well, there was just no telling. I knew that by no stretch of the imagination was I qualified for any rank higher than that of lieutenant, but I wanted to be that with all my heart. And I suspected that because of the speech and because it had become known that I was an ex-Senator's son I would realize my ambition. But this being a mere suspicion, I relaxed my efforts no whit.

Crit and Emmet, however, had made no speech and had no ex-Senator for father. Their sole qualification was excellence, and, they being peewees, that had gone unobserved. The three of us had known each other and been friends always. Now the bonds between us were so close they hurt. The night study-hour was the period of our chief terror, because toward its close an orderly would enter the cold windy mess-hall where we hunched over our books and announce: "The following student officers will report to the Captain's room." He would then read the list of the condemned. Either those named would disappear next morning, sneaking home with the conviction they were failures, or they would be subjected to some public test that always broke them. Only a certain number of us could be given commissions and therefore hundreds of us would have to be broken. The officers increasingly looked for signs of weakness or ineptitude. Theirs had to be a superficial hit-or-miss judgment, and peewees were their natural prey.

One morning Emmet was called out to lead a platoon in setting-up exercises. He did it hesitantly and without style. Crit and I thought he was gone. But he was Irish and red-headed and mean-looking. You could tell at a glance that his was the face that launched a thousand revolutions, not to mention uprisings, brawls and free-for-alls. I think the officers lost their nerve. They probably figured that if they ordered him home he would then and there draw a shillelagh and lay the camp waste.

Emmet and I worried continually about Crit. He was the best soldier in the company, but he just soldiered. We would rage and condemn, but Crit never complained or criticized and day by day he seemed to get smaller and paler and more little-boy-looking. The three of us were intact the beginning of the last week of camp. We thought we had won through. But that night Crit's name was called out.

Emmet and I went to our bunks. Taps sounded. We undressed and lay down and waited for Crit. Lights were out so fortunately we couldn't see each other. About midnight Crit came in and sat on the edge of my bunk. He said simply:

"Well, Bill, I've got to go."

"When?" we asked.

"First thing in the morning."

"It's impossible," I stormed. "You're the best soldier of the whole bunch. Something's got to be done. It's an outrage, a disgrace to the camp."

"Whatever is done has to be done now, tonight," said Crit.

I got up and put on my uniform, rebellious, impotent, and crying.

"Do your best, Percy," came from Emmet's bunk.

I left the barracks and stood in the dark before the Captain's door. At last he came out and I asked permission to speak to him. I am certain that I made the most eloquent plea I ever made or ever will make. I would have lied willingly, but all I needed to do was to tell the truth, all of it. Finally the Captain said, more in sympathy than in encouragement: "Well, I'll give him a chance—tomorrow morning."

The three of us lay in our bunks with the news, with the hope. We didn't do any talking. I guess we prayed most of the night.

Next morning we went through the usual routine. Neither Emmet nor I could look at Crit or speak to him. One formation after another was lived through and nothing happened. At last, just before mess time, the Captain called out: "Mr. Crittenden, take the company." He stepped out of the ranks and stood before the company, so small, so quiet, so beyond anyone's help. It was unbearable. Then the officers fell on him with intricate directions which he must translate into commands and must see that the company execute. He had never drilled the company before. First one officer and then another took up the goading. No one else in our company had been subjected to such a grueling. But Crit never wavered or slipped. His voice with the correct commands rang out clear and self-possessed and stern, but pitifully young. He was magnificent. It was a triumph of nerve. Emmet and I in our squad stumbled along blindly, as proud as if we'd been presented with a helmet full of D.S.C.'s.

So the three of us received our commissions and we'd rather have had those single bars on our shoulders than celestial wings.

The first person to congratulate me was Captain Harris, who observed sourly but with a twinkle: "Well, Lieutenant, you made it, didn't you?" Even I had come to love him. What he knew he knew thoroughly; what he didn't know he made no pretense of knowing. He never bluffed and he never played favorites. Those of us who received commissions gave him a banquet and I made the speech telling what we thought of him. We were all pretty broken up and moist, and he had to leave the room, because of course top sergeants don't cry.

It wasn't easy for us three buddies to part, but the first chapter was ended, and honorably. I started for France, Crit for Oklahoma, and Emmet began his adventurous trek toward the First Division. We never met again till the war was over. And now a bit wizened, like picked chickens, I suppose, peewees still, our exploits forgotten except by us, our world slipping away, we hear the younger generation demanding peace and isolation and we feel sorry for them, knowing they missed a lot of fun and a lot of grief that was better than fun.

CHAPTER XVI

Getting to the Front

On the camouflaged but unconvoyed vessel that bore me to England, I met Gerstle Mack, sat with a life-preserver in my lap anticipating doom, and read *She* (forbidden by Father) to keep from being seasick. Ours was a shipload of casual officers, unassigned, ignorant, cheerful, and complete strangers to one another. We landed in Liverpool the day a transport was torpedoed in the Irish Sea and without delay were whisked across England, lovely even at that drab wintry season. To survive the rest-camp in which we were deposited required real stamina. We lasted out an all-night dash across the Channel, herded standing in the hold of a mouse of a boat that jumped and shied and all but turned over. Curled up in a baggage rack on the wall I watched between paroxysms of nausea the pale flower of the American army wilt with seasickness. Another rest-camp, half completed, leaking the ample French rain, slathered with mud, awaited us in Le Havre. There our individual assignments to posts of duty reached us and we dribbled out apprehensively to our various locations. I drew Tours via Blois.

Tours had not yet become the Sargasso Sea of sunk military careers, but the basin of the watery graves was in the building, though they hadn't started hauling in the seaweed. I reached there about the second day of creation and was immediately made a billeting officer. The job required a little tact, a little French, and considerable energy. It could have been done as well by a civilian.

All morning I would inspect and grade rooms offered by the townsfolk to the American army for its officers and non-coms. The rooms were usually tousled and always smelly, for the French are pretty bitter against fresh air and consider night air fatal. All afternoon I would assign the rooms I had inspected to officers applying for billets. A general rated a bathtub, a lieutenant anything that was left. I did well by myself, but only after tricking my conscience.

A middle-aged woman, pretty and chic, came into the office to offer the Americans a room in her home. She was obviously a lady and scared to death. You could tell her decision to permit a stranger under her roof had been an ordeal, and it must have taken sleepless nights to find the courage to invade this office full of uniformed men who couldn't speak her language and might not realize she was a gentlewoman. On seeing her I decided hers was the house in which I wished to be quartered. Three hours later, without inspecting her room (so that I could assure my conscience I didn't know whether it was good or bad), I drove up to 18 rue de Clocheville, deposited my baggage on the steps, dismissed the driver, and rang the bell. Mme Thierry opened the door, surprised at seeing me so soon and flustered at recognizing me. I said I wanted to move into the room she had offered. She objected that I hadn't seen it. I countered I had seen her. She was horrified at my impertinence and admitted me dubiously. Of course it was a delightful room, fit for a major general.

Mme Thierry's husband was the best doctor in Tours and one of the kindest men in the world. Her nineteen-year-old son, Jean, was at the front. It was the only time I ever lived in a French family—French families being notoriously partial to leaving the stranger at the gate. After two months of it I not only tolerated but applauded the French lack of interest in other peoples and their exclusive and passionate love of the French. Although realists and rationalists, they treasure sentiment as décor, and irony as wit and not as bitterness. I could never understand how a people could be so disillusioned and yet retain so bright a zest for living. They seem to consider life a raw deal and within limits very agreeable.

It was the winter of our discontent, that winter of 1918, full of foreboding, almost of despair. We thought Amiens would fall before the Americans could arrive in numbers, and after Amiens, Paris—in which event our army would have to scuttle over the Pyrenees to safety and disgrace. The Thierrys were heavy-hearted for their boy and saddened daily by news of some friend's death at the front.

To cheer them up two old friends of theirs came down from Paris for a visit, Rodin's rival, the great sculptor Sicard, and his beautiful Russian wife. They were often joined by an army chaplain, his uniform plastered with medals and a black patch over one eye. The five of them would while away the depressing winter evenings by reading aloud eighteenth-century memoirs, those just a little naughty. The chaplain was a wag as well as a hero, and his remaining eye burned with life and malice. Sicard, broad-shouldered and dour-looking, could be roused to memorable gaiety. Charming people, and so civilized. Their breed is not increasing.

I was often invited to family dinner, which would have been more than acceptable even without that miraculous Vouvray from the doctor's own vineyard. I should probably have been invited oftener had my French been house-broken. It took a sudden turn for the worse at the biggest party of the winter.

For the occasion the usual number of aunts and a grand-mère or two had been hauled from the attic, brushed off, and freshened up with ruching at the wrists of their black basques. They made me homesick: they looked like Aunt Fanny, their appetites were gargantuan like Aunt Nana's, and though entirely worldly-wise, their manners were delicately jeune-fille and conventual like those of old maids in Charleston. By the end of the soup course (served with Barsac) the interchange of chirpings had reached such a tempo I gave up trying to follow the sense and was sitting peacefully and contentedly thinking how nice they all were, and how alike nice people were the world over, when an Aunt Fanny, remembering it wasn't well-bred to omit the stranger from the conversation, asked across the table: "And now, Lieutenant Pairsee, won't you tell us something of the fauna and flora of your dear Southland?"

All French ladies are impervious to the facts of geography. You can do nothing about their impression that the Mississippi is a branch of the Amazon, and the Delta borders Tierra del Fuego on the north. I ransacked my brain for a topical theme. Or should it be tropical? Panic enfolded me. What can you say about the Delta? I became distraught in my search for a Southern theme. Rattlesnakes! Oh, how I hated them! But they were pretty Southern and not in the least French. I tried to dismiss them. They became an idée fixe. At the same time my French vocabulary suddenly wasted away. Slowly and pausefully I began on rattlesnakes. This is the information I imparted: "In my country there lives a serpent." Mild ah's. "He is three or four kilometers long." The ah's pick up. "He always carries little chimes." Great flurry of ah's and extraordinaire's. I ceased, but Aunt Fanny, unhappily roused to enthusiasm for natural history, insisted on knowing where this amazing reptile carried his chimes. On his head? What in heaven's name was the word for tail? I lunged and missed by a bare inch. Out of my naïve mouth leaped that most shocking of French words, a word which sounded to an American ear like the one I sought. A snowfall of silence covered the company. Aunts and grandmères tilted their eyes to the ceiling, saint-wise. Then the aumonier choked, threw his napkin over his head, and burst into a bellow of laughter. The rest followed suit. They rocked and wept and choked and stopped and started again. I, still guiltless as a clam, sat unnerved to the point of catalepsy. Clochettes dans le —— oh Lord!

No sooner had I become proficient at billeting than I was yanked out of it and assigned as flunky and handy man to the post commandant, Colonel B. We didn't take to each other. I recognized in him the regular-army outline without its content. He knew but two verbs: pass-the-buck and get-by-with-it. Having nothing for me to do, he made up things. The only definite assignment I received was to fix a smoking stove in the office. Two moronic doughboys were donated as my assistants. I knew if I booed at them they'd run into the woods and start whinnying. After two days of tussle with that stove-pipe we succeeded in blackening the office so completely it seemed paneled in ebony and looked rather handsome. The Colonel asked what progress we were making. I explained it was the nature of that stove to smoke out generals, and personally I couldn't do anything about it. He wanted to bawl me out, but decided it wasn't any use—and it wasn't.

Those would have been wretched days under Colonel B. had it not been for occasional glimpses of Gerstle and Frank Hoyt and an unexpected visit from Father.

Despairing of active service, Father had joined the Y.M.C.A. as one of an advisory committee of three and was making speeches at the canteens throughout the American sector. In his Y uniform he looked so strikingly like General Pershing he was always being embarrassed by salutes from green doughboys and embarrassing them in turn by his dreadful return salute, as sketchy as a general's. Some divine innocence in him made him believe nothing was too intelligent or too idealistic for our soldiers and they responded by loving his speeches. That same quality led him to regard me as a hero, though I had never seen a trench.

The Thierrys and the Sicards were great friends of Anatole France, who was living that winter in Tours. They must have mentioned me to him because he sent me an English translation of *Thaïs* with a charming inscription and a sheaf of American periodicals, the most unlikely imaginable, such as the *Ladies' Home Journal.* Twice he invited me to his Sunday levée and I longed to attend, but when I asked permission of Colonel B. he was so irritated at never having heard of Anatole France that he refused. So he was glad when a hurry-up order came from Paris for a lieutenant who could speak French. Protesting, I told him I wanted to go to the front and not to Paris. He observed that as far as he was concerned I could go to hell, but for the present I might try the next train to Paris and report to the purchasing agent of the American army, Colonel Charles Dawes. I tried the next train to Paris.

Colonel Dawes's small office contained two straight chairs, the Colonel, and a desk, on which reposed the Colonel's feet. I came snappily (I hope) to attention, saluted, and said: "Sir, Lieutenant Percy begs to report." He gazed at me anxiously but without interest. "Oh, for God's sake, Lieutenant, don't stand at attention! It worries me." I relaxed, almost crumpled. "All this saluting and carrying on gives me the fidgets. Now, Lieutenant, what do you want?"

"Nothing, sir. I thought you wanted me."

"What to hell do I want with you?"

"I can't imagine, sir. You sent for me in a hurry from Tours. I speak French."

"Good God," he burst out, "and now I've forgotten what I wanted you for. Sit down, sit down, Lieutenant, and help me remember."

I sat down and was about to suggest that anywhere he might send me, just so it was farther, might satisfy us both, when he exclaimed: "Old Jones, that's it, old Jones (Major Jones, I should say) needed you. Do you know Jones? Nice chap. You'll like him. Know where he is? Well, I'll take you down to him. Hell, what a mind I've got, what a mind! This goddamn army!" He led me down three flights of dark stairs and turned me over to old Jones. I batted my eyes to collect myself and stood at attention.

Major Jones was oldish and amiable and had the sort of face you couldn't possibly remember. I would scrutinize him, wishing he had one eye or three ears or a long scar so I could recognize him tomorrow. But it wasn't necessary. He was so pleased with the girls and the liquor and the safety of Paris he had little time to interfere with my work, much less to supervise it.

It was curious work for an infantry officer. My duty was to supply civilian labor for the American army, usually for Gerstle, who apparently was running engineer headquarters round the corner. The only civilian labor left in Paris was apaches, pickpockets, gutter-snipes, and syphilitics. I operated through the French Bureau of Labor in this manner: Gerstle would order ten carpenters, fifteen masons, twelve plasterers, six painters, and one cabinet-maker (never more; I wonder why); the Bureau would summon the scum of Paris into my presence; I would sift it for the craftsmen requisitioned and direct them to meet me at the railroad station next morning. They would be booked to build a hospital at Saint-Etienne or barracks at Bordeaux. I would secure their reservations, meet them in front of the station, call the roll, get their tickets, and put them into their compartments. In this way I became thick and friendly with the underworld of Paris. No one ever came to tell them good-by except me (perhaps because no train in any direction could be induced to leave later than six a.m.) and they were always in high spirits. Their baggage consisted of a long loaf of bread, a large bottle of pinard, a cigarette behind one ear and a flower behind the other (by preference a carnation). For traveling costume they wore big baggy corduroys, tight at the ankles, a shirt without a collar, a black skimpy muffler, and a wide red sash yards long. Their hair was always dripping wet and carefully parted, with an elaborate spit-curl on the forehead. They would greet me loudly with "Hé là, mon lieutenant, ça va?" and when I put them on the train I would shake hands with them all, down to the last ax-slayer.

After they had been on their jobs a week, the Bureau

of Labor would receive from them an indignant telegram saying that they were rioting, that American food was impossible, fit for swine but not for civilized Parisians, that they demanded return fare to Paris immediately. About the same time Major Jones would hand me a telegram from the commanding officer of the camp to which they had gone to this effect: "Labor rioting. Fantastic complaints concerning American food. Riot quelled. Can't understand your selection. Labor shortage continues. Situation acute. Do you call this co-operation? For God's sake rush labor less epicurean and revolutionary who will work." The Bureau would treat the incident as if the Bastille was about to fall again and would confidentially implore me to reform the American army's cuisine. In a few days the rioters would all be back, delighted with the trip, glad to see me, ready to go elsewhere. I would again hire and ship them, they would again riot and return. The French never did come to think it was funny, or place the blame on those charming cut-throats of mine. We became so chummy I would take them cigarettes as a good-by present. I wished for a bitter enemy so they could do him in for me, ferociously and with gusto, just for sentiment's sake.

Although these goings-on occupied my waking hours amusingly enough, that spring in Paris was not a happy one. The marronniers bloomed sullenly under sunless skies, there was no heat in any hotel, Big Bertha boomed by day and planes dropped their loads by night, news from the front was increasingly terrifying—fear clung to Paris like mold. But these were not the true causes of my restlessness and unhappiness. Poilus from the trenches walked the boulevards, thick and stocky, dowdy in their horizon-blue uniforms, and sad-eyed. Spruce Australian, English, and New Zealand officers, on leave from the front, filled the bars and cafés. I began to believe these true soldiers knew I worked in an office, in a safe place, like a damn civilian. To men from the line an assignment in Paris was a badge of disgrace. No use to argue that it wasn't your fault, you were obeying orders, orders you hadn't asked for—I became convinced that without suffering there was no real soldiering and that the eye of every real soldier accused me of being an embusqué. An embusqué, everyone knew, was an officer who had got himself a soft safe berth by pull.

To let things take their own course meant to remain in the Labor Bureau for the duration. I brooded miserably on the situation and finally spied a faint ray of hope. The only "pull" I could possibly have would be through Huger Jervey, who at the time was in Saint-Aignan acting as chief of staff of the replacement division. I wrote and begged him to get me out of the S.O.S. and toward the front. He knew me and he knew how any soldier would feel under the circumstances, but, thinking of Father and Mother, he hated to help me out of safety and toward possible danger. Being a Southerner, a Sewanee man, and one of my oldest and dearest friends, however, he couldn't refuse. Major Jones received a request for my transfer to Saint-Aignan. The Major summoned me to his office and said affably: "Lieutenant, I have received a request for your transfer to the replacement division. You are indispensable to my department. I have recommended you for promotion. I have refused the request for transfer." My only chance to be a real soldier gone, gone because of this lazy old embusqué! Merciful anger saved me from tears. In Homer's phrase, I summoned my stout heart and spoke wingèd words:

"Major Jones, you've been good to me. May I speak to you man to man? I have watched you here in Paris doing your duty efficiently and on the surface cheerfully. But you haven't fooled me: I know you have been eating your heart out. The one thing in the world you want is to get to the front. You are soldiering, but it's killing you. Major, if you feel that way, think how I must feel, so many years younger than you. This is my only chance. My whole future is in your hands. You can keep me here for the rest of the war or you can let me do what you want to do, what every real American wants, what I want. Don't deprive me of my one chance. Major, let me go."

I almost believed my own eloquence and my voice was trembling. The Major's eyes became moist and he murmured emotionally: "Go, my boy, go. I understand. I can't hold you here. God bless you."

Although I knew they were crocodile tears, I felt like busking that old man on his bald spot. I had always considered Machiavellian tactics abominable, and guile and flattery the most contemptible of the survival virtues, but I had not one regret, no remorse, no repentance. I was spilling over with happiness. I wanted to share it with Gerstle and Charlotte and Frank Hoyt, but I couldn't locate any of them. So I walked on air down the Champs-Elysées repeating: "My heart is like a singing bird whose nest is in a watered shoot" and wondering what a watered shoot might be. I floated up the grands boulevards like a very luminous jack-o'-lantern, found by instinct the Café de la Paix, pulled out an iron chair that felt like down, took a seat, and ordered a whisky and soda.

It was at this point that I beheld an apparition of joy which almost floored me: Lieutenant McCloud of Leon Springs came sauntering down the boulevard. He had been the orneriest, wildest backwoodsman in camp and he hailed from Sullivan's Hollow, than which there is no more blood-spilling, moonshine-drinking, tobacco-spitting nest of outlaws in all the South, no, not excepting Louisiana's Tangapahoa or Kentucky's Harlan. When I had known him he couldn't speak English, much less French. But here he was strolling in front of the Café de la Paix in the snappiest of uniforms, with the sauciest of overseas caps over one eye, and on his arm the most flamboyant little cutie in Paris. He approached with a dazzling grin, as if we'd just finished squads-right together: "Hey, Percy, what's the French word for bolts?" "Bolts and shackles?" I ventured. "No, just bolts. My job is buying bolts for this man's army." He strode off in male grandeur, his little sweetie nestling warmly, but kicking up one heel behind her à la Moulin Rouge and giving me a wink as they faded out. Shades of Sullivan's Hollow!

Saint-Aignan was the liaison between the front and rear of our army, and Huger, apparently, was its presiding deity. Very splendid and dignified, he asked me where I wanted to go from there. I had had three months within which to learn the duties of an infantry officer and six months within which to forget them. Obviously I still wasn't fit to handle a platoon, so we decided the place for me was the officers' school of the line at Gondrecourt, completing which, one would be sent to the trenches as a replacement.

Gondrecourt was much like Leon Springs, but less taxing physically and unendearing. The officers taking the course were from line outfits to which they would be returned. I was an outsider and beneath notice. So I studied hard while they went through the motions, and for my virtue was rewarded as virtue is so often rewarded —instead of being sent to a division in the line as platoon leader I was made an instructor. I protested passionately and was told to shut up and report immediately to General Hay of the Ninety-second Division.

I had never heard of General Hay or the Ninety-second and I scoured France looking for them with the least possible enthusiasm. When I finally entered the division area, looking out of the train window, I decided that in a fit of homesickness I had lost my mind—the landscape was speckled with Negro soldiers! The Ninety-second was the much publicized Negro division, in which all officers except supply officers and those above the grade of captain were Negroes. Not knowing whether to laugh or cry and wishing I could see somebody from Trail Lake, I located the inhospitable division headquarters and asked for General Hay. They pointed him out, entering his car, a bleak, austere man with a hurt, forbidding look and a cold voice drained of color by the long giving of commands.

Standing on the sidewalk at attention, I introduced myself by the usual formula.

"What are you reporting for?" he demanded harshly.

"As instructor, sent from Gondrecourt."

"I didn't ask for an instructor and I don't want one," said the General. (I've sometimes thought the army's manual of manners must be *Alice in Wonderland* instead of Emily Post.) I was fed up with bad manners and bawlings out.

"Sir, I didn't ask to be sent here and I don't want to be here."

"Why?" he snapped.

"Sir," I proceeded as if he liked me, "can you imagine anyone *choosing* to be an instructor, particularly to an outfit that doesn't want him?"

He sized me up grimly and I didn't feel big.

"What have you learned over here that may help my men?"

"Map- and compass-reading, message-sending, and the

new French open-order formations." (I refrained from saying reeling, writhing, and fainting in coils.)

"Can you teach these subjects?"

"Yes, sir."

"Do you know anything else?"

"No, sir, I'm one of these new officers out of civilian life. I know nothing at all, sir, except a little human nature and good manners when I see them." I smiled cheerfully.

He meditated: "Hard on both of us."

"Not so very," I answered sincerely.

"Well, get in the car. We'll try it," said the General.

General Hay's headquarters were in a hovel of a village where the remaining civilians were shockingly poor and dirty-looking. Next morning I felt at home when upon asking a Negro orderly for some warm water he averred there warn't none and you couldn't git none. I suggested borrowing from the house across the street. He sighed and commented: "Lawd, that woman ain't seen no warm water since the last time she cried."

For a few days I drove with the General over his brigade on inspection trips. He was grim and aloof, but I noticed he inspected closely and asked me many questions, none personal. One night he knocked at my door and said: "Lieutenant, I'd like you to come to my room."

I went, puzzled and curious. He sat down stiffly but wearily and motioned me to a chair. "Lieutenant, I notice you are not afraid of me."

"No, sir, not a bit."

"I have an unfortunate manner. I appear cold and stern. My officers are afraid of me, all of them. For that reason they will not talk to me candidly. I am responsible for seventy-five hundred men, a whole brigade, and in all my army life, ever since I graduated from the Point, I have never commanded more than a hundred. For many years I have been a desk officer. I need to learn everything anyone can teach me. We are all like that, we ranking officers of the old army. Your first duty, Lieutenant, is to instruct me and to protect me from mistakes so I may protect my men. Will you promise to criticize me and give me any information you have and I haven't, as if we were of equal rank?"

I promised.

"I am making you brigade instructor. Half of your time will be spent in one regiment, half in the other. Any officer you recommend for demotion I shall demote. I will trust the honesty of your judgments."

I felt like putting my hands between his and swearing fealty. Without the oath, I was his man. He carried out his promise to the letter and I never tried harder not to fail a man. He was promoted before the war ended and I rejoiced, knowing he merited it. Only divine devotion to duty could have induced so self-contained and proud a man to open his heart and call for help to a shrimp of a lieutenant.

My classes were held for Negro officers, the majority of whom outranked me. I knew they would be looking out for slights and condescensions, especially after they recognized me as a Southerner. I wanted to give them their every due, to pay them their every military respect, but at the same time I was not going to permit them to be familiar. So I was punctilious about saluting them first, and for the rest I knew that nothing keeps one at arm's length so effectively as meticulous politeness. To satisfy their curiosity they tried me out once by inviting me to mess with them, but when that failed, our relations became cordial and natural. We treated one another with deserved deference which satisfied us both.

I don't like to say anything disparaging about the Ninety-second Division, because an outside instructor is helpless unless the outfit's regular officers co-operate with him, and the officers of General Hay's brigade co-operated with me to the limit. But believing that the Negro's first need is not sympathy or patronizing or even help, but the truth, I must set down here what I believe to be true of the division's Negro officers. Those who came from the regular army, where they had been sergeants, made splendid officers; those who came from civilian life by way of training camps were lazy, undevoted, and without pride. Both dressed well, but the latter were peacocks in splendor and strut. I couldn't judge the enlisted personnel—I liked them of course, they reminded me of home, but I feared for them under test.

After I'd been teaching four or five weeks, two of the Negro captains took me aside and did me the honor to unburden themselves to me. Earnest men of innate dignity, they were able, devoted officers. They asked if anything could be done to keep the division out of the line. They insisted it was unfit for line service. Without bitterness but with profound sorrow they confessed that under battle conditions it would disgrace our country. I was distressed for them and inquired the reason for their fears.

"Lieutenant," said the more articulate of the two, "you know. Don't make us say. These men are not going to follow us into battle because we are Negroes. You say we are able officers. That makes no difference. A Negro won't follow a Negro. We have enough pride in ourselves and in our race not to want to see that happen. Try to do something about it, Lieutenant."

I did try. I wrote Colonel Quekemeyer, General Pershing's aide and an old Delta boy, and told him what I had observed and learned, what these officers had told me, and what I feared. I suppose sending such a letter broke all rules and regulations. Of course I received no answer. I expected none. But, after the Armistice, Quackmeyer told me that General Pershing appreciated the facts, shared my fears, but because of political pressure could do nothing about it. He was forced to give them their chance in the line.

The Ninety-second Division returned to New York in splendor, marched down Fifth Avenue and was applauded and publicized as heroes. Its only major engagement had been in the Argonne. Of its exploits there General Pershing wrote: "The 92nd Division attacked but did not hold all its gains." His words win my admiration as a masterly example of the glacial tact of understatement, the polar pity of reticence.

I have another reason for disliking to criticize the Ninety-second: it was with them I got my break. The Colonel of the regiment in which I was instructing was promoted. He was a kind and intelligent gentleman, with a drooping mustache and an air like the White Knight's. A general's first need is an aide. White lieutenants being practically non-existent in these parts, General Jackson called me to his room and said in his pleasant, informal way: "Percy, how'd you like to be my aide-de-camp?"

Thanking him, I said I understood an aide was the lowest form of military life and all I aspired to be was a platoon leader at the front.

He laughed. "I have just seen the order for your reappointment as instructor, Percy. You will be teaching in the training area till peace is signed and you'll be so deep in the woods you won't know it. My brigade is at the front now and I'm joining it Wednesday."

I gulped and sat down. "General, I'll join you Wednesday."

CHAPTER XVII

At the Front

25 Sept. 1918–9 p.m.
With the Armies

Mother dear:

Just a hurried line. Unless the order is changed we're going into a gorgeous big battle in a few hours, of which you'll know the full results long before this reaches you. I've no premonitions and few apprehensions, though battles of course aren't safe things. And for good luck, letters came from you and Father today. I'm glad he liked my little "Squire's Song." It was written at Tours with Frank Gailor in mind as he was going off to the Messines show, but it holds true for any soldier fighting in the great cause. One must be a soldier these days—there is no other part a man may play and be a man. Should anything ever happen to me over here, you and Father must, and I know you will, feel that it was a great privilege for us to be allowed to go forth with the heroes. I've had too much and too keen happiness out of this life to want to leave it or to leave it without regret, but this cause is too great to count the cost or speculate on the outcome to the individual. All that's good in me comes direct from you and Father, and my only ambition in this business is not to be unworthy of you. And whatever happens we'll be together in the end.

. . . I'll write you in a few days. Now for a little much-needed sleep.

All my love to you both.

Your devoted son,
W. A. Percy

O.K.–W. A. Percy,
1st Lt. Inf.

[*After the Argonne*]
October 4, 1918

Dear Father:

I have been through hell and returned without a scar. Already it seems a lifetime distant. I cannot recall the sensations clearly, the sheer relief of getting away from it is so great that it will be impossible to give any vivid account of the experience. Here I've a room to myself, a bed, we've just finished a hot supper served on plates with knives and forks and spoons, and we are so happy to be alive that the nightmare we've just left seems unreal, a thing that could not actually have been experienced.

We were rushed up the night before the attack and at midnight the barrage commenced. Although it was a fearful din I was somehow disappointed in it; in fact, slept from sheer exhaustion through most of it on the concrete floor of our dugout. At dawn we attacked. I went to an O.P. (observation post) in the woods to watch, but the mist was so thick I could see nothing and my only sensation as the sun came up was listening to the wild canaries which were suddenly and strangely moved to music that could be heard above the thunder of the guns. The General and I started forward in side-cars, but the roads were so choked with traffic that we abandoned them and followed the assaulting lines on foot. Our first experience of battle was in a shattered hull of a town on the edge of our side of No Man's Land. Troops, wagons, guns, ambulances were surging through in inextricable confusion when suddenly a shell fell on the crossroads, 50 yards ahead of us. An ambulance went up in a puff of cotton, horses and men fell; then another shell. One of our batteries on a slope at the crossroads was replying, and as a third shell fell who should rush down from it, to grab my hand, sing out hello, and rush back, but Gus? I haven't seen him since.

We finally got out of town and into the torn and scarred region between the lines, where already the engineers were attempting to build back the roads. Our troops had swept at once into the woods and were going forward under the barrage with little opposition. We followed them and their wake was clear from the rubble and refuse of battle—abandoned packs and guns, rarely a dead German, ammunition, helmets, then trenches and shelters that had been "cleaned out," as the saying is, for throwing grenades into them. The enemy, holding the first few kilometers lightly, had evidently been surprised by the onslaught. We lunched in a German kitchen off of German food—tea, coffee, potatoes, cabbages, purple and white, and, most surprisingly, good bread and fifty pounds of lump sugar. The day was clear and cool —picnic weather—and that first day was like a picnic. At leisure we examined the marvelous German system of defense, dugouts fifty and sixty feet deep, many of them concrete, often comfortable, sometimes even elegant, for one had a shower-bath and another was papered with burlap. The fine German equipment was scattered broadcast for the troops coming on in reserve to choose souvenirs from, knapsacks, warm socks, helmets (all camouflaged), big blankets, grenades and ammunition galore, shoes, underwear, personal property of all kinds, letters, pictures, books (I found a copy of Scott's *Waverly*), bottles of mineral water, canteens, and pistols. All the resistance that first day was made by machine-guns, which were cleaned up without much difficulty. It was rather a rollicking army that went forward those first six or seven kilometers. But that night it rained.

Next night as I rode forward in the darkness the roads over which all our food and supplies had to come were already becoming muddy and the mud from that time on was one of the things we had to fight. Perhaps you'd like to know what I wore and carried into the affray. A helmet, a gas mask, your field glasses, a heavy cane, a case, a pistol, belt and canteen, a trench coat, a musette bag containing one loaf of bread, a can of corned beef, a pair of socks, a toothbrush (never used), a few letters, a compass, the *Oxford Book of Verse,* and a shaving set. It's easy to tell these simple things, but I can't catalogue the sensations or the events of the next two or three days.

I once wrote Mother not to pity the soldier. Well, now I think the infantryman is the most to be pitied person in the world. The sheer misery he endures is not approached by men in any other branch of the service. He not only fights, but he marches unending miles, carries all he has to eat or keep himself warm with on his back. The artilleryman rides with his guns and sees little of the actual horror, the airman is just a mad adventurer, but these doughboys! I don't see how they do it. If there were no such thing as bullets and shells and bayonets, what they suffer in hunger and cold and exhaustion would earn them eternal reverence.

The second day was cold and rainy. I was detailed at a crossroads behind the assault echelons to direct the wounded and send back the stragglers. It developed into a big undertaking. The wounded themselves were tractable enough—many bad cases and some hit by shrapnel and machine-gun bullets—but every litter had extra volunteers as carriers whom I had to send back and all the unheroic of the battle came my way—the cowards and deserters and malingerers. The drawn faces of these were more awful than those of the wounded. Once a whole line broke and came tumbling back, led by an officer gone mad with shell-shock. I ordered and pleaded and threatened and just as things were at their worst there was the sound of horsemen galloping to us up the road from the rear and it was our artillery coming up to support us, headed by Colonel Luke Lea.

That day was bad enough, but the next was worse. The generals rode up to the front lines to investigate and encourage the men. I followed on foot, and on reaching the forward dugout was told my General had gone forward, so without orders I started out to find him. As I wandered along wondering vaguely where he was, the enemy's barrage suddenly opened up and I was caught in it. I had no duties of any kind, so I hopped into a shell-hole for a minute and waited; then, thinking that was poor business, went on. To be shelled when you are in the open is one of the most terrible of human experiences. You hear this rushing, tearing sound as the thing comes toward you, and then the huge explosion as it strikes, and, infinitely worse, you see its hideous work as men stagger, fall, struggle, or lie quiet and unrecognizable. I was on a wide reverse slope, where there was no timber or shelter, and where the shells were falling ceaselessly in groups of three. Suddenly over the crest a company broke and I saw their Colonel single-handed trying to rally and direct them. So I joined him and took over the company. A fine young chap by the name of McSweeney (General Farnsworth's aide) joined me. It was a vivid, wild experience and I think I went through it calmly by refusing to recognize it was real. You couldn't bear to see men smashed and killed around you and know each moment might annihilate you, except by walking in a sort of sleep, as you might read Dante's *Inferno.* The exhilaration of battle—there's no such thing, except perhaps in a charge. It's simply a matter of will-power. As for being without fear, I met no such person under this barrage, though most played their parts as if they were without it. When we had rallied the men and put them in shell-holes, I went up to the crest and as our advance had ceased sat down in a fox-hole which a soldier had dug the night before, next to that of a French lieutenant. With slight intermissions the barrage continued for four hours. We sat there laughing and talking and wondering if the next one would get us. He had a wife and child and had seen four years of this hell; once he remarked: "Oh, we will never leave here," but he was coolness and politeness itself. Hits within twenty yards almost deafened us, but we both escaped without a scratch.

That night the two of us and some twenty more passed in a dugout listening to the shells and awaiting the counter-attack, which did not develop. That dugout I shall never forget. It was about ten feet wide and forty feet long. The two sides were of mud, dripping and shiny, likewise the floor. The roof was a few logs and a layer of elephant iron which, far from furnishing protection from shell bursts, did not even keep out the rain which all night long trickled through onto our faces and hands and down our backs. We sat shoulder to shoulder on the floor in two rows, our backs against the mud of the walls, our feet against the feet of the man opposite. One candle made visible our weariness and discomfort. I've never seen such tired men. We'd all been a bit gassed and during the night four mustard shells fell at the door and forced us to climb into our masks (all but me, who was in charge and answering the telephone all night). The features of the men had sagged and run together with fatigue; it was cold and they had no blankets; our only food for two days had been bread and corned beef. The horror of the impending destruction tortured them while it could not hold them from sleep. They slept prone in the mud or propped up against each other; clothes, helmets, hands, faces, and hair all one color—mud. There was no complaining, little talking, and no thinking. Fatigue, cold, and hunger quickly made of us mere animals. It was a long night and outside the soldiers were lying under the rain and bitter wind, unfed, but holding.

The next morning the General and I went back to the elegant dugout of the artillery and Luke Lea served us a meal which was so good it almost brought tears to my eyes; no other meal will ever be as good. Coffee, broiled bacon, hot cakes, and syrup. I may sometimes forget Luke's cordiality, but his breakfast never.

Well, we're out of it all now. Most of the mud is scraped off. I've washed my face again and brushed my teeth and slept in a bed. The hardships and miseries are almost forgotten and we're looking forward to several weeks of training and instruction in this pretty country, almost within sight of the cathedral and moated town you visited.

Nuff said. I'm living and awfully glad to be alive. I've gone through unforgettable experiences and I have nothing to regret. Will write again shortly. Best love to you and Mother.

Your devoted son,

W. A. Percy

1st Lt. inf.

On the Lys
4 November 1918

Mother dear:

The shells have stopped. It's just this side of midnight, everyone except the telephone man and myself has rolled into blankets on the floor or into bunks left by the Boche; there's still three inches of candle left. It's Sunday night —so I'll drop you a line about our recent doings. Our second battle is over and we've done well, advancing some seventeen kilometers, crossing the river and rather leading the divisions on either side of us. Things have run more smoothly than in our first attempt, and for us back at headquarters there have been less fatigue, less excitement, and fewer personal adventures.

Our start was really a rather beautiful thing—and that is noteworthy as there's so little beauty—at least, physical beauty—in a battle. For a P.O. we'd taken a small farmhouse with a red roof and drying tobacco hanging like a frieze under the eaves. Just at dawn our barrage started under a faintly pink sky. You could see endlessly in every direction, for the country is flat as ours and without woods, just miles of turnip, beet, and cabbage fields, little orchards, and quiet homey farmhouses. When the big guns started we seemed to be in the midst of an amphitheater, and all around us clear to the horizon we could see them flame and hear them roar. And they'd hardly started when, suddenly, against the forward skyline where the enemy lay, rockets began to leap of all colors and kinds, the enemy's signals of distress and vain calls for assistance.

We went forward almost at once across the river with the lovely lily name to follow the advancing infantry, and selected as our new P.O. what had been a charming home, sitting back in a small park with trees and flower-beds and a small artificial lake. Its owners had fled only a few days before, leaving their personal effects scattered wildly about (Delft china plates still on the walls, an old cashmere shawl hung over one chair, a woman's hat on another), but shells had dashed out the windows, torn the roof, smashed the piano, and littered the place with debris. It wasn't a nice neighborhood. The civilians remaining, after their days of hiding from bombardment in the cellars, were too dazed to rejoice at their deliverance. When we moved into the town, the Boche proceeded to shell it, and the bleak streets were only too often horrible with the evidence of his accuracy.

But the second day was rather a triumphal procession. After a bitter rear-guard resistance, the enemy retired, and we pursued him through a town where, in one of those fine bursts of patriotism small towns are sometimes capable of, all the civilians had refused to leave, and when our troops entered, they rushed out from their cellars and hiding-places wild with joy. We were the first friends they'd seen in four years, and our presence was the first news they'd had of the coming of Americans. Flags, so long forbidden, were hung in all the windows, and, lining the streets, they waved and cheered us as we passed. . . . We need to remember that day of glory now, for today and yesterday have been pretty bitter. We reached our objective, a river-bank, and were later under a hail of lead and gas while we attempted a crossing. I've suffered personally none of the agony that the men and line officers have been called on to endure; and they only a small part of what these French and British have been enduring for four years. Certainly, no one can ever hate war as a soldier does: it is the wickedest, most hateful thing man was ever guilty of.

I don't remember these last days as a connected story:

most of the time I wasn't doing anything except thinking and observing, the former not apt to make one buoyant, the latter not fruitful. But I've a few vivid impressions of unimportant incidents. You never realize how many different kinds of soldiers are called on for heroic, unrewarded tasks, just as a matter of course. A truck-driver wouldn't occur to you as a subject for song or story, yet there's something almost epic in seeing a train of provisions or ammunition moving up to supply the front line at night. The road is spotted by enemy artillery, and all night the shells fall on it or near it, and, when the shells stop, there's a dreadful whir overhead, and you know a plane with bombs is searching for the best place to drop them. Yet these men drive on in the pitchy darkness, in terror doubtless, but without halting. A shell catches them: men and horses are killed; but the rest of the train moves on, for without them the infantry could not carry on. . . .

The first night we reached the river, I went down to get a report from the Major and to see what was doing. It's a mystery how our army ever gets to its destination. All movements are at night, over an absolutely strange country, only the officers can read maps, and most of them have a fearful time with French maps; when you come to a crossroads and stop to locate yourself, you either find your searchlight refuses to work, or an enemy bombing-plane is in the neighborhood and you don't dare use it; and if by good luck you find a native and ask him the way, you almost blow up to discover he doesn't speak French. Well, as I started to say, I roved down toward the river—I'm always remembering a magic line of Verhaeren's: "Toujours l'énorme Escaut roule dans mes pensées"—and on the way stopped by the P.O. of a battalion. It was in the kitchen of a farmhouse just off the road. In the wide low-ceiled room one candle was burning, in the shadows about the big Flemish fireplace clustered two peasant women and four children, all quiet and watching, still with wonder, the Americans. The Major and another officer were studying a map and sending occasional messages to units scattered somewhere out in the night—where the guides would meet them, which one should move up, where the kitchens had been left, whether the ammunition train had arrived, etc., etc. These days the work of an officer, when his troops are not actually engaged, is getting them fed, clothed, supplied, moved without too great exhaustion and without being detected. There's no drill or instruction and little discipline. While we were discussing the orders for next day, one of the women set down on our table three cups and a pitcher of steaming milk. She couldn't speak a word of French or English, but she had a cheery, brave, bustling way about her, and in sign of friendship she was giving us all she had. In the old days, when Beowulf fought dragons and fly-by-nights, it was always the wife of the king who poured the mead cup for the heroes before battle, but her gesture could never have been as simple and fine as that peasant woman's. And the milk was delisch—the first I'd had in four months.

The hamlet on the river-bank was the peacefulest place you ever saw, the curé and a few civilians still remained, and under a velvet sky, all stars, our soldiers drifted about almost carelessly. Twenty-four hours later the hamlet was not on the map; it had vanished and in its place lay a rubble heap.

On my way back they began shelling the roads, which makes the going fairly interesting. They say English officers never duck shells, and it's probably true. I don't know of any rule in our army, but there's the universal custom for all ranks and grades, when you hear the scream coming your way, to dive into the nearest ditch, or, if none's handy, flat on your stomach. Well, I was flat a considerable portion of that night, and twice it seemed as if that would surely be my permanent position. But I guess you and Adah and Janet and Miss Carrie have worried the good Lord into taking care of me personally. . . .

Well, I'll stop. Lots of love to you and Father.

Your devoted son,

W. A. Percy

Monday, November 11, 1918

Mother dear:

Today is the impossible great day for which the world has been waiting four years and which it seemed we'd never see arrive. The armistice is signed and peace now is a matter of putting terms on paper. For us it came just in time. We'd started an advance of very great difficulty, with the enemy holding the heights on the other side of a bridgeless river and scourging our men, as they tried to cross, with high explosives, shrapnel, and machine-guns. Last night I was wrapped up in Father's Alaskan robe and trying to sleep in a corner between bursts from a long-range big-caliber battery stationed in our garden. Sleep wasn't easy as a window crashed in at every burst, and the air displacement almost blew us off the floor. The telephone was constantly ringing—Where were the engineers with the pontoon material? Could we give a carrying party for the infantry? Last attempt to cross had failed; machine-gun fire unceasing; the French on our left held up: gas shells falling in the town. And there was the weary confusion of mid-battle as seen from brigade headquarters, when suddenly at

2.10 in the morning I heard Moore—the other aide—gasp: "What's that?" And it was the Armistice! Signed, sealed, and delivered! Stop the artillery, no further advance necessary; wake up the General; the hubbub outside is only the French returning from the line singing and calling to our men: "La guerre est finie!" It's morning now, and we are loitering around waiting for our next orders. We don't know the terms, we don't know where we are going, we can't realize the immensity of this news. We can step out the door without fear of a shell, we can walk down the road without a gas mask, I can sit in comfort by a fire or a desk and not be haunted by the thought of men lying out under the wintry sky, hungry and riddled by shell and bullets. This physical relief is so great that I can't begin to appreciate the enormous spiritual results, this wave of gladness sweeping over the world, the home-turning of those who have fought, "the tears of recognition never dry."

I haven't got a captaincy, for which the General recommended me. So I'll bring home no honors. But I didn't go into it with the hope of getting any, and rewards given by other men have never impressed me. I've seen unforgettable sights. I've done my part to the best of my ability in a great cause, my life has been spared—certainly it would be churlish to ask more or to do other than to thank the merciful God for what He has granted. . . .

Well, it's all very wonderful: the times are so much greater than I am. I can't realize that I am playing in the last act of the world's greatest tragedy. Love to you and Father. Letters should go to and fro without trouble now. Watch for the fro.

Devotedly your son,
W. A. Percy

This is what my letters home said. But soldiers' letters from the front, if I may judge from my own, are gauche outpourings, too hot and too cold, too eloquent in a distressing amateurish fashion and too reticent, at once accurate and misleading. Their deficiency springs not so much from the haste of their composition as from the soldier's effort to express enough of the truth to give a glimpse of what he is going through, yet not enough to distress the devoted reader to whom he is writing. Rereading mine, after these twenty-two sobering years, I find they record all I have forgotten and omit all that I remember, all that made my stay at the front a test and a turning, the most memorable and maturing experience of my life. What soldiers write home about must be supplemented by what soldiers do not write home about, if one is to gain an inkling of why a soldier is more and less than a man.

When we were pulled out of the quiet Baccarat sector, where I had joined General Jackson and the Thirty-seventh Division, we knew we were in for trouble. You could feel it in the air, electric with hurry and secrecy. The first great battle of the massed American army was imminent, the battle of the Argonne. We were to be a part of it. Green as we were, General Pershing had assigned to us a sector near the center of the line to the west of Montfaucon, which, washed in yellow sunlight on its rise above the tree-tops, glowed like a Maxfield Parrish dream of a fortress.

On the second night before the Argonne I lodged in the small first-floor room of a two-story house that opened on the road. It was a poor little house that was home to poor people. I lay in my narrow bed by the open window and couldn't sleep. It was deep quiet night and the village was still as death. I listened to the ominous dull thunder from the front. I was tired. Then I heard upstairs above me a couple in bed making loud love. It should have seemed ribald and amusing; it seemed only obscene and pitiful. That poor poilu home on two days' leave and his shapeless, hard-working wife! This was love, this animal-sounding thing. I remembered that love had once seemed tender and beautiful. It wasn't any more. The sounds died down. I hoped they had enjoyed themselves and wondered if they were crying now, clinging to each other whimpering. I closed my eyes and the sleepless hours began.

After midnight I heard on the road the tramping of feet. It was soldiers marching with the snap gone out of their rhythm and that sound of shifting and bumping of gear a jaded outfit makes. As they paused outside my window a young voice, frayed and listless, called: "Platoon—halt. Left face. At ease." They shifted their feet and sighed, cleared their throats to spit, and cursed a little. The platoon leader's voice said drearily:

"Check up on 'em, sergeant. Where's Smithy?"

"Dropped out, sir," answered a steadier voice.

"And Weems?"

"Taken sick, sir."

"And Odell?"

"Guess he couldn't make it."

"Well, we got to go on, sergeant. Right face. Forward march."

Where were they going this time of night? Did they know themselves? Were they lost? A battle was ahead. They had to get there. But where or why? They were too tired, they couldn't remember. I lay still and listened to them tramping into the wide night. They were so much younger than French soldiers.

The next night my billet had no bed and the roof had

been torn away, but there were walls and a floor. I lit a candle, hunted for a clean corner, and spread my blanket. Then my eye fell on a small print pinned loosely to the wall, the only object in a naked room. It was an Italian Madonna. As I looked at it dully, knowing it was familiar and trying to remember the artist's name, a wave of anger and nausea swept over me. Art? What was art, painting, music, poetry, all that stuff? Child's play, the pastime of weaklings, pointless, useless, unmanly, weak, weak, weak—I had loved it once and men had wasted their lives on it. I blew out the candle, lay down in my blanket, and shook in the darkness. It took me a year to remember it was a Luini.

When the first picnic day of the Argonne had closed in rain, four or five of us started to our new headquarters on horseback. The darkness had substance; it touched you. We could not discern the country through which we were passing, we could only sense the deeper darkness of trees on each side of the road and the silence, as if no one was there or had ever been there or ever would be there. A weeping rain fell, cold, eternal, inconsolable. It had been a long, exciting, exhausting day, our first day of battle, and it followed three nights of half-sleep. We let the horses guide themselves and in our saddles fought sleep. Each man wondered wildly within himself how long he could last. This was always the inner terror—would the sleeplessness and exhaustion be too much for the frail machine that was a man? Would the machine break? We rode in silence through a nightmare of silence. It was broken wildly by a long-drawn animal scream. But we knew the animal was a man. It was repeated and repeated, full of torture and fear. We realized it was trying to talk, to talk to us, from out there in the woods alone. We rode on and said nothing; we didn't dare. We learned next day it was a German soldier with his jaw shot away.

About two o'clock we found our overnight headquarters, a hole in the earth, but it had chicken-wire bunks. I fell into one and was immediately asleep. In fifteen minutes the General shook me awake: "Sorry, Percy. You must walk back a mile and a half to the crossroads and wait for the second battalion. Show them to their positions. You're the only person handy who knows them." I grabbed the short staff with a leather thong which I had found in a shell-hole and stumbled out. Somehow I reached the crossroads, meeting no one, hearing nothing, the only living creature on that vast battlefield. I was sure if I sat close to the road I couldn't miss them and if I sat up straight I couldn't fall asleep. I sat down on the muddy bank of the road with my knees drawn up, stuck the staff in the ground between my feet, and leaned my chin on it. The rain dribbled down my neck. When I awoke I was sitting in the same position and it was light. Asleep at the post of duty! The road was empty. Stiff with cold and desperate, I stood in the rainy half-light and prayed that the battalion had not passed. In a few minutes I saw it marching up the road toward me, beautiful as marching seraphim. For such a dereliction ordinary soldiers, yokels who didn't know or care why they were fighting, had been shot at dawn. I led the battalion to its position.

Next night our headquarters was that deep dugout which I shall never forget, as familiar to me still as my own bedroom. It was a German dugout and for our purposes faced the wrong way: it gaped to receive a shell. Sixty precipitous steps led down to its interior, dripping and dark like a cave. Two tiers of chicken-wire bunks flanked its long narrow corridor, and mine was a top one, so close to the ceiling you had to slide in sideways. Its last occupant, troubled by a dribble of water from above that leaked on his throat, had ingeniously attached a tin can to the ceiling and it required some skill and no thickness to sidle in and out without striking it and dousing yourself with the icy contents. Whenever I fell asleep, the telephone would ring or my name would be called, and, starting up, nervously, I'd hit that can and be splashed into cold bright consciousness. In spite of its convenience, I never grew to like it, but I grew more and more fond of that unknown predecessor of mine. He became a mystical bunkie, and I hoped we hadn't killed him.

Water stood on the floor of the dugout and there was no room to move about. The steps, steep as a ladder, were slick with slime, and some soldier, awkward in his heavy gear and sloppy with mud, would always be slipping and crashing down them heavily to our feet. He would lie there moaning a little or cursing softly and none of us would help him up or notice him. We were all holding more than we could contain, like a glass of water too full and held from spilling by tension. The slightest jar, even a sigh, would break it into overflowing. We didn't know what form the overflow might take—tears, hysteria, madness—but we knew laughter could be the jar and pity the sigh, and we couldn't risk either. For our protection we substituted dull anger.

From where we were, the forest stretched darkly behind us to the rear, and before us flowed undulations of open country as far as Ivoiry, our immediate objective. Everything happened under a morose dripping sky. In my recollection I seem always to have been standing in front of that dugout of ours. I watched little groups at the edge of the woods burying their comrades, just to get them out of sight. Around a shell-hole, half full of brown water, another group knelt with safety razors, making a woebegone effort to clean up and feel less lousy and less forgotten of God. Once a squadron of American planes in V formation roared over us toward the front, but from above, from nowhere, dropped an enemy squadron. The sky was littered with dog-fights. One American plane after another burst into flames and corkscrewed down, screaming like a siren in anguish, while the victors re-formed and darted proudly homeward. You could almost see them wag their tails.

But it was all unreal, like a slow-motion nightmare, and unreal incidents kept happening. You would see a regiment in extended formation, wide space between each two men, and from the look of them you couldn't tell what outfit they were, the 147th or the 148th or some unknown brown army from another planet. They marched stiffly down the slope in front of us and up the bare wide hillside to the lighter east. As they reached the crest each man against the sky became a giant twenty feet tall. They would seem to linger without stopping in the silver light of the top, still giants, and suddenly disappear down the farther slope. In the top of your brain you knew it wasn't true, they were only our men going into action against the brighter skyline, but in your darker deeper brain you noted the miracle and cringed.

That was the hill-crest where the best-known man in the division lay (for the roads crossed there), only he wasn't a man. I saw the thing as I passed with the General and, not recognizing it, went back and poked with my stick. It was a torso, a big one, without arms or legs or head, its lower part obscenely naked, the rest dressed in a German officer's uniform. Under a sack lay the mess of his spare parts. It couldn't be real. If it was real, you'd scream or burst into tears or shoot somebody.

The Italian boy with the long ugly face and the enormous dark eyes, speechless from the shell-splinter in his back—he wasn't real as I leaned over him, and his eyes drew all the strength from his dying body into one stare's terrified question: "Am I going to die?"

It couldn't be real. Under the barrage that creature wrapped in white cerements from his waist up his body and over his face and head, who would rise from the shell-hole suddenly and wave his stiff arms—he was Lazarus. The sharp thin sound stabbing the roar of the shells—that wasn't the crack of a rifle, and the boy screaming: "What am I going to tell my papa? What am I going to tell my papa? I shot myself in the hand!"—that didn't happen, the red hole in his palm wasn't a bullet-hole, it was something else, perhaps the stigmata.

And I walking quietly under the rain of shells from one shell-hole to another saying: "Get your heads down. Keep under cover. Relief's coming up in a minute. Hold on," knowing I bore a charmed life and couldn't be hit, knowing everyone else would be killed, but not I, smiling to know I would sit down again in the sun-parlor at home with the summery wind blowing the fresh curtains and Mother serving me breakfast as she laughed and talked and the water clean and cold in the sweating glass—I wasn't real. When Colonel Galbreath cited me because I strolled up to him through the leaping geysers and called: "Pretty warm day, Colonel, but you can't stay here. Get back where you belong. You've no right to be here," he thought I was gaily self-possessed and efficient—but I wasn't even there, I was lying in the bottom of a dark well shaking with horror.

The other battles in which our division engaged varied in detail from the Argonne, but varied not at all in those essentials that concerned the pitiful creatures who did the killing and were killed. For them every battle was merely strain and keeping on in spite of strain, merely fear and fear overcome, horror and horror made casual. For them after the battle there was no exhilaration but only animal exhaustion. Each man had had his own little adventures, desperate and precious to him—I had mine—but they were less desperate and less precious to him than the adventures of his squad or his company or his division. To each man battle was horrible and innocent, despicable and divine, torture but so austere and exalted that it invested the lowliest rumpled, unshaven participant with a fierce dignity, an arrogant worth. Although you felt like a son-of-a-bitch, you knew you were a son of God. A battle is something you dread intolerably and for which you have always been homesick.

After the Argonne our division fought honorably on the Belgian fronts out from Ypres between the Scheldt and the Lys. I remember it all. But over and above more important events I remember one inconsequential morning because somehow it seemed a symbol or an allegory. I had gone through the town of Olsene afoot and alone, carrying a message to the 148th, which was attacking. I found the Colonel in the ticket office of an abandoned railway station. A gloomy room and gloomy soldiers gathered there, for things were going badly and the shells fell like slow large snowflakes. My message delivered, as I started on my return trip and stepped from the doorway, one of them crashed a few yards from me and ripped the belly from a friend of mine. They tended him, and I went on across the turnip fields alone. A young soldier with a smashed ankle hobbled up and asked for a drink of water. That cold feeling was in my stomach's pit. I reached the village of Olsene again, desolate and gray as an hour before. Its single street was straight, narrow, and cobblestoned; its small stone houses, touching one another, stood flush with the road, dripping wet, blank-faced. Now, though, the village was not unoccupied as I had left it. But it was as silent. The bodies of forty-two Americans, my comrades, lay on the cobblestones in two short parallel rows, one behind the other. Their guns were in their hands. Their packs were on their backs. They had not fired a shot. They were not yet cold. They lay in uncouth attitudes, though I saw no blood. They did not seem asleep, but frozen in some profound discomfort, their faces yellow-green and strangely old. I walked between their short and sprawling rows and I was afraid. I wanted to run, to hide in a house, to escape this unending nightmare. Then the shelling began. It watered the road I was walking. The shells fell thickest ahead, near the crossroads I had to pass. The cold was now in my throat. I must not run, even to get by the crossroads. There was no one anywhere, but the shells kept falling ahead, they were finding the range of the crossroads. At last I reached them. I would soon be past and safe. I wanted to break into a run and not be left battered and nasty on the naked cobblestones. I was halfway across. And I stopped. There in the very middle, sitting on the ground with a broken telephone wire across his lap, a kit of tools by his side, busy with his task, was a single doughboy. No officer was near, no buddy was helping him. But about him the shells were falling and they gouged the shaking earth. I paused by him and said: "Hey, buddy, you've got pretty good nerve." He looked up, dirty, hard-boiled, absorbed: "Hell, somebody had to do it." And I went on, ashamed, knowing we were gods.

The matter which with the least decency you could have written home about would have been how we really felt

hat day when war stopped. In the tender aimless sun-
hine, in the incredible silence, we roamed the little town
ingly, like drifting shades. The physical relief, the ab-
ence of apprehension, brimmed us with ease and thanks-
;iving, but for each of us our bliss and serenity were only
he superstructure over a hidden tide of desolation and
lespair. Each of us was repeating to himself in his own
lim words something I heard crying out in me:

"It's over, the only great thing you were ever part of.
[t's over, the only heroic thing we all did together. What
:an you do now? Nothing, nothing. You can't go back
o the old petty things without purpose, direction, or
ınity—defending the railroad for killing a cow, drawing
leeds of trust, suing someone for money, coping again, all
›ver, with that bright rascal who rehearses his witnesses.
You can't go on with that kind of thing till you die."

That short period of my life spent in the line is the
only one I remember step by step—as if it moved *sub
specie æternitatis.* Not that I enjoyed it; I hated it. Not
that I was fitted for it by temperament or ability, I was
desperately unfitted; but it, somehow, had meaning, and
daily life hasn't: it was part of a common endeavor, and
daily life is isolated and lonely.

On my way home I landed in New York and found
Mother and Father at the dock waiting for me. I had
on a rakish overseas cap, a snappy uniform with Sam
Browne belt, gold service stripes on the cuffs, a captain's
silver bars on the shoulders, and on the breast a Croix de
Guerre with a gold and a silver star. They were so happy,
so filled with pride and thanksgiving, it was embarrassing. I tried, too, to be glad and proud and thankful, but
I have never before or since felt so incapable of emotion,
so dead inside. A chapter was ended which had been
written in capital letters of red and purple with Gothic

curlicues of gold, but ahead lay other chapters, and
knew they were written in fine black print, too small t
read without glasses, preferably rose-colored ones. It wa
as if in the midst of a reading from Homer you turne
the page and your eye met the society column of th
Daily Democrat.

CHAPTER XVIII

The Ku Klux Klan Comes and Goes

Gervys Lusk left home a wastrel and returned a hero; he departed with a black eye and came back with a D.S.C. During that spiritual interregnum when both of us were fumbling to become good citizens (an undertaking in which he was entirely successful) Gervys confided to me that the home town had felt distinctly let down when I returned from the wars intact. It reasoned that not having been outstandingly useful—"indispensable" would have been Major Jones's adjective—I could have afforded to be ornamental by making "the supreme sacrifice." I was cast for the role—a poet (so they had heard), young (at least youngish), slender (thin, in moments of non-exaltation). It seemed churlish of me not to have seized the opportunity. I felt rather the same way about it, now that the opportunity was safely out of hand.

My destiny apparently is to pick up the pieces and start over. A lame start it was in 1919. I spent the first few months tinkering with the manuscript of *In April Once* and almost ruined it—April was over; I made numerous speeches over the state for something like the Second Liberty Loan;

for six months I again taught at Sewanee, and would probably be teaching there now had not one or two of the dignitaries questioned my papist affiliations. Briefly I did a deal of floundering before I could settle down all over again to living, mere living.

During that period I evidently did some thinking about our Southern race problem because I recently came across this letter addressed to the *New Republic* (though of course never published nor acknowledged):

Sewanee, Tennessee
September 6, 1919

The New Republic
New York City
Sirs:

Your intellectual fearlessness and sincerity prompt me to write you regarding the recent outbreak of lawlessness in Knoxville, Tennessee, which the newspapers have delighted to call a "race riot." I am an average educated Southerner and I want to give you the point of view of my class. The Northern press will doubtless see in this occurrence merely another instance of what it imagines to be the South's hostility and cruelty to the Negro, its inability to deal justly with him without Northern interference. But the moral is not so stereotyped. Viewed in its true relations, the Knoxville outrage is indicative of a situation more complex, and full of pathos, and difficult of adjustment, than any our well-meaning Northern friends conceive. This was no race riot. It was a burst of hoodlumism which protected itself under the local excitement and indignation at a ghastly and terrifying crime committed by a Negro.

It is clear from the newspaper reports that the mob at first made no attack on the Negroes, but turned against the jail from which they knew the Negro they wanted had been taken. The jail was wrecked, the criminals within released, jail records and property destroyed or stolen, and finally the house of the sheriff, who at that time was on his way to Chattanooga with the prisoner, ransacked and rifled. Hardware stores were next broken into for ammunition and arms. Thereafter conflicts between these hoodlums and terrified blacks were inevitable. A good Southerner considers this incident, as does any other good American, a national disgrace.

You in the North always assume there are two attitudes toward the race question—one pre-empted by the enlightened benign citizen of Northern birth, the other peculiar to the narrow heartless citizen of Southern birth. There is no such difference. I live in the Mississippi Delta, where a full half of the white population, outnumbered ten to one by the Negro population, is Northern by birth and rearing. Yet the attitude of that one half differs in no wise from the attitude of the other half born and bred in the South. Under similar conditions, and it matters not where those conditions arise, it may be Chicago, South Africa, Washington, or Knoxville, white men of Anglo-Saxon descent, whether Northern or Southern born, act in precisely the same way toward the Negro. Inhabitants of Maine, and France and Finland, can afford to toy mentally with the race problem and the theories they arrive at may be widely divergent. But among white men for whom the problem is a bitter and pressing fact, who live with it, there is no difference of opinion as to the problem's solution, based on difference of place of birth or of education. There is only a difference on this as on all questions between those Southerners who through poverty, lack of inheritance, and ignorance misunderstand and dislike the Negro, and those who by training and opportunity feel themselves his friend and protector.

Here are the two questions, or rather the two phases of

one question, with which we live: first, how best to protect and educate and deal fairly with a race which at its present stage of development is inferior in character and intellect to our own (this is the phase of the question in which the North is perennially interested); second, how best to develop so upright a character in our own people that they will resist the ever present temptation to prey and batten on this inferior race (this is the phase of the question in which the North is never interested, of which indeed it is hardly cognizant). To solve these questions in wisdom, justice, and kindness is difficult under any circumstances, but there are thousands of unadvertised leaders of thought in the South capable of working out such a solution if left to themselves —not quickly nor easily, but through the years. And they are the only people who can: it is their problem, their burden, their heavy heritage.

And the Knoxville crime illustrates the strongest force against which these leaders have to fight; to wit, the lawlessness and hoodlumism of our uneducated whites. The same force at work in politics produces vicious unworthy Southern governors and congressmen. Our fight to protect the Negro is merely part of our fight for decency in politics, for law-enforcement. The fight is often lost, but it never ceases; indeed, it gains in strength and in the end it is certain of victory.

You will wonder perhaps why I am telling you our troubles. My reason is quite simple: I want you to know why it is that we whose hearts are essentially as yours in this matter fear unjust criticism, unwise advice from the North. It makes a good Southerner's task only the harder. We could afford to be indifferent to your misunderstanding were it not that the inflammable, uneducated whites whom the best part of our lives is spent in controlling and teaching seize on the indiscreet utterances and unmerited strictures of the

Northern press as excuses for their own excesses and injustices. Nor is the effect on the Negro himself less deplorable. Doing no good in themselves, these utterances and strictures greatly lessen our force for good.

To you our tragic situation, calling for courage and wisdom and unselfishness and patience, is a theory, a subject for criticism, suggested panaceas, scorn. We know the solution, the only one; for there is no short cut. It is in the first place education for the whites and in the second education, simple and practical, for the Negro. For the rest common kindness must be the guide in this as in all human affairs. My plea to you is that you trust us who are fighting the fight in the South, and that you accept my assurance we are not a corporal's guard.

Respectfully yours,
W. A. Percy

I drag in this communication because after twenty years it still seems to me to point out the South's two major deficiencies—character and education—which, after all, are world deficiencies, and to indicate the lines along which the "solution" of our race problem must proceed. Of course the letter expresses the Southern point of view of a so-called conservative, which is deplored to the point of tears by the so-called liberals. There's an enduring quality to truth exceedingly irritating to fidgety minds. In the South our anxiety is not to find new ideas, but to bring to realization old ones which have been tested and proved by years of anguish—a far more difficult undertaking. We Southerners aren't as bright as we are right. But when we do hit on a new idea, it's not only wrong, it's inconceivable.

The years following the war were a time of confusion not only to ex-soldiers but to all Americans. The tension of high endeavor and unselfish effort snapped, and Americans went "ornery." In the South the most vital matter became the price of cotton, in the North the price of commodities. Idealism was followed by the grossest materialism, which continues to be the order of the day.

Our town of about ten thousand population was no better or worse, I imagine, than other little Southern towns. My townsfolk had got along pretty well together—we knew each other so well and had suffered so much together. But we hadn't suffered a common disaster, one that was local and our very own, like a flood or a yellow-fever epidemic, since the flood of 1913, and that had failed as a binder because it didn't flood the town. Unbeknownst, strangers had drifted in since the war—from the hills, from the North, from all sorts of odd places where they hadn't succeeded or hadn't been wanted. We had changed our country attractively for them. Malaria had been about stamped out; electric fans and ice had lessened the terror of our intolerable summer heat; we had good roads and drainage and schools, and our lands were the most fertile in the world. We had made the Delta a good place in which to live by our determination and our ability to endure hardships, and now other folks were attracted by the result of our efforts. The town was changing, but so insidiously that the old-timers could feel but could not analyze the change. The newcomers weren't foreigners or Jews, they were an alien breed of Anglo-Saxon.

Although I was always traveling to strange places, I loved Greenville and never wanted any other place for home. Returning to it was the most exciting part of a trip. You could find friendly idlers round the post-office steps pretending they were waiting for the mail. You could take a coke any time of day with someone full of important news. There'd be amiable people running in and out of the house, without knocking, for tennis or golf or bridge or poker or to join you at a meal or just to talk. It was a lovable town

I suppose the trait that distinguished it from neighboring towns was a certain laxity in church matters. We didn't regard drunkenness and lechery, Sabbath-breaking and gambling as more than poor judgment or poor taste. What we were slow to forgive was hardness of heart and all unkindness. Perhaps we were overstocked with sinners and pariahs and publicans, but they kept the churches in their places and preserved the tradition of sprightliness. Of course we had church folk, plenty of them—Episcopalians, not numerous but up-stage, whose forebears came from Virginia, Kentucky, or South Carolina; Catholics from Italy or Ireland or New Orleans; Methodists, indigenous and prolific; Baptists, who loved Methodists less but Catholics least, swarms of them; Presbyterians, not directly from Geneva or Edinburgh, but aged in the wood, fairly mellow considering they were predestined; and Jews too much like natives even to be overly prosperous. There were bickerings and fights during election time, but day in and day out we were pretty cozy and neighborly, and nobody cared what to hell was the other fellow's route to heaven. There was no embattled aristocracy, for the descendants of the old-timers were already a rather seedy remnant, and there was no wealth. White folks and colored folks—that's what we were—and some of us were nice and some weren't.

I never thought of Masons. Most of my friends wore aprons at funerals and fezzes (over vine leaves) at knightly convocations. Even Père had been a Mason, to the scandal of the Church and the curtailment of his last rites, but he took it easy. I thought Masonry a good thing for those who liked that sort of thing.

We had read in the newspapers that over in Atlanta some fraud was claiming to have revived the old Ku Klux Klan which during reconstruction days had played so desperate but on the whole so helpful a part in keeping the peace and preventing mob violence. This Atlanta monstrosity was not even a bastard of the old organization which General Forrest had headed and disbanded. This thing obviously was a money-making scheme without ideals or ideas. We were amused and uninterested. Even in Forrest's day the Klan had never been permitted to enter our county. It couldn't happen here. But reports of the Atlanta organization's misdeeds—masked night parades to terrorize the Negro, threatening letters, forcible closing of dance-halls and dives, whippings, kidnappings, violent brutalities—crowded the headlines. As citizens of the South we were ashamed; as citizens of Greenville we were not apprehensive.

Then in the spring of 1922 a "Colonel" Camp was advertised to speak in our courthouse for the purpose of forming a branch of the Klan in Greenville. Thoroughly aroused, we debated whether to permit the speech in the courthouse or to answer it there. We couldn't learn who had invited him to speak or who had given him permission to use the courthouse, but evidently some of our own people were already Klansmen—fifth-column tactic before there was a Hitler. Our best citizens, those who thought for the common good, met in Father's office and agreed almost unanimously that the Colonel should be answered and by Father.

The Klan organizer made an artful speech to a tense crowd that packed every cranny of the room; and every man was armed. Who killed Garfield? A Catholic. Who assassinated President McKinley? A Catholic. Who had recently bought a huge tract of land opposite West Point and another overlooking Washington? The Pope. Convents were brothels, the confessional a place of seduction, the basement of every Catholic church an arsenal. The Pope was about to seize the government. To the rescue, Klansmen! These were statements which any trained mind recognized as lies, but which no man without weeks of ridiculous research could disprove. It was an example of Nazi propaganda before there were Nazis. The very enormity and insolence of the lie carried conviction to the simple and the credulous. The Colonel was listened to with courtesy.

To his surprise, Father answered him: he had never been answered before. I have never heard a speech that was so exciting and so much fun. The crowd rocked and cheered. Father's ridicule was amusing but bitter; and as he continued, it became more bitter, until it wasn't funny, it was terrifying. And the Colonel was terrified: he expected to be torn limb from limb by the mob. I don't blame him. At the close of Father's speech the crowd went quite mad, surging about, shouting and cheering, and thoroughly dangerous. A resolution was passed condemning the Klan. Colonel Camp scuttled out of a side door, appealing to a passing deputy for protection. The deputy, an Irish Catholic and the kindliest of men (out of *Henry IV*), escorted him ceremoniously to his hotel.

It was a triumphant meeting, but for the next two years our town was disintegrated by a bloodless, cruel warfare, more bitter and unforgiving than anything I encountered at the front. In the trenches soldiers felt sorry for one another, whether friend or enemy. In Father's senatorial fight, we were surrounded by ferocious stupidity rather than by hatred. But in the Klan fight the very spirit of hatred materialized before our eyes. It was the ugliest thing I have ever beheld. You didn't linger on the post-office steps or drink cokes with random companions: too many faces were hard and set, too many eyes were baleful and venomous. You couldn't go a block without learning by a glance that someone hated you.

The Klan did not stand for, but against. It stood against

Catholics, Jews, Negroes, foreigners, and sin. In our town it chose Catholics as the object of its chief persecution. Catholic employees were fired, Catholic businessmen were boycotted, Catholic office-holders opposed. At first this seemed strange to me, because our Catholics were a small and obscure minority, but I came to learn with astonishment that of all the things hated in the South, more hated than the Jew or the Negro or sin itself, is Rome. The evangelical sects and Rome—as different and uncomprehending of each other as youth and old age! One seems never to have glimpsed the sorrowful pageant of the race and the other, profoundly disillusioned, profoundly compassionate, sees only the pageant. One has the enthusiasm and ignorance of the pioneer, the other the despair of the sage. One's a cheer-leader, the other an old sad-eyed family doctor from Samaria. We discovered that the Klan had its genesis, as far as our community was involved, in the Masonic Temple. The state head of that fraternal organization, a well-meaning old simpleton, had been preaching anti-Catholicism for years when conferring Masonic degrees. He joined the Klan early and induced other Masonic leaders to follow his example. These composed the Klan leadership in our county, though they were aided by a few politicians who knew better but who craved the Klan vote. It was a pretty leadership—fanatics and scalawag politicians. But not all Masons or all the godly were so misguided. The opposition to the Klan at home was led by a Protestant committee (and every denomination was represented in its ranks), who fought fearlessly, intelligently, and unceasingly this evil which they considered as unchristian as it was un-American. Father was not only head of the Protestant anti-Klan committee but of the anti-Klan forces in the South. He spoke as far north as Chicago and published probably the first article on the Klan in any distinguished magazine. It was reprinted from the *Atlantic Monthly* and distributed over the whole country. He felt the Klan was the sort of public evil good citizens could not ignore. Not to fight it was ineffectual and craven.

It's hard to conceive of the mumbo-jumbo ritual of the Klan and its half-wit principles—only less absurd than the Nazi principles of Aryan superiority and lebensraum—as worthy of an adult mind's attention. But when your living, your self-respect, and your life are threatened, you don't laugh at that which threatens. If you have either sense or courage you fight it. We fought, and it was high time someone did.

The Klan's increasing atrocities culminated in the brutal murders at Mer Rouge, where Skipwith was Cyclops. Mer Rouge is across the river from us, on the Louisiana side. It is very near and the murders were very ghastly. The Klan loathed and feared Father more than any other man in the South. For months I never let him out of my sight and of course we both went armed. Never before nor since have our doors been shut and locked at night.

One Sunday night of torrential rain when Father, Aunt Lady, and I sat in the library and Mother was ill upstairs I answered a knock at the door. It was early and I opened the door without apprehension. A dark, heavy-set man with two days' growth of beard and a soft-brimmed black hat stood there, drenched to the skin. He asked for Father and I, to his obvious surprise, invited him in. He wouldn't put down his hat, but held it in front of him. I didn't like his looks, so while Father talked to him I played the piano softly in the adjoining room and listened. The man's story was that he came from near our plantation, his car had run out of gas a few miles from town, he'd left his sister in the car and walked to town, he couldn't find a service station open, and would Father help him? Father, all sympathy, started phoning. The stranger seemed neither interested nor appreciative. I watched him with mounting suspicion. Father's effort to find a service station open having failed, he said: "My car is here. We might run out and get your sister—I suppose you can drive my car?" The stranger brightened and observed he could drive any make of car. The two of them were still near the phone when Father's three bridge cronies came stamping in, laughing and shaking out the rain. As they came toward Father, the stranger brushed past them and had reached the door when I overtook him. "Say, what's the matter with you?" I asked. "Wait a minute and some of us will get you fixed up." He mumbled: "Got to take a leak," walked into the rain, and disappeared.

We waited for him, but we did not see him again for two years. Then he was in jail charged with a string of robberies. When he saw I recognized him, he grinned sourly and remarked: "Old Skip nearly put that one over." He refused to enlarge on this statement, which presumably referred to Skipwith, Cyclops of Mer Rouge. We found from the neighbors that the night of his visit to us he had arrived in a car with another man and parked across the street from our house.

It looked too much like an attempt at kidnapping and murder for me to feel easy. I went to the office of the local Cyclops. He was an inoffensive little man, a great Mason, and partial to anti-Catholic tirades. I said: "I want to let you know one thing: if anything happens to my Father or to any of our friends you will be killed. We won't hunt for the guilty party. So far as we are concerned the guilty party will be you."

There were no atrocities, no whippings, no threatening letters, no masked parades in our town. The local Klan bent all of its efforts toward electing one of its members sheriff.

If they could have the law-enforcement machinery under their control, they could then flout the law and perpetrate such outrages as appealed to them. Our fight became a political fight to prevent the election of the Klan's choice for sheriff. The whole town was involved and the excitement was at fever heat. What appalled and terrified us most was the mendacity of Klan members. You never knew if the man you were talking to was a Klansman and a spy. Like German parachute jumpers, they appeared disguised as friends. For the Klan advised its members to lie about their affiliation with the order, about anything that concerned another Klansman's welfare, and about anything pertaining to the Klan—and its members took the advice. The most poisonous thing the Klan did to our town was to rob its citizens of their faith and trust in one another. Everyone was under suspicion: from Klansmen you could expect neither frankness nor truth nor honor, and you couldn't tell who was a Klansman. If they were elected judges and law-enforcement officers, we would be cornered into servility or assassination.

Our candidate for sheriff was George B. Alexander, a powerful, square-bearded, Kentucky aristocrat drawn by Holbein. He was one of those people who are always right by no discernible mental process. His fearlessness, warmheartedness, and sheer character made him a person you liked to be with and for. He was Father's favorite hunting companion and friend.

On election night the town was beside itself with excitement. Crowds filled the streets outside the voting booths to hear the counting of the ballots as it progressed. Everyone realized the race was close and whoever won would win by the narrowest of margins. The whole population was in the street, milling, apprehensive, silent. When the count began, Father went home and started a bridge game. I waited at the polls. About nine o'clock a sweating individual with his collar unbuttoned and his wide red face smeared with tears rushed out on the steps and bellowed: "We've won, we've won! Alexander's elected! God damn the Klan!" Pandemonium broke loose. Men yelled and screamed and hugged one another. Our town was saved, we had whipped the Klan and were safe. I ran home with the news and Father's bridge game broke up in a stillness of thanksgiving that was almost religious.

Mother was away. Being a Frenchwoman, she had been neither hysterical nor sentimental during the months and months of tension and danger. But none of us knew what she went through silently and it was then her health began to fail.

While we were talking about the victory, a tremendous uproar came to us from the street. We rushed out on the gallery. From curb to curb the street was filled with a mad marching crowd carrying torches and singing. They swarmed down the street and into our yard. It was a victory celebration. Father made a speech, everybody made a speech, nobody listened and everybody cheered. Klansmen had taken to cover, but the rest of the town was there, seething over the yard and onto the gallery. They cut Mr. Alexander's necktie to bits for souvenirs. And still they cheered and swarmed.

Father, nonplussed, turned to Adah and me and laughed: "They don't seem to have any idea of going home and I haven't a drop of whisky in the house—at least, I'm not going to waste my *good* liquor on them." Adah and Charlie dashed off in their car and returned with four kegs. Father called to the crowd: "Come on in, boys," and into the house they poured. That was a party never to be forgotten. While Adah was gone, Lucille and her band appeared, unsummoned save by instinct. Lucille, weighing twenty stone, airily pulled the grand piano into her lap, struck one tremendous chord—my Steinway's been swayback ever since—and the dancing began. Adah never touches a drop, but she mixes a mighty punch. Things got under way. There were few inhibitions and no social distinctions. Dancers bumped into knots of heroes who told one another at the same time their harrowing exploits and unforgettable adventures. A banker's wife hobnobbed with the hot-tamale man, a lawyer's careened with a bootlegger. People who hadn't spoken for years swore deathless loyalty on one another's shoulders. The little town had come through, righteousness had prevailed, we had fought the good fight and for once had won. Everybody was affectionate with everybody else, all men were equal, and all were brothers-in-arms.

Hazlewood, the gentlest and most courageous of men, kept on making speeches from the front gallery long after his audience had adjourned to the dining-room and were gyrating like flies around Adah. He was so mortified at this treatment (when it came to his attention) that he joined them and was consoled and liberally refreshed. When at a late hour he started to leave, he couldn't find his hat and became whimpery. After discovering it under the radiator, he couldn't pick it up. When he was hatted at last and started on his way, Fletcher met him on the steps, gasped: "Oh, Hazlewood!" and kissed him. Hazlewood exclaimed: "Fletch, Fletch, you shouldn't have done that," burst into tears, and walked home down the middle of the street, sobbing bitterly.

From down Lake Washington way the swarthy tribe of Steins journeyed in, all seven of them, one behind another, the old man, broad-shouldered, arrogant, and goateed, leading the advance through the side door. You felt certain they'd left a tent and a string of camels under the porte-cochere. Solemnly they shook hands with everyone down the line, curved into the dining-room around the punch bowl, shook hands again, told everyone good-night, and left through the front door. We had barely recovered from this princely visitation when they again hove into view through the side door, went through the same exchange of courtesies, pausing a bit longer at the punch bowl, and disappeared out the front door. All during the evening, just about time you were getting settled in your mind, this apparition of a Tartar tribe would materialize, unhinge you, and withdraw, always with decorum but with mounting elation. The last time I expected them to produce cymbals and go to it, but instead Mrs. Stein staged a thrilling fandango with Mr. George B.

Old man Finch, bolt upright in a throne-like chair, fell sound asleep in the very center of the revelry. Well-wishers bore him to a car, drove him home, and deposited him with the greatest tact in the swing on his own front gallery. Later he fell off and cut his forehead. Wakened by the bump, his daughters swarmed out, found him unconscious and bathed in blood, summoned half the doctors in town, and went to keening. Next morning Louise telephoned asking if I'd found Papa's teeth. I'm afraid another guest wore them off.

Long after midnight I looked into the pantry and beheld my favorite barber, a plumber acquaintance, an ex-sergeant, and the hot-tamale man seated at the pantry table eating supper. They'd raided the ice-box and found besides a bottle of liquor. They graciously invited me to join them. Instead I routed out my husky soldier friend, Howard Shields, and admonished him to get those people out of the house, one way or another. Howard bowed stiffly and answered: "Certainly, leave it to me." A bit later I again looked into the pantry; Howard was standing with a glass full of straight whisky in his hand making an undisciplined speech about the virtues of his squad. His four listeners beamed foolishly. One of them managed to observe: "Didn't know Howard waised squabs," and went off into giggles, then into hiccups, then into tears. I addressed Howard sternly: "Go to bed," and he disappeared upstairs. On the way to my room I looked in on him: he was sound asleep. Actually, he hadn't taken off a stitch, he was lying under the sheet fully clothed and anticipating my inspection. The coast being clear, he slipped out, found his buddy, George Crittenden, knocked him cold, and lit out in his car for Clarksdale.

It was a memorable evening. On the way home people fell off bicycles and into gutters, ran over street signs and up trees—and all happy (except Hazlewood). The police radiantly gathered them up and located their destinations.

We decided it was just as well, after all, that Mother had been out of town. It wasn't her sort of party. She'd have started clearing the house at the first drunk, victory or no victory.

Our Ku Klux neighbors stood on their porch watching—justified and prophesying Judgment Day.

It had been a great fight. It was also a ruthless searchlight on character, of one kind or another. My generation still remembers it, though it all happened eighteen or nineteen years ago, and that's a century of any other time. An old Klansman, one who, being educated, had no excuse for being one, asked me the other day why I'd never forgiven him. I had to answer: "Forgiveness is easy. I really like you. The trouble is I've got your number and people's numbers don't change."

CHAPTER XIX

Hell and High Water

Forty-seven years ago—to be accurate, on May 13, 1893—the Greenville *Democrat* carried this appeal:

> ON GUARD—This week guard duty has been continued, and the need of it, we may briefly tell thus: As long as there is a foot of water against our levees there is danger.
>
> The Levee Board has done well, and at the approach of high water of this year they could say with a confidence, never possessed before, "We turn over to you earth works sufficient to withstand the strain of any previous flood and ask you as citizens to guard them from unforeseen foes."
>
> To refuse or neglect to do your individual duty proclaims you wanting in those characteristics which would prove your patriotism in a time when your country is threatened. . . .
>
> Capt. LeRoy Percy relieved Capt. Alexander at Camp Cousens and now has charge with J. H. Wynn, Alf H. Stone, Van B. Boddie, H. T. Ireys, Jr., A. Lewenthall, David Stone, Harvey Miller and Edgar Baker.

The levee at Camp Cousens, which Father's guard protected in 1893, was about four feet high, had been built by Irishmen with wheelbarrows and paid for by local taxation; it always broke. The levee of today is forty feet high, has been built by caterpillars and drag lines and paid for by the United States government; it sometimes breaks. The old guards were volunteers; guards nowadays are hired by the Levee Board.

The new levee is stronger, but the old guards—well, perhaps I exaggerate their excellences, but to me their names are innocent and idolized and more familiar than those of my fellow Rotarians I lunch with every Thursday. All of them except two are dead. When they were doing their turn at guard duty they were undistinguished citizens of the countryside, but the roster of the dead includes a captain in the Spanish-American War, a circuit judge, a leader in the state legislature, two sheriffs, a distinguished Cincinnati attorney, and a United States Senator. Of the living, one is a Major General in the United States Army, and Mr. Alf, of course, is not only an author and an ex-president of the National Tax Association, but the most trusted and beloved public citizen in the state. Guard duty or something in the Delta way of life must have made men strong in those days or else they came of strong stock.

I asked Mr. Alf the other day if he remembered old Camp Cousens and, as I expected, he remembered it all, in detail. While off duty the guards played freeze-out poker for licks administered by the winner with Mr. Cousens's broad, water-soaked razor strop to the squinched posterior of the loser as he bent miserably over a log. No winner ever stayed his arm because of friendship or compassion. The game was gay and brutal. Hotspur and the heroes beneath Troy would have joined it and have been companionable in that company. It attracted participants from the whole neighborhood. One planter, affable and tipsy, rode up on his fine five-hundred-dollar mare as the players were recovering from the last game in a swim. Without dismounting he whipped his snorting mount into the thick of the swimmers, roaring out the while: "Gotta head like a fish and a tail like a man. I'm a mare-maid." Evidently the Delta gentry of fifty years ago were not effete or decadent. I like to hear about them—theirs was such a magnificent male combination of gentleman and pioneer—but I doubt if I should have been at ease living among them. They were a bit too lusty and robustious; that good rough streak of Rabelais in them was unfortunately omitted from my make-up.

The low levees of 1893, ineffectual as they were to keep the Mississippi off the cotton fields, themselves had certain real advantages. When they broke, the water trickled in gradually, stood quietly over the land two or three weeks, deposited a fine nutritious layer of sediment, and withdrew without having drowned anybody or wrecked any buildings or prevented a late planting of the crop. You called that an overflow. Our great dikes of today, when once breached, hurl a roaring wall of water over the country, so swift, so deep, so long-lasting, it scours the top soil from the fields, destroys everything in its path, prevents crop-planting that year, and scatters death among the humble, always unprepared and unwary.

My first overflow I recall as a very jolly affair. In town the water was only two or three feet deep and by picket fences and floating board-walks you could climb and slither from the north end of Walnut Street, where the levee now stands, to Washington Avenue, where Rattlesnake Bayou once ran. Crawfishing was super-excellent, and if you fell in, it was adventure enough for a lifetime.

It must have been during this overflow that Father permitted me to go with him in a skiff from Greenville to the old Percy plantation ten miles to the east, where stands now the town of Leland. Overflow water is depressingly brown, the glare was terrible, and from trees and bushes hung snakes, which I loathed and which loved to fall into boats. I was utterly bored and despondent. Sitting in the bow I sought refuge from the dreary present in the thrilling pages of *The Last of the Mohicans.* Father was disgusted with me: here I was mid-stage in drama and romance and I preferred reading about them! I sensed distinctly he wanted to box my ears, but I kept on reading. He was diverted by sight of the old Hood house, forlorn in the watery desolation. When we toured the county together, he could never resist talking about the old times and he repopulated it with the rash amazing folk by whom it had been settled. His were often rip-snorting yarns of killings and poker games and duels, more thrilling than any Western and not unlike them. But this time he was merely laughing at his recollection of Major Hood.

A testy old gentleman who lived a few miles from the Major had named his plantation Ararat because, situated on the high banks of Deer Creek, it had never been overflowed. They were great friends though rarely on speaking terms. During an unprecedentedly high water in which even Ararat had gone under, Major Hood rowed over to the house, where his old crony was sitting in a rocking-chair on his veranda, comforting himself with a long toddy as he scanned venomously the surrounding waste of water. Without getting out of his skiff the Major drew alongside and snickered maliciously: "Ararat?" (only he pronounced it "Arry-rat"). "Should have called it 'Nary-rat.' " Without another word he rowed home, leaving his old friend apoplectic. For months they never spoke; then the master of Ararat dropped over to call on the Major and they went off together on a famous jamboree.

Now a battlement of levees extends for a thousand miles

on each side of the river from Memphis to New Orleans, without break in the battlement except where the hills crowd down to the bank for a glimpse of the old yellow snake or where tributaries like the Arkansas, the White, the Yazoo, and the Red join it with their own mighty contents. It towers forty feet above the country it protects and its sloping thickness is a hundred feet wide at the base.

All of us who grew up in the Delta have had experience aplenty in guard duty, or "walking the levee," as we call it. The earliest reason given for this custom was the fear that folks from the other side of the river would sneak over in a dugout and dynamite our levees in order to relieve the pressure on theirs. I doubt if anyone on either side ever attempted such a crime, but, the tradition having been established, armed citizens must guard the levee all night, listen for marauders in the willows, and shoot to kill. A soberer reason for the custom was to discover weak spots in the levee, particularly "boils."

A boil is a small geyser at the base or on the berm of the levee, on the land side, of course. It is caused by the river's pressure fingering out some soft stratum in the soil of the levee or by a crawfish hole. If the geyser runs clear, it is being filtered and is comparatively harmless; but if it runs muddy, it is in direct contact with the river and you'd better shoot your pistol, yowl to the next guard, and do something quick. What you do, if you have the gumption of a catfish, is build with sacks of earth a little "run-around"—that is, a small levee around the geyser to the height of its jet. That stabilizes the pressure, and the boil is safe, but should be flagged and watched. The levee generally breaks from boils enlarging themselves and not from the river running over the top.

So during every high-water scare Delta citizens walk the levee all night with pistol and lantern, nowadays with flash-light. If you won't volunteer for that duty, you should return to the hills from which obviously you came. If a guard gets lonesome he may gig a frog, whose croaking makes everything lonesomer, or take a little drink. During these times the river is a savage clawing thing, right at the top of the levee and sounding at night like the swish of a sword or the snarl of a beast. It puts ice in your heart when you're trudging the darkness on the slippery berm and hoping not to step on a snake. Each guard walks alone, and the tiny halo of his lantern makes our fearful hearts stouter.

I'd done so much guard duty during the years that I gave myself a holiday in April 1927. The American Legion boys had taken over the job and were handling it conscientiously and efficiently. Besides, during the three rainy nights preceding the break, I was in a writer's tantrum, the remaining proofs of which are *Three April Nocturnes*. But all good men and true except me were at Scott, fifteen miles above town. There five thousand Negroes, innumerable army and Levee Board engineers, plantation-owners, managers, old-time high-water fighters were battling with sandbags and willow mats to save a weak section of the levee. It was cold and a steady rain fell, freezing the workers and softening the levee. The greatest flood in the history of the Mississippi was roaring south between levees that trembled when you walked on them. The workers knew the fight was well-nigh hopeless, but there was nothing else to do but fight. They knew that if they lost, terror and desolation and death would spread over the hundred miles of thickly populated country from Cleveland to Vicksburg, over the fifty miles from Greenville to Greenwood. In the glare of improvised flares and flood-lights they swarmed over the weak spot like ants over an invaded ant-hill. But about daylight, while the distraught engineers and labor bosses hurried and consulted and bawled commands, while the five thousand Negroes with croker sacks over their heads and hundred-pound sandbags on their shoulders trotted in long converging lines to the threatened point, the river pushed, and the great dike dissolved under their feet. The terrible wall of water like an imbecile blind Titan strode triumphantly into our country. The greatest flood in American history was upon us. We did not see our lands again for four months.

If the Lord was trying to cement us with disaster, He used a heavy trowel that night.

CHAPTER XX

The Flood of 1927

The 1927 flood was a torrent ten feet deep the size of Rhode Island; it was thirty-six hours coming and four months going; it was deep enough to drown a man, swift enough to upset a boat, and lasting enough to cancel a crop year. The only islands in it were eight or ten tiny Indian mounds and the narrow spoil-banks of a few drainage canals. Between the torrent and the river ran the levee, dry on the land side and on the top. The south Delta became seventy-five hundred square miles of mill-race in which one hundred and twenty thousand human beings and one hundred thousand animals squirmed and bobbed.

In the thirty-six hours which the river required after its victory at Scott to submerge the country, panicky people poured out of Greenville by the last trains and by automobiles over roads axle-deep in water. These were mostly frantic mothers with their children, non-residents from the hills who regarded the river hysterically and not devotedly, and the usual run of rabbit folk who absent themselves in every emergency. During the same hours of grace panicky people poured into Greenville. These were mostly Negroes in dilapidated Fords, on the running-boards of trucks, or afoot carrying babies, leading children, and pulling cows, who are always at their worst in crises. Outside of town stock was being rushed cross-country to the levee, and Negroes were being piled into lofts, gins, and compresses by plantation managers. For thirty-six hours the Delta was in turmoil, in movement, in terror. Then the waters covered everything, the turmoil ceased, and a great quiet settled down; the stock which had not reached the levee had been drowned; the owners of second-story houses with their pantries and kitchens had moved upstairs; those in one-story houses had taken to the roofs and the trees. Over everything was silence, deadlier because of the strange cold sound of the currents gnawing at foundations, hissing against walls, creaming and clawing over obstructions.

When at midnight the siren of the fire department by a long maniac scream announced to the sleepless town that the water had crowded over the town's own small protection levee, we knew the last haven of refuge had been lost. In each home the haggard family did its hysterical best to save itself and to provide for the morrow. Outside on the sidewalks you heard people running, not crying out or calling to one another, but running madly and silently to get to safety or to their loved ones. It was a sound that made you want to cry.

At home Mother, Father, and I had been waiting for that signal, like zero made audible. When it came we telephoned a few friends and then half-heartedly began dragging upstairs such furniture as we could manage and Father filled the bathtubs with water. No one knew how high the flood would rise. By breakfast time it had still not entered our neighborhood. We stood on the gallery and watched and waited. Then up the gutter of Percy Street we saw it gliding, like a wavering brown snake. It was swift and it made toward the river. It spread over a low place in the yard and covered Mother's blue larkspur. We said nothing, but suddenly Mother called the terrified little Negro chauffeur and jumped into the car. She had forgotten to buy an oil stove. Our protests were useless. She was in one of those intrepid moods when Frenchwomen had best not be crossed. Up the street a truck-driver was abandoning his truck and splashing wildly home through the water. It was three months before we saw it again. When Mother and the car reappeared, it was between two flanges of spray and hub-deep. Father looked somberly over the drowning town. I think he was realizing it was the last fight he would make for his people. He was sixty-seven and though unravaged by age he was tired. But he only said: "Guess you'd better go while you can. I'll be along." I waded to relief headquarters.

Our kindly old Mayor had appointed me chairman of the Flood Relief Committee and the local Red Cross. I found myself charged with the rescuing, housing, and feeding of sixty thousand human beings and thirty thousand head of stock. To assist me in the task I had a fine committee and Father's blessing, but no money, no boats, no tents, no food. That first morning when the water reached Greenville we of the committee traipsed through the mounting flood to the poker-rooms of the Knights of Columbus, hung out a sign labeled "Relief Headquarters," installed a telephone, and called on the Lord. That calling on the Lord was a good idea, for our first job was to get people out of trees and off of roofs, which, in addition to good will and heroism, of which we had plenty, required motor boats, of which we had none. We were desperate, but the Lord, overlooking our lack of faith, performed one of His witty, whimsical miracles: out of the White River poured a daring fleet of motor boats—the bootleggers! They shot the rapids of the break and scattered into the interior. No one had sent for them, no one was paying them, no one had a good word for them—but they came. Competent, devil-may-care pariahs, they scoured the back areas, the forgotten places, across fences, over railroad embankments, through woods and brush, and never rested until there was no one left clinging to a roof or a raft or the crotch of a tree.

The next problem up for immediate solution was how to stop the looting and burglarizing which had already begun. Without boats the small force of local law-enforcement officers was cooped up impotently in the courthouse and the police station. We telephoned the Governor and asked him to send us National Guards. They arrived, a gay, busy bunch, ably officered and inveterate saluters. With their breeches rolled up to their thighs and their cheeks and legs pink with cold, they splashed about through the icy water trying to look military and succeeding in looking like an army of Kewpies. But their mere presence restored and maintained order.

Our first acts, though in defiance of all law, were effective: we seized and manned all privately owned motor boats, skiffs, pleasure craft, wagons, and trucks (with these we had the nucleus of a transportation system); we confiscated all stocks of food and feed stuff in the local stores (with these, even beleaguered as we were, we shouldn't starve to death for the immediate present). However, for the indefinite future our need of money, tents, and motor boats was desperate. We sent out a nation-wide appeal. The response was immediate and on a grand scale. Friends from the North wired me ten thousand dollars, local citizens raised an equal amount, and through the Red Cross campaign, headed by Mr. Hoover, the people of America gave millions. Whenever you are just about to decide that Americans are selfish, unpatriotic, and unintelligent, they always prove themselves the most liberal and lovable people in the world. You simply can't stay disgusted with them. What a pity they are not disciplined enough to survive!

With Red Cross funds came the Red Cross personnel from Washington, trained, patient, and easy to work with.

Perhaps these early accomplishments of ours sound routine and inevitable, but in fact they taxed our ingenuity, our strength, and our judgment. At headquarters we slept three or four hours a night and, when not sleeping, lived in bedlam. It fell to my lot as chairman to make hundreds of decisions each day and the impossibility of investigation or second thought made every decision a snap judgment. Of necessity I became a dictator, and because the Red Cross controlled the food supplies and transportation I could enforce my orders. The responsibility didn't daunt me, but the consciousness that my judgments were often wrong was a continuing nightmare. If I had to be a despot I was very anxious to be a beneficent one.

At headquarters we couldn't have functioned except for the telephone. Our lives seemed to be one long conversation with Washington or Memphis or Vicksburg, while people seethed in and out of the office with every imaginable request, well-wishers from Biloxi to Memphis insisted on tendering their heroism personally and in detail, and the local phone gabbled like a half-wit:

From Miss Lou: "A man just turned over in front of my house; he nearly drowned and he is now on my front gallery. Send a motor boat for him right away." All boats are more fruitfully occupied. "Miss Lou, have you a man in the house?" "Will, you know I haven't." "Well, you need one, keep him."

From the hospital: "Get some anti-typhoid serum at once, by plane."

From the sheriff's office: "The five hundred darkies in this courthouse can't be fed and the place smells like a slaughter-pen. Get them out of here and up to the levee." How deep is the water between the courthouse and the levee? We have only two motor boats available. "Chippy" (my junior law partner, proper peewee size), "get them to the levee somehow." It was an inspiring sight to see him leading his black army in single file through the water, he spectacled like an owl, bald and chin-deep in the current, they trailing behind him, moaning and shuddering—a small heroic Moses for whom somebody had forgotten to part the waters.

From an unknown hysterical lady: "There's a dead hog on my back porch; come and get him quick."

From an exasperated committeeman: "Those rations for the Mound turned over in twenty feet of water. Must we let them have another load?"

From a bootlegger: "Ain't you got any mash for chickens? My chickens goin' ter starve."

From doctors' headquarters on the levee: "Another Negro baby has just been born. Mother says it's got to be named after you, but it's a girl. How about Wilhelmina instead?"

From Tommy: "Our wagon full of milk for those babies started floating and turned over. The horses were drowned, the milk-cans were lost, and the babies still need milk."

From an Avon committeeman: "The truck goin' down the levee with rations fell off in the river." "Did the driver drown?" "I forgot to ask." Something always happening at Avon—rations get stolen, committeemen fight and resign, and now their truck in the river!

Voice from the Alfalfa Mill, where four hundred Negroes are conglomerated: "A woman done died out here." (What a selfish time to die!) "All right, I'll send a boat out." Hours later the same voice: "That woman out here's still dead." "All right!" (Dying, with all we've got to do!) Next day the same voice tearfully: "If that woman stays here, us kaint." "Chippy, that wretched woman is still dead. Please do something about her." After three hours of battling currents Chippy returns, bustling and competent: "Everything's fixed. All we need's a shroud." Good God! I might just as well be asked for a Poiret model. I spied the sheet which covered a poker table. "Chippy, look! a perfect shroud." "Never had a better one," agreed Chippy sardonically, and disappeared with it. He supervised the rites in the river, but the Negroes maintained that such watery graves were what kept the river up.

Whatever we had accomplished, recklessly and chaotically, those first few days of the flood, one problem, the vital problem of our whole situation, had not been solved: how could we feed the whites and the blacks scattered broadcast through the town in second stories, in attics, in office buildings, mills, and hallways, in inconceivable nooks and crannies? We did not know who or where they were; they could not get to us and we could not get to them. Our problem was essentially a choice between mass feeding and evacuation. For the whites we chose evacuation. I issued an appeal very much in the nature of a command, I am afraid, for the old, the women, and the children to leave town and proceed by boat to Vicksburg. We begged the necessary boats and barges from the Standard Oil Company. They landed at the foot of Washington Avenue and blew a long blast to their prospective passengers as solemn and mandatory as Gabriel's trump. Everything that could float was mustered into service, and from the interior of the town to the levee the flotilla wobbled and ricocheted its way with its freightage of the old and ailing, women and children.

When they had reached the wharf there was a scene of desperate confusion: invalids on cots, old people, querulous and uncomfortable, whining children, addle-pated mothers, squalling babies, having been got to the levee with the utmost difficulty and with great reluctance on their part, tried suddenly to board the boats at the same time. Everybody was short of money, short of temper, short of reasonableness. They milled and stampeded. The space available on the boats was limited and reserved, but in the confusion there were able-bodied men who tried to slip on, pleading sickness or urgent business or what not. We turned them back. It was horrible to see them plead and to hear the crowd from the boats hiss and jeer them. Cowards are not numerous, but they generally manage to be wretchedly conspicuous.

Mother was not among those present. After issuing the evacuation order, I asked her if she was not going to co-operate with the chairman, who happened to be her son. She looked at me as if she had seen me for the first time and was not gladdened by the sight. A Gallic "Psct" of contempt made itself unmistakably audible and she announced: "Adah and I have no idea of leaving. I should like to know how you and LeRoy and Charlie could manage without us!" As the chairman had not envisaged such a calamity he withdrew with some hauteur but without dignity. Many of the older women, those who had seen floods come and go, were similarly disdainful and insubordinate.

What should we do with the Negroes: evacuate them in the same manner or feed them from centralized kitchens as the Belgians had been fed? There were seventy-five hundred of them. It was raining and unseasonably cold. They were clammy and hungry, finding shelter anywhere, sleeping on any floor, piled pell-mell in oil mills or squatting miserably on the windy levee. The levee itself was the only dry spot where they could be assembled or where tents by way of shelter could be set up for them. In spite of our repeated and frantic efforts we had been unable to procure a single tent. We feared disease and epidemics. Obviously for them, too, evacuation was the only solution. Therefore the Red Cross prepared them a camp in Vicksburg and procured two large steamers with barges. At last the innumerable details for their exodus were arranged and the steamers, belching black smoke, waited for them restlessly at the concrete wharf.

It was at this juncture that the Negroes announced they did not wish to leave and a group of planters, angry and mouthing, said they should not and could not leave. I was bursting with fury when Father overtook me on the levee. I explained the situation and he agreed I should not, of course, be intimidated by what the planters said, but he suggested that if we depopulated the Delta of its labor, we should be doing it a grave disservice. I insisted that I would not be bullied by a few blockhead planters into doing something I knew to be wrong—they were thinking of their pocketbooks; I of the Negroes' welfare. Father intimated it was a heavy decision, one I should not make alone. He suggested that I call into consultation the heads of all of my committees. I said they had been consulted and were of one mind: as we couldn't provide an adequate camp for the Negroes, we must evacuate them. Father urged that in fairness to everyone I should recanvass the situation and abide by the decision of my committee. Although nothing new had happened to cause them to change their minds, I promised Father I would call them for a last consultation that evening. The boats in the meantime were tied up and their captains were glowering at the delay. At the meeting of the committeemen I was astounded and horrified when each and every one of them gave it as his considered judgment that the Negroes should remain and that we could provide for their needs where they were. I argued for two hours but could not budge them. At the end of the conference, weak, voiceless, and on the verge of collapse, I told the outraged captains that their steamers must return empty.

The next day the Lord again assisted, this time with two miracles—the sun came out warm and the tents arrived. Seven miles of encampment were set up on the levee, kitchens were established, the doctors devised a sanitary system that worked—the Negroes stayed home and everyone was satisfied. After Father's death I discovered that between the time of our conversation and the committee meeting he had seen each committeeman separately and had persuaded him that it was best not to send the Negroes to Vicksburg. He knew that the dispersal of our labor was a longer evil to the Delta than a flood. He was a natural gambler: he bet on warm weather and tents. Knowing that I could not be dissuaded by threats or even by his own opposition, he had accomplished his end in the one way possible and had sworn the committee to secrecy. Of course, none of us was influenced by what the Negroes themselves wanted: they had no capacity to plan for their own welfare; planning for them was another of our burdens.

Those first weeks the citizens of my little town were magnificent: they relearned friendliness; they re-established unity; they cleansed themselves of some of the venom and nastiness left by the Ku Klux Klan; they worked without pay for the general good, and no work was too hard and no hours too long. Those I had not placed on committees lent a hand independently and made jobs for themselves wherever they saw there was a need. Even Klansmen cooperated, even doctors worked together. Lawyers, ministers, insurance men, dentists, merchants, salesmen, cotton factors, hotel men, slaved at unaccustomed tasks—cooking for the Negro kitchens, convoying women and children from their homes to outbound boats, guarding warehouses, issuing clothes and rations, erecting wooden walkways above the flooded sidewalks, building camps and latrines, assembling data for Mr. Hoover, supervising and checking the loading and unloading of supplies from the steamers, caring for ten thousand head of stock on the levee, sending fleets of motor boats to the beleaguered inland towns. Once more I was proud of my people. My old army buddy, Emmet Harty, was my personal assistant, and Father, though he was not a member of the committee, was the brains and the faith back of everything, the strong rock on which we leaned and in whose shade we renewed our strength. He was our liaison with the outside world and most of his time was spent in arduous trips through the flood waters to meetings and consultations held from New Orleans to Washington. For eight weeks we were as heroic a people as you would wish to find. Then came the June rise.

In June the river was supposed to fall; that was its unbroken custom and surely its clear duty. Indeed, it started to fall. It fell possibly a foot. Home-folk outside the flooded area immediately went into tantrums of homesickness and made life for us at headquarters miserable by their pleas for return transportation. Negroes dropped apparently from the sky and insisted on going to their cabins (standing nine feet deep instead of ten) to see about their "thangs." Then the river rose again and fell no more until the last week of August.

Undoubtedly the flood should have ended in June. If it had, we could have remembered ourselves as paragons of unselfishness and devotion. But it didn't and, descending precipitously from our heights, we lapsed into true, everyday sons of Adam. We were tired out; we wanted to think of our own troubles; we longed to get back to our own concerns. We had risen to an emergency, but we couldn't stay risen. Perhaps the June rise had nothing to do with our lamentable reversion to type. Perhaps the cause was less picturesque and more depressing. I have noticed that if you afford people a chance to give, they are little less than angels; but if you afford them a chance to receive, they almost convince you somebody is right about the need of a hell. The shabby truth is that in June the Red Cross began its campaign of rehabilitation, and people began to receive —food and clothing of course, but in addition household goods, farm supplies, and money. Not only did the Red Cross do a magnificent job of giving, but I don't think there was a church, a fraternal organization, or an organized charity in America that did not donate almost prodigally. Particularly I recall the generosity of the Masons and the Christian Scientists. Our heroic people became mere people: they not only received, they grabbed. Everybody wanted what was coming to him and a little more. The deterioration of the populace affected even our workers: committeemen sulked or fought among themselves or resigned; everybody criticized everybody else; from whites and blacks alike came improper demands, and here and there we discovered simple undiluted dishonesty. It was a wretched period.

One evening I motored home through the rasping currents particularly depressed. It had been one of those days that turn Spartan souls into fidgety, irascible old men. Besides, my boat had torn into my favorite crape myrtle and almost turned turtle. Mother gave me a helping hand as I stepped unsteadily from the bow to the gallery. But I noticed her air was remote and determined and boded no good. Father and Charlie Williams were taking a drink in the library, both looking haggard. I joined them, but in spite of Father's Four Roses we all remained exhausted and depressed. As we sat down to dinner Mother looked us over and announced:

"We've got a crawfish bisque tonight, a good one. . . . You men have got on my nerves. I know you come home every night tired out, worried sick, and all in. But do you think Adah and I are enjoying ourselves? Adah works hard all day on the concrete wharf and I don't have a pleasant time keeping this house going with water all around, the servants scared to death and worthless, Will not letting me have anything that even smells of Red Cross, and all of you hauling in people to meals without a minute's warning. Now I want you to stop looking like sick kittens. Nobody has a right to act down just because he is down. Buck up!"

And we bucked up, believe me. It was a princely bisque.

A few days later she was almost in tears when she confided to me that Minerva, the cook, had struck and refused any longer to serve breakfast for Charlie and me at six o'clock. I asked her to leave Minerva to me and stomped off to the kitchen. I faced that saddle-colored mountain of laziness, that iniquitous amorist, that awful genius of the domestic hinterland, and addressed her spleenfully:

"Just one more word from you about not getting breakfast at six o'clock and I'll haul you out of those comfortable rooms of yours over the garage and deposit you on the levee. I'll give you a tent that leaks and put you on half rations. Also I'll bring back that worthless husband of yours so he can beat the hell out of you every night."

The insurrection collapsed.

I suppose the June rise was responsible also for one of the most memorable and least important incidents of that unhappy time. Early in the flood an ancient brownie appeared at headquarters and without explanation asked to be made the official feeder of all stock marooned on dredge banks. As I had overlooked the appointment of such a dignitary, I cheerfully inducted him into office by presenting him with a bale of hay. I was not certain he wouldn't use it as a personal nest, for he was four feet tall, bewhiskered, toothless, and incredibly dirty. Nobody had ever seen him before the flood and nobody ever saw him after the water subsided. Apparently a kind-hearted water-gnome. Weekly he entered the office without knocking, sat on an imaginary chair (he accomplished this unusual feat by crossing one leg over the other and balancing himself against the wall on his diminutive rump), grinned, and announced: "Here I is." I never questioned him, but always gave him a ration of four bales of hay and a sack of oats.

One of his ports of call was "Dredge Ditch No. 9" or "No. 9," as the Negroes called the drainage canal a few miles east of town through whose spoil-banks we had dynamited a passage for boats to and from Leland. The cross-currents at that point were terrifying. To navigate the opening was an aquatic feat, a sort of shooting the rapids which we Delta land-lubbers found disconcerting in the extreme. If a motor went balky it meant certain disaster, and even under the best conditions there were frequent upsets, rescues, and hair-breadth escapes. That passage was our Scylla and Charybdis. On the embankment overlooking it lived one solitary mule. His interest in seeing whether a boat maneuvered the rapids or turned over was extreme and personal. He would come down from his perch to the water's edge and watch quizzically, ears forward. He was not hysterical or even sympathetic, but distinctly he was interested. Everybody in the county knew that mule.

In June a wild-eyed Negro rushed into the office wailing that his mule had been stolen. Impossible! You couldn't take a mule anywhere if you stole it. The Negro insisted he had seen the marks of a barge on the mud of the embankment. I shuddered with premonition. What embankment? Yes, it was No. 9, and *his* mule was *the* mule. Here was not only wickedness but impiety. Boatloads of the mule's outraged friends and well-wishers scoured the county for three days in search of him or his abductor. In vain. At the gnome's next visit I advised him of the monstrous occurrence. He sat on the wall, frowned, and cogitated darkly, his finger against his forehead. Then I heard a chuckle and a series of "Umph! Umph! Umph!s" Still chuckling mysteriously he left without his hay and oats and disappeared in his rickety bateau up Poplar Street. Guided doubtless by some terrene telepathy, he discovered that sprightly quadruped standing shoulder-deep in water in his own back yard. In a sudden attack of nostalgia he had swum the three miles to the cabin where he lived. Evidently he was not expecting the June rise. I am told he leered at the gnome when they met and followed him jocosely back to No. 9, snorting like a hippo.

It was also about this time that the Negro press of the North, led by the *Chicago Defender*, started an eight weeks' campaign of vilification directed at me. I had been rather amused at Mr. Hoover's pain when his devout efforts and the Red Cross's extraordinary accomplishments had elicited no word of praise or appreciation from that press. So I had to take lightly their accusations that I had dumped the town's sewage into the Negro residential section while the white folks were playing golf at the Country Club, and they were easy to take lightly because the golf-links at the moment were still four feet under water and the town sewerage system never ceased to function. I was even rather thrilled when the *Chicago Defender* climaxed an eloquent editorial by observing that until the South rid itself of its William Alexander Percys it would be no fit place for a Negro to live. But I ought to have been as pained as Mr. Hoover by these libels, because the Negroes at home read their Northern newspapers trustingly and believed them far more piously than the evidence before their own eyes.

The Negroes had behaved admirably during the first weeks of the flood. The camp life on the levee suited their temperaments. There was nothing for them to do except unload their rations when the boats docked. The weather was hot and pleasant. Conditions favored conversation. They worked a little, talked a great deal, ate heartily of food which somebody else had paid for, and sang at night. During the recent clamor for greater leisure for the children of men, I have often wondered what men are worthy of leisure. As far as I have been able to observe, only saints, a few aristocrats, and Negroes. These adorn what to the generality is deteriorating. But perhaps to be an ideal adept in idleness one should be illiterate. At any rate it was unfortunate that the Delta Negroes could read Negro newspapers during the flood.

I sensed this dimly when, as houses began to emerge from the water, we felt the need of a committee to list, by a personal house-to-house inspection, the individual losses in household goods. At the suggestion of a charming and idealistic Red Cross worker from Washington we decided to appoint for this purpose a committee of Negroes, thinking such a show of confidence would appeal to the Negro's pride and to his possible aspiration to do his part. I selected for the committee a doctor's widow, a dentist, a mail-carrier, and two other intelligent and trustworthy residents. They accepted their assignment of duties enthusiastically and we felt sure our experiment would be a success. But we could get no report from the committee. After waiting ten days we called them in for an explanation. We all felt desperately sorry for them: in tears they explained that the Negroes would not permit them to enter their homes, but slammed the doors in their faces, accusing them of having "sold out" to the whites. Regretfully we had to replace them with white committeewomen, who after weeks of hard work assembled the necessary information, on the basis of which we issued to the Negroes household goods to replace those they had lost.

I feel sure that the most painful incident of the flood would not have occurred had it not been for the embittering influence of the *Chicago Defender.* It was a general rule of the Red Cross that recipients of its bounty should unload it gratis. This meant in our instance that meal, flour, meat, sugar, and tobacco, ninety-five per cent of which went to the Negroes, must be unloaded by them without pay. When the water began to fall, the Negroes in the levee camp, where they were housed and fed under sanitary conditions, began to steal back to their soggy, muck-filled homes in the town. They always chose the hour of a boat's arrival for their sentimental journey rather than meal time. It became increasingly difficult to collect an unloading crew. If there was no such crew waiting, the steamer would immediately proceed with its sacred cargo to some more interested port. For that reason we had already lost one boat-load of provisions and our stocks were running low. Mr. Davis, in charge of the wharf, grew daily more frantic. At last he asked my permission to get the police to round up a gang of laborers to unload the next boat. I refused, because that meant forcing labor to work and the Northern press would surely accuse the Red Cross of peonage. Mr. Davis insisted that in no other way could a crew be assembled—he had tried every other method permitted by the Red Cross and had failed. I still refused, and he angrily and properly resigned. I gave up. The police were sent into the Negro section to comb from the idlers the required number of workers. Within two hours the worst had happened: a Negro refused to come with the officer, the officer killed him. The details were obscure and irrelevant. The Negro was a good man, the policeman young and inexperienced. It was no consolation to remember that we were not the first who with the best meaning had incurred the worst.

The next day my trusted Negro informant told me the Negroes had worked themselves into a state of wild excitement and resentment. He feared an uprising. They far outnumbered the whites, and when aroused they are not cowardly. Keeping the peace under these circumstances was my responsibility. I told my informant I would call a meeting of the Negroes for that night and speak to them in one of their churches. He vehemently opposed this course, saying the Negroes were all armed and all of them blamed me for the killing. Nevertheless I called the meeting and requested that no white person except myself be present.

At the designated hour the church was lighted but completely empty except for Mr. Davis and his wife, who to my surprise were seated in the front row. One by one, glum and silent, the Negroes trickled in, all men. As they entered, there was none of the confabulating and handshaking customary on such occasions. I waited in the ominous silence for the church to fill. It was the surliest, most hostile group I ever faced. A massive black preacher rose and announced starkly: "I will read from the Scripture." Without comment, he read the chapter from Genesis on the flood. It was as impressive as ice-water. Then he said: "Join me in a hymn." It was a hymn I had never heard, a droning, monotonous thing that swelled, as they repeated verse after verse, from an almost inaudible mutter to a pounding barbaric chant of menace. I could feel their excitement and hate mount to frenzy. In the quivering silence that followed the last defiant roar from those dusky throats and deep chests, the preacher turned toward me, and I wondered if he would dare introduce me to this audience with the usual fulsome phrases. Instead his words were gaunt: "I present Mr. Percy, chairman of the Red Cross." I knew there was no chance here to appeal to reason. Retreat was out of the question. Attack was imperative. Unapplauded I mounted the pulpit and spoke slowly and bitterly:

A good Negro has been killed by a white policeman. Every white man in town regrets this from his heart and is ashamed. The policeman is in jail and will be tried. I look into your faces and see anger and hatred. You think I am the murderer. The murderer should be punished. I will tell you who he is. . . . For months we Delta people have been suffering together, black and white alike. God did not distinguish between us. He struck us all to our knees. He spared no one. He sent His terrible waters over us and He found no one of us worthy to be His friend as Noah was. He found no one of us worthy to be helped by Him, so we had to help ourselves. For four months I have struggled and worried and done without sleep in order to help you Negroes. Every white man in this town has done the same thing. We served you with our money and our brains and our strength and, for all that we did, no one of us received one penny. We white people could have left you to shift for yourselves. Instead we stayed with you and worked for you, day and night. During all this time you Negroes did nothing, nothing for yourselves or for us. You were asked to do only one thing, a little thing. The Red Cross asked you to unload the food it was giving you, the food without which you would have starved. And you refused. Because of your sinful, shameful laziness, because you refused to work in your own behalf unless you were paid, one of your race has been killed. You sit before me sour and full of hatred as if you had a right to blame anybody or to judge anybody. You think you want avenging justice, but you don't; that is the last thing in the world you want. I am not the murderer. Mr. Davis is not the murderer. That foolish young policeman is not the murderer. The murderer is you! Your hands are dripping with blood. Look into each other's faces and see the shame and the fear God has set on them. Down on your knees, murderers, and beg your God not to punish you as you deserve.

They went on their knees and we prayed. The danger was averted, but when I called for volunteers to unload the next boat only four stood up—a friend of mine, a one-armed man, and two preachers who had been slaves on the Percy Place and were too old to lift a bucket.

During the last week of August the river crawled back to its bed through the trail of its slime and desolation. The Red Cross settled down to intelligent, constructive routine, performed largely by its own personnel. I was exhausted and I felt I had the right to resign as chairman. Having persuaded my friend Hazlewood Farish—later my law partner and the grandfather of my namesake—to take my place, I sailed for Japan. I had never imagined I was naturally given to attacks of hubris, but the painful truth is that when I left the work to which I had devoted myself exclusively for four months, I was convinced it would suffer because of my absence. I suspect I even hoped it would. Human beings are engagingly absurd, we oscillate between being insignificant and imagining ourselves God. It is a small man indeed who is not made big by a big job, but never as big as he imagines. I returned from Japan to find that the relief work had proceeded distressingly well without me. Actually the two really great contributions made to the Delta by the Red Cross had been made without me and without my connivance: we learned to conquer pellagra and to raise alfalfa. The Red Cross had substituted in the plantation ration salmon for salt meat because salmon was cheaper, and so we stumbled on the fact that you can't have pellagra if you eat enough fish. Since the flood did not permit us to plant our usual spring and summer crops, Mr. Hoover hit on alfalfa as a fall crop and distributed free alfalfa seed. Now alfalfa is our standard hay and our best soil-builder.

If out of the 1927 flood our people learned mutual helpfulness instead of the tenets of the Klan, our farmers learned the cultivation of alfalfa, our Negroes learned how to avoid pellagra, and our government learned the necessity for flood control, we Delta folks will have to pronounce that flood an unqualified success. If I learned from it due humility as to my own indispensability and due wonder at that amazing alloy of the hellish and the divine which we call Man, I, too, should recall it only with gratitude, though I hope even the liveliest appreciation would not require me to want to go through it again.

CHAPTER XXI

Planters, Share-Croppers, and Such

Father was the only great person I ever knew and he would not have been great without Mother. They died two years after the flood, mercifully within a few weeks of each other. Without them my life seemed superfluous.

Holt, a hunting partner of Father's and an ex-slave, came up to the office to express his grief. I met him in the hall, but he motioned me to Father's desk, saying: "Set there where he sot. That's where you b'long." He took the chair across the desk from me, filling it and resting his strong hands on the heavy cane he always carried and needed. He was a magnificent old man with massive shoulders and a noble head. For some minutes he struggled silently, sitting there in what had been Father's office, then he let the tears gush unhindered from his eyes and the words from his heart: "The roof is gone from over my head and the floor from under my feet. I am out in the dark and the cold alone. I want to go where he is." He rose and hobbled out. Many of us felt that way.

From Father I inherited Trail Lake, a three-thousand-acre cotton plantation, one of the best in the county and unencumbered. I was considered well-to-do for our part of the state. Father loved the land and had put into it the savings of a lifetime. Perhaps he loved it because he and his brothers and sisters had been born on it and had passed their childhood among country things. His grandfather had obtained title to the Percy Place about 1850. It was a patch of woods then and many slaves had to labor many months before it could properly be termed a cotton plantation. This grandfather, whom the family affectionately, but rather disrespectfully, referred to as Thomas G., had been the favorite son of old Don Carlos and had married a famous beauty from Huntsville named Maria Pope. If you had lived as long as I have with that oil painting of him in the library over the fireplace, you could easily deduce why Maria and Don Carlos loved him. It reticently and through a fume of chiaroscuro reveals a personable young chap in a black stock and a black waistcoat adorned with four stylish brass buttons. At first perhaps you won't notice his smile, but it's there, all right, at the corner of his mouth, very shadowy and knowing, a little hurt but not at all bitter. It's by that smile I really know him, and not by his descendants, who mostly are the kind you like to descend with, or by the tender trusting references to him in Don Carlos's will. Though I've always lived with the remnant of his brown English library (each leather volume numbered and marked with the book-plate bearing his name sans crest or escutcheon) and always loved his enormous mahogany dining-room table with its carved legs and brass claws, around which all of us have eaten meals together going on six generations now, it's not they but his smile that makes him a familiar and a confidant of mine—that and the fact he cut no very great figure in the world. He isn't a demanding ancestor.

He seems to have felt that if he raised his sons to be gentlemen he would have done his full Christian duty by them and indeed by life. Training in a profession, though ornamental, was unnecessary for a gentleman, but of course you couldn't be one at all unless you owned land. Therefore, Thomas G. casually made doctors of his two older boys, Walker and LeRoy, and a lawyer of Fafar, after whom I was named, but having done that, without, of course, expecting them to practice medicine or law, he settled down gravely to the really serious business of getting them a plantation. He decided on a place in the Delta, paid for it, manned it with enough slaves to clear and cultivate it, and shipped his sons, all three of them, down to live on it.

When I was a youngster, I quite often spent the week-end on this plantation of theirs, which is still called the Percy Place. Already the slave quarters looked ramshackly, the woods had disappeared, the loamy creek land seemed thin, and the residence, from which the ells had fallen away, was ugly and plain, more full of room than anything else and split amidships by an enormous drafty hall, a very cave for coolness and emptiness.

I am sure in these days and times no wise father would dare bundle off three sons, two of them married, and expect them to live forever after under the same roof without kicking it off. Uncle Walker was married to Aunt Fannie, Fafar to Mur, and Uncle LeRoy (whom everybody loved and the youngsters called Uncle Lee) was the bachelor—scholar and gallivanter of the trio and so destined to endure gracefully occasional admonitions and rakings over the coals from his young sisters-in-law. Yet all reports agree that the Percy household was not only amiable but full of fun. Apparently they were a cheery lot who liked life.

Then the war came, and everything changed. By the

time of the surrender Uncle Walker had died, Uncle Lee had been stricken with paralysis, and when Fafar, the youngest and the soldier of the three, returned, it was to a diminished and penniless household of which he found himself the head and the bread-winner. The women and children and sick were still clinging to the place, but there wasn't a servant or a field-hand on it. All the slaves had left. I suppose he and Mur must have done some pretty tragic planning together the night he got home. Mur brought out from hiding the last of the plantation's horses, Fafar mounted this priceless, unlovely steed—his name was Bill Jack—and jogged off to Greenville, which then was a mere river-landing at the end of ten miles of impassable road. Fafar was over thirty years old and a Colonel of a defeated army. He hung out a shingle announcing to the bankrupt countryside that W. A. Percy had opened offices for the practice of law. In time he became one of Mississippi's famous lawyers, but Father said that right from the start he always managed to collect more clients than fees.

Fafar was fifty-five years old when he died. Long before his death people had been calling him "Old Colonel Percy" and "The Gray Eagle." His life had been crowded with usefulness and honor, but it ended when he was fifty-five. That is my age now. When I consider all he did and all I haven't done, I feel the need of taking a good long look at Thomas G., debonair and wistful, expecting nothing.

Of course the stage that Fafar trod after the war was no ordinary stage, and the play no ordinary play. Those days you had to be a hero or a villain or a weakling—you couldn't be just middling ordinary. The white people in the whole Delta comprised a mere handful, but there were hordes of Negroes. Poor wretches! For a thousand years and more they had been trained in tribal barbarism, for a hundred and more in slavery. So equipped, they were presented overnight with freedom and the ballot and told to run the river country. They did. They elected Negroes to every office. We had a Negro sheriff, Negro justices of the peace, Negro clerks of court. There were no white officials, not even carpetbaggers. It was one glorious orgy of graft, lawlessness, and terrorism. The desperate whites though negligible in number banded together to overthrow this regime and chose Fafar as their leader. His life work became the re-establishment of white supremacy. That work required courage, tact, intelligence, patience; it also required vote-buying, the stuffing of ballot-boxes, chicanery, intimidation. Heart-breaking business and degrading, but in the end successful. At terrific cost white supremacy was re-established. Some of us still remember what we were told of those times, and what we were told inclines us to guard the ballot as something precious, something to be withheld unless the fitness of the recipient be patent. We are the ones I suppose who doubt despairingly the fitness of Negroes and (under our breath be it said) of women.

Father considered Fafar superior to any human being he had ever known: he insisted he had a finer mind, a greater gusto, a warmer love of people, and a more rigid standard of justice than any of his sons. But for Fafar's efforts at running the plantation Father had only amused and tolerant scorn.

It appears that Fafar practiced law in order to be able to practice husbandry. He retained title to the Percy Place by paying its taxes with fees. But never, never, during all the years he managed it, did it yield one penny of profit. Father contended the reason for this deplorable result was Fafar's inability to say no to any Negro in wheedling mood. I suspect, however, the main reason was the low price of cotton and the South's economic collapse following Gettysburg.

After the first fine frenzy of emancipation, although Negro politicians and carpetbaggers were riding high and making prosperity look like sin, the rank and file of ex-slaves, the simple country Negroes, found themselves faring exceedingly ill. They had freedom, but nothing else. It's a precious possession, but worthless commercially. The former slave-holders had land, but nothing else. It's as precious, nearly, as freedom, but without plow and plow-men equally worthless. On ex-slave and ex-master it dawned gradually that they were in great need of one another—and not only economically, but, curiously enough, emotionally. Holt killed a Yankee officer for insulting Colonel Howell Hines, his old master. Fafar had Negro friends without whose information and advice he and the other political rebels of the time would have suffered under this reign of scalawaggery even more grievously than they did. To each plantation drifted back puzzled, unhappy freedmen who had once worked it as slaves and who were discovering that though slaves couldn't go hungry, freedmen could and did. Ex-slaves returned to the Percy Place and asked for a chance to make a crop on it. Fafar had little to offer them except good land and leadership. He puzzled over what was just to do and what he could do. He concluded by offering his ex-slaves a partnership with him. The terms of it were simple.

In simple words, about like these, he explained it to them:

I have land which you need, and you have muscle which I need; let's put what we've got in the same pot and call it ours. I'll give you all the land you can work, a house to live in, a garden plot and room to raise chickens, hogs, and cows if you can come by them, and all the wood you want to cut for fuel. I'll direct and oversee you. I'll get you a doctor when you are sick. Until the crop comes in I'll try to keep you from going hungry or naked in so far as I am able. I'll pay the taxes and I'll furnish the mules and plows and gear and whatever else is necessary to make a crop. This is what I promise to do. You will plant and cultivate and gather this crop as I direct. This is what you will promise to do. When the crop is picked, half of it will be mine and half of it yours. If I have supplied you with money or food or clothing or anything else during this year, I will charge it against your half of the crop. I shall handle the selling of the cotton and the cottonseed because I know more than you do about their value. But the corn you may sell or eat or use for feed as you like. If the price of cotton is good, we shall both make something. If it is bad, neither of us will make anything, but I shall probably lose the place and you will lose nothing because you have nothing to lose. It's a hard contract these hard times for both of us, but it's just and self-respecting and if we both do our part and have a little luck we can both prosper under it.

This was the contract under which Fafar operated the Percy Place during his lifetime, under which Mur operated it after his death, under which Father operated it from the time of her death to the time it was sold. It changed in no essential during all those years except that with better times the promise to keep the Negroes from going hungry and cold became a fixed obligation to lend them a stated amount of money each month from the first of March, when planting started, to the first of September, when cottonseed money began coming in. After the place had been worked for years under this arrangement—years during which nobody grew rich and nobody suffered for necessities—Father decided that it was getting run down, it was too old, it was worn out. Miserable, but feeling foresighted and awfully business-like, he sold the Percy Place.

I rode through it last week and the crop was twice as big as either Fafar or Father had ever raised on it. Modern methods of farming, government-inspired diversification of crops, and the use of fertilizer have made it more productive than when Thomas G.'s sons planted their first cotton crop in its virgin soil with slave labor.

Let no one imagine that because Father sold the Percy Place he was landless. Far from it. Instead, he'd been watching longingly the new part of the county, the Bogue district, and little by little, bit by bit, over a period of ten years, he'd been buying a plantation there. It was his very own, his creation, and he loved it. He started with a batch of virgin timber and cleared that. Next he won in the cotton market and put the winnings into that section of Doctor Atterbury's, good land and mostly in cultivation. Then he added the desolate-looking deadening along Deep Slough. At last he bought the Cheek Place and the Ross Place. In all he finally acquired title to a single block of land of over three thousand acres—some cleared, some half-cleared, some in cultivation, part of it paid for, part mortgaged, most of it magnificent ridge-land, a few hundred acres swampy and sour. He named it Trail Lake after a singularly dilapidated-looking slough which meandered half-heartedly into the center of the place before petering out from sheer inertia. When I was going to Sewanee the whole property looked ragged and unkempt, full of fallen logs and charred stumps, standing and prone. It was at the end of the world, in a turkey and panther country. You could reach it only by a rocking impromptu trainlet called the Black Dog. The trip from Greenville and back required twenty-four hours.

Trail Lake was so far from anywhere, so inaccessible to "the law" and to the infrequent neighbors, that the Negroes ran off one manager after another and terrified the whole countryside. Father almost lost the place because the Negroes wouldn't let any white man stay on it. At last, in desperation, he sent down a young manager from Arkansas, Billy Hardie, who shot a tenant the day of his arrival and single-handed dispersed a crap game his first Saturday night. Quiet ensued. It's a pleasant country, but even now not safe. If you haven't got a few pioneer virtues thrown in with the run-of-the-mill sort you'd better move on to a more cultured environment.

I have no love of the land and few, if any, pioneer virtues, but when Trail Lake became mine after Father's death, I must confess I was proud of it. I could reach it in three quarters of an hour. It was a model place: well drained, crossed by concrete roads, with good screened houses, a modern gin, artesian-well water, a high state of cultivation, a Negro school, a foolish number of churches, abundant crops, gardens and peach trees, quantities of hogs, chickens, and cows, and all the mules and tractors and equipment any place that size needed.

Father had operated it under the same contract that Fafar used on the Percy Place. The Negroes seemed to like it and I certainly did. I happen to believe that profit-sharing is the most moral system under which human beings can work together and I am convinced that if it were accepted in principle by capital and labor, our industrial troubles would largely cease. So on Trail Lake I continue to be partners with the sons of ex-slaves and to share fifty-fifty with them as my grandfather and Father had done.

In 1936 a young man with a passion for facts roved in from the University of North Carolina and asked to be allowed to inspect Trail Lake for the summer. He was Mr. Raymond McClinton, one of Doctor Odum's boys, and the result of his sojourn was a thesis entitled "A Social-Economic Analysis of a Mississippi Delta Plantation." That's coming pretty stout if you spend much of your time trying to forget facts and are stone-deaf to statistics. But some of his findings were of interest even to me, largely I suspect because they illustrated how Fafar's partnership-contract works in the modern world. In 1936, the year Mr. McClinton chose for his study, the crop was fair, the price average (about twelve cents), and the taxes higher than usual. Now for some of his facts:

Trail Lake has a net acreage of 3,343.12 acres of which 1,833.66 are planted in cotton, 50.59 are given to pasture, 52.44 to gardens, and the rest to corn and hay. The place is worked by 149 families of Negroes (589 individuals) and in 1936 yielded 1,542 bales of cotton. One hundred and twenty-four of the families work under Fafar's old contract, and twenty-five, who own their stock and equipment, under a similar contract which differs from the other only in giving three-fourths instead of one-half of the yield to the tenant. The plantation paid in taxes of all kinds $20,459.99, a bit better than $6.00 per acre; in payrolls for plantation work $12,584.66–nearly $4.00 an acre. These payrolls went to the Negroes on the place. The 124 families without stock of their own made a gross average income of $491.90 and a net average income of $437.64. I have lost Mr. McClinton's calculation of how many days of work a plantation worker puts in per year, but my own calculation is a maximum of 150 days. There is nothing to do from ginning time, about October the first, to planting time, about March the fifteenth, and nothing to do on rainy days, of which we have many.

These figures, as I read them, show that during an average year the 124 families working on Trail Lake for 150 days make each $437.64 clear, besides having free water and fuel, free garden plot and pasturage, a monthly credit for six months to cover food and clothing, a credit for doctor's bills and medicine, and a house to live in. The Negroes who receive this cash and these benefits are simple unskilled laborers. I wonder what other unskilled labor for so little receives so much. Plantations do not close down during the year and there's no firing, because partners can't fire one another. Our plantation system seems to me to offer as humane, just, self-respecting, and cheerful a method of earning a living as human beings are likely to devise. I watch the limber-jointed, oily-black, well-fed, decently clothed peasants on Trail Lake and feel sorry for the telephone girls, the clerks in chain stores, the office help, the unskilled laborers everywhere—not only for their poor and fixed wage but for their slave routine, their joyless habits of work, and their insecurity.

Even with a place like Trail Lake, it's hard to make money farming. Although I kept myself helpfully obscure during the first years of my plantation-ownership, retaining the same excellent employees and following Father's practices, I began losing money almost at once, and in two years (they were depression years for everybody, I must confess) I had lost over a hundred thousand dollars and Trail Lake was mortgaged to the hilt. For the next four or five years I was in such a stew and lather getting that mortgage reduced and taxes paid, I lost track of goings-on in the outside world and missed the first tide of talk about share-croppers. Those hundred and twenty-four families of mine with $437.64 in their jeans worked "on the shares" and called themselves "croppers," but I wasn't familiar with the term "share-croppers." As used by the press, it suggested to me no Delta group and I assumed vaguely that share-croppers must be of some perverse bucolic genus that probably originated in Georgia and throve in Oklahoma. But one day I read that the President of the United States had excoriated bitterly and sorrowfully "the infamous share-cropper system." I asked a Washington friend of mine in what locality that system of farming prevailed. He knocked the breath out of me by answering: "On Trail Lake." I woke to the discovery that in pseudo-intellectual circles from Moscow to Santa Monica the Improvers-of-the-world had found something new in the South to shudder over. Twenty years ago it had been peonage. In the dark days when the collapse of the slave-trade had almost bankrupted good old New England, it had been slavery. Now it was the poor share-croppers—share-croppers over the whole South, but especially in the Delta. That very partnership of Fafar's which had seemed to me so just and practical now was being denounced as avaricious and slick—it was Mr. Roosevelt's "infamous system." We who had operated our plantations under it since carpetbag days were taunted now with being little better than slave-drivers by the carpetbaggers' progeny and kin. Obviously we are given to depravity down here: the South just won't do. In spite of prayers and advice from the "holier-than-thou's" it's always hell-bent for some deviltry or other. At this moment there's another of those great moral daybreaks on, and its east is Washington. In the glow I realize that Fafar and Mur, Father and I suffered from moral astigmatism—for all I know, from complete moral blindness: we were infamous and didn't even suspect it. Well, well, well. That makes a Southerner feel pretty bad, I reckon.

Notwithstanding an adage to the contrary, truth, as I've observed it, is one of the least resilient of herbs. Crushed to earth, it stays crushed; once down, it keeps down, flatter than anything except an oat field after a wind-storm. The truth about share-croppers has been told and retold, but, being neither melodramatic nor evidential of Southern turpitude, it isn't believed. I am not a well-informed person, but I know the truth about share-cropping and in this chapter I have told enough for earnest seekers to infer what it is; I have not done this, however, in the naïve hope that my words will do the slightest good or change the views of a single reader; my reason is other and quite unworthy: there's a low malicious pleasure in telling the truth where you know it won't be believed. Though rightly considered a bore and a pest in the best Trojan circles, Cassandra, no doubt, had her fun, but, at that, not nearly so much as the Knights of the Bleeding Heart who in politics and literature years from now will still be finding it fetching and inexpensive to do some of their most poignant public heart-bleeding over the poor downtrodden share-croppers of the deep South.

Share-cropping is one of the best systems ever devised to give security and a chance for profit to the simple and the unskilled. It has but one drawback—it must be administered by human beings to whom it offers an unusual opportunity to rob without detection or punishment. The failure is not in the system itself, but in not living up to the contractual obligations of the system—the failure is in human nature. The Negro is no more on an equality with the white man in plantation matters than in any other dealings between the two. The white planter may charge an exorbitant rate of interest, he may allow the share-cropper less than the market price received for his cotton, he may cheat him in a thousand different ways, and the Negro's redress is merely theoretical. If the white planter happens to be a crook, the share-cropper system on that plantation is bad for Negroes, as any other system would be. They are prey for the dishonest and temptation for the honest. If the Delta planters were mostly cheats, the results of the share-cropper system would be as grievous as reported. But, strange as it may seem to the sainted East, we have quite a sprinkling of decent folk down our way.

Property is a form of power. Some people regard it as an opportunity for profit, some as a trust; in the former it breeds hubris, in the latter, noblesse oblige. The landed gentry of Fafar's time were of an ancient lineage and in a sober God-fearing tradition. Today many have thought to acquire membership in that older caste by acquiring land, naked land, without those ancestral hereditaments of virtue which change dirt into a way of life. On the plantation where there is stealing from the Negro you will generally find the owner to be a little fellow operating, as the saying goes, "on a shoe-string," or a nouveau riche, or a landlord on the make, tempted to take more than his share because of the mortgage that makes his title and his morals insecure. These, in their pathetic ambition to imitate what they do not understand, acquire power and use it for profit; for them the share-cropper system affords a golden opportunity rarely passed up.

Two courses of action would be effective against unworthy landlords: the Negroes could and should boycott such landlords, quietly and absolutely; the government could and should deny government benefits to the landlord who will not put the terms of his contract in writing, who will not carry out those terms and who will not permit the government to prove by its own inspection that they have been carried out. In place of these suggested remedies, I can only recommend changing human nature. All we need anywhere in any age is character: from that everything follows. Leveling down's the fashion now, but I remember the bright spires—they caught the light first and held it longest.

So much that was fine and strong went into the making of this Delta of ours! So much was conquered for us by men and women whose names we have forgotten! So much had to be overcome before ever this poor beautiful unfinished present was turned over to us by the anonymous dead—malaria and yellow fever, swamp-water and rain-water and river-water, war and defeat, tropic heat and intemperate cold, poverty and ignorance, economic cruelty and sectional hatred, the pathos of a stronger race carrying on its shoulders a weaker race and from the burden losing its own strength! They must have been always in the front line fighting for us, those builders of the Delta; they could never have stopped long enough to learn of leisure and safety the graces of peace. But there are those who live in fear as in a native element, and they are beautiful with a fresh miraculous beauty. It is watching for unseen death that gives a bird's eyes their glancing brilliance. It is dodging eternal danger that makes his motions deft and exquisite. His half-wit testament to the delight of living, terror has taught him that, shaking the melody from his dubious innocent throat. Perhaps security is a good thing to seek and a bad thing to find. Perhaps it is never found, and all our best is in the search.

CHAPTER XXII

Fode

People are divided into Leaners and Leanees: into oaks more or less sturdy and vines quite, quite clinging. I was never a Leaner, yet, although seldom mistaken for one, I find people are constantly feeling impelled to protect me. Invariably they are right and I accept their proffered ministrations gratefully. I cannot drive a car or fix a puncture or sharpen a pencil or swim or skate or give a punch in the jaw to the numerous parties who need punching. My incompetency is almost all-inclusive, but it must have a glow, for it attracts Samaritans from miles around. I have been offered a very fine, quick-working poison for use on my enemies or myself; I have had my rifle carried by a soldier who disliked me, just because I was all in; a bootlegger once asked me to go partners with him because I looked seedy; a top sergeant, icy with contempt, put together my machine-gun when its disjecta membra unassembled would have returned me in disgrace to America; a red-headed friend of mine had to be restrained from flinging a red-headed enemy of mine into the river for some passing insolence; an appreciable percentage of the hard-boiled bastards of the world have patched tires, blown life into sparkplugs, pushed, hauled, lifted, hammered, towed, and sweated for me because they knew that without their aid I should have moldered indefinitely on some wretched, canstrewn landscape. If you mix incompetency with a pinch of the wistful and a heap of good manners, it works pretty well. Men of goodwill are all over the place, millions of them. It is a very nice world—that is, if you remember that while good morals are all-important between the Lord and His creatures, what counts between one creature and another is good manners. A good manner may spring from vanity or a sense of style; it is a sort of pleasant fiction. But good manners spring from well-wishing; they are fundamental as truth and much more useful. No nation or stratum of society has a monopoly on them and, contrary to the accepted estimate, Americans have more than their share.

The righteous are usually in a dither over the deplorable state of race relations in the South. I, on the other hand, am usually in a condition of amazed exultation over the excellent state of race relations in the South. It is incredible that two races, centuries apart in emotional and mental discipline, alien in physical characteristics, doomed by war and the Constitution to a single, not a dual, way of life, and to an impractical and unpracticed theory of equality which deludes and embitters, heckled and misguided by pious fools from the North and impious fools from the South—it is incredible, I insist, that two such dissimilar races should live side by side with so little friction, in such comparative peace and amity. This result is due solely to good manners. The Southern Negro has the most beautiful manners in the world, and the Southern white, learning from him, I suspect, is a close second.

Which reminds me of Ford. (He pronounces his name

"Fode" with enormous tenderness, for he is very fond of himself.)

In the South every white man worth calling white or a man is owned by some Negro, whom he thinks he owns, his weakness and solace and incubus. Ford is mine. There is no excuse for talking about him except that I like to. He started off as my caddy, young, stocky, strong, with a surly expression, and a smile like the best brand of sunshine. For no good reason he rose to be my chauffeur; then house-boy; then general factotum; and now, without any contractual relation whatever, my retainer, which means to say I am retained for life by him against all disasters, great or small, for which he pays by being Ford. It was not because of breaking up the first automobile, coming from a dance drunk, or because of breaking up the second automobile, coming from a dance drunk, that our contractual relation was annulled, but for a subtler infamy. I was in the shower, not a position of dignity at best, and Ford strolled in, leaned against the door of the bathroom, in the relaxed pose of the Marble Faun, and observed dreamily: "You ain't nothing but a little old fat man."

A bit of soap was in my eye and under the circumstances it was no use attempting to be haughty anyway, so I only blurted: "You damn fool."

Ford beamed: "Jest look at your stummick."

When one had fancied the slenderness of one's youth had been fairly well retained! Well, taking advantage of the next dereliction, and one occurred every week, we parted; that is to say, I told Ford I was spoiling him and it would be far better for him to battle for himself in this hostile world, and Ford agreed, but asked what he was going to do "seeing as how nobody could find a job nohow." As neither of us could think of the answer, I sent him off to a mechanics' school in Chicago. He returned with a diploma and a thrilling tale of how nearly he had been married against his vehement protest to a young lady for reasons insufficient surely in any enlightened community with an appreciation of romance. With Ford's return the demand for mechanics fell to zero—he always had an uncanny effect on the labor market—so he took to house-painting. His first week he fell off the roof of the tallest barn in the county and instead of breaking his neck, as Giorgione or Raphael would have done, he broke only his ankle and had to be supplied with crutches, medical care, and a living for six weeks. It was then that I left for Samoa.

But I should not complain. Ford has never learned anything from me, but I am indebted to him for an education in more subjects and stranger ones than I took at college, subjects, however, slightly like those the mock-turtle took from the Conger eel. The first lesson might be called "How Not to Faint in Coils." Ford observed:

"You don't understand folks good as I does." I was appalled. "You sees what's good in folks, but you don't see what's bad. Most of the time I'se a good boy, then I goes nigger, just plain nigger. Everybody do that, and when they does, it hurts you." I was pulverized. It may not have taken a wicked person to think that, but it certainly took a wicked one to say it.

That I have any dignity and self-respect is not because of but in spite of Ford. We were returning from a directors' meeting in a neighboring town and he was deeply overcast. At last he became communicative:

"Mr. Oscar Johnston's boy says Mr. Oscar won't ride in no car more'n six months old and he sho ain't goin' to ride in nothin' lessen a Packard."

I received this calmly, it was only one more intimation that my Ford was older than need be and congenitally unworthy. Ford continued:

"He says Mr. Oscar says you ain't got near as much sense as your pa." I agreed, heartily. "He says you ain't never goin' to make no money." I agreed, less heartily. "En if you don't be keerful you goin' to lose your plantation." I agreed silently, but I was nettled, and observed:

"And you sat there like a bump on a log, saying nothing, while I was being run down?"

"Well, I told him you had traveled a lot, a lot more'n Mr. Oscar; you done gone near 'bout everywhere, en he kinder giggled and says: 'Yes, they tells me he's been to Africa,' en I says: 'He is,' en he says: 'You know why he went to Africa?' en I says: ''Cause he wanted to go there,' en he says: 'That's what he tells you, but he went to Africa to 'range to have the niggers sent back into slavery.'"

I exploded: "And you were idiot enough to believe that?"

"I'se heard it lots of times," Ford observed mildly, "but it didn't make no difference to me, you been good to me en I didn't care."

Having fancied I had spent a good portion of my life defending and attempting to help the Negro, this information stunned me and, as Ford prophesied, it hurt. But hiding my wounded vanity as usual in anger, I turned on Ford with:

"You never in your life heard any Negro except that fool boy of Oscar Johnston's say I was trying to put the Negroes back in slavery."

"Lot of 'em," reiterated Ford.

"I don't believe you," I said. "You can't name a single one."

We finished the drive in silence; spiritually we were not en rapport.

The next morning when Ford woke me he was wreathed in smiles, suspiciously pleased with himself. He waited until one eye was open and then announced triumphantly:

"Louisa!" (pronounced with a long *i*).

"What about Louisa?" I queried sleepily.

"She says you'se goin' to send the niggers back into slavery!"

Louisa was our cook, the mainstay and intimate of the household for fifteen years.

"God damn!" I exploded, and Ford fairly tripped out, charmed with himself.

I dressed thoughtfully and repaired to the kitchen. My intention was to be gentle but desolating. Louisa weighs over three hundred, and despite a physical allure I can only surmise from the stream of nocturnal callers in our back yard, she distinctly suggests in her general contour a hippopotamus. When I entered the kitchen I found her pacing ponderously back and forth through the door that opens on the back gallery. It seemed a strange procedure—Louisa was not given to exercise, at least not of that kind. The following colloquy ensued:

"Louisa, what are you doing?"

"I stuck a nail in my foot."

"Why don't you go to the doctor?"

"I'se gettin' the soreness out."

"You can't walk it out."

"Naw, suh, the nail is *drawing* it out."

"What nail?"

"The nail I stepped on."

"Where is it?"

Louisa pointed to the lintel of the door. A nail hung from it by a piece of string; under it Louisa was pacing. I left her pacing. I didn't mention slavery then or later.

My bitter tutelage didn't conclude here. In late autumn we drove to the plantation on settlement day. Cotton had been picked and ginned, what cash had been earned from the crop was to be distributed. The managers and bookkeeper had been hard at work preparing a statement of each tenant's account for the whole year. As the tenant's name was called he entered the office and was paid off. The Negroes filled the store and overflowed onto the porch, milling and confabulating. As we drove up, one of them asked: "Whose car is dat?" Another answered: "Dat's *us* car." I thought it curious they didn't recognize my car, but dismissed the suspicion and dwelt on the thought of how sweet it was to have the relation between landlord and tenant so close and affectionate that to them my car was their car. Warm inside I passed through the crowd, glowing and bowing, the lord of the manor among his faithful retainers. My mission concluded, I returned to the car, still glowing. As we drove off I said:

"Did you hear what that man said?"

Ford assented, but grumpily.

"It was funny," I continued.

"Funnier than you think," observed Ford sardonically.

I didn't understand and said so.

Ford elucidated: "He meant that's the car *you* has bought with *us* money. They all knew what he meant, but you didn't and they knew you didn't. They wuz laughing to theyselves."

A few days later the managers confirmed this version of the meaning of the phrase and laughed. I laughed too, but not inside.

Yet laughter singularly soft and unmalicious made me Ford's debtor more even than his admonitions and revelations. I still think with gratitude of an afternoon which his peculiarly Negro tact and good manners and laughter made charming. I was in what Ford would call "low cotton." After a hellish day of details and beggars, my nerves raw, I phoned for Ford and the car. On climbing in I asked dejectedly:

"Where shall we drive?"

Ford replied: "Your ruthers is my ruthers" (what you would rather is what I would rather). Certainly the most amiable and appeasing phrase in any language, the language used being not English but deep Southern.

"Let's try the levee," I suggested.

Although nothing further was said and Ford asked no questions, he understood my depression and felt the duty on him to cheer me up. He drove to my favorite spot on the levee and parked where I could watch across the width of waters a great sunset crumbling over Arkansas. As I sat moody and worried, Ford, for the first and only time in his life, began to tell me Negro stories. I wish I could imitate his exact phrases and intonations and pauses, without which they are poor enough stories; but, in spite of the defects of my relaying, anyone can detect their Negro quality, care-free and foolish and innocent—anyone, that is, who has lived among Negroes in the South.

Here are the three I remember in something approximating Ford's diction:

"There wuz a cullud man en he died en went to hevven en the Lawd gevvum all wings, en he flew en he flew" (here Ford hunched his shoulders and gave a superb imitation of a buzzard's flight). "After he flew round there fur 'bout a week he looked down en saw a reel *good*-lookin' lady, a-settin' on a cloud. She wuz *reel* good-lookin'. En he dun the loop-the-loop.

"The Lawd cum en sez: 'Don't you know how to act? There ain't nuthin' but nice people here, en you beehavin' like that. Git out.' But he told the Lawd he jest didn't know en he wuzzent never gonner do nuthin' like that no mo', en please let him stay. So the Lawd got kinder pacified en let him stay. En he flew en he flew. En after he had been flying round fur 'bout a week, he ups en sees that same good-lookin' lady a-settin' on a cloud en he jest couldn't hep it—he dun the loop-the-loop.

"So the Lawd stepped up en he sez: 'You jest don't know how to act, you ain't fitten fur to be with decent folks, you'se a scanlus misbeehavor. Git out.' En he got.

"He felt mighty bad en hung round the gate three or four days tryin' to ease up on St. Peter, but St. Peter 'lowed there wuzn't no way, he jest couldn't let him in en the onliest way he might git in wuz to have a *conference* with the Lawd. Then the man asked if he couldn't 'range fur a conference en they had a lot of back-and-forth. En finally St. Peter eased him in fur a conference." (Ford loved that word, it made him giggle.) "But the Lawd wuz mad, He wuz mad sho-nuff, he wuz hoppin' mad en told him flat-footed to git out en stay out. Then the cullud man sez:

" 'Well, jest remember this, Lawd: while I wuz up here in yo' place I wuz the flyin'est fool you had.' "

Since the thirteenth century no one except Ford and his kind has been at ease in heaven, much less confident enough of it to imagine an aeroplane stunt there. And I do hope that good-looking lady saw the loop-the-loop.

The second story is just as inconsequential:

"A fellow cum to a cullud man en promised him a whole wagen-load of watermelons if he would go en set by hisself in a hanted house all night long. Well, the man he liked watermelons en he promised, though he sho didn't like no hanted house, en he sho didn't wanter see no hants. He went in en drug up a cheer en set down en nuthin' happened. After so long a time, in walked a black cat en set down in front of him en jest looked at him. He warn't so skeered because it warn't much more'n a kitten, en they both uvvem jest set there en looked at each uther. Then ernurther cat cum in, a big black 'un, en he set by the little 'un en they jest set there lookin' at him, en ain't sed nothin'. Then ernurther one cum en he wuz big as a dawg en all three uvvem jest set there en looked at him en sed nuthin'. Ernurther one cum, still bigger, en ernurther, en ernurther, en the last one wuz big as a hoss. They all jest set there in a row en sed nuthin' en looked at him. That cullud man he wuz plum skeered en he had ter say sumpin so he 'lowed all nice en p'lite:

" 'Whut us gwiner do?'

"En the big 'un sed: 'Us ain't gwiner do nuthin', till Martin comes.'

"The cullud man says reel nice en p'lite: 'Jest tell Martin I couldn't wait,' en he busted out the winder en tore down the big road fast as he could en faster, en he ain't never taken no more interest in watermelons since."

"But, Ford," I asked, "who was Martin?"

"I dunno," said Ford and chuckled, "but I reckon he wuz big as er elly-fant."

I reckon so too, and twice as real, so far as I am concerned.

And now the last:

"A cullud man cum to the white folks' house in the country en sed to the man:

" 'Boss, I'se hongry; gimme sumpin t'eat.'

"The man sed: 'All right, go round to the back do' en tell the cook to feed you.'

"The cullud man sed: 'Boss, I'se neer 'bout starved, I ain't et fur a whole week.'

"The man sed: 'All right, all right, go round to the kitchen.'

"The cullud man sed: 'Boss, if you gimme sumpin t'eat

I'll split up all that stove wood you got in yo' back yard.'

"The man sed: 'All right, all right, go en git that grub like I tole yer.'

"So he went. After 'bout three hours the man went to his back yard en saw the cullud man, who wuz jest settin'. So he sed:

" 'Has you et?'

"En he sed: 'Yassir.'

"En he sed: 'Has you chopped up that wood-pile?'

"En he sed: 'Boss man, if you jest let me res' round till dinner time, after dinner I'll go en chop out that patch of cotton fur you.'

"So the man sed: 'All right, but don't you fool me no more.'

"After the cullud man had et him a big dinner he started out to the cotton patch en he met him a cooter [a mud-turtle] en the cooter sed to him:

" 'Nigger, you talks too much.'

"The nigger goes tearin' back to the big house en when he gits there the man cums out en sez:

" 'Nigger, has you chopped out that cotton?'

"En the nigger sez:

" 'Lawd, boss, I wuz on my way, fo' God I wuz, en I met a cooter en he started talkin' to me en I lit out from there en here I is.'

"The boss man was plenty riled and he sez:

" 'Nigger, take me to that cooter en if he don't start talkin', I'se goin' to cut your thoat frum year to year."

"So they bof uvvem started fur the cotton patch en there in the middle of the big road set that cooter. En he never opened his mouth, he ain't sed nuthin'. So the man hopped on the nigger en whupped him sumpin' scand'lous en left fur the big house mighty sore at niggers en cooters. Well, the cullud man wuz neer 'bout through breshing hisself off en jest fo' moseying on off when the cooter poked his head out en looks at him en sez:

" 'Nigger, I tole you you talks too much.' "

Can it be wondered at, now that Ford is sojourning in the North beyond the infamous housing conditions of the South, comfortable and healthy in his own little room with four young Negro roommates, a single window to keep out the cold and a gas burner for cooking and heat—can it be wondered, if now when the phone rings and the operator's voice says: "Detroit, calling collect," that I accept the charge, although I know who it is and why he is calling? It is Ford and he is drunk and he is incoherently solicitous for me and mine and for his mother and wants to come home and needs five dollars. I reply I am glad to hear his voice, which is true, and hope he is well, and advise him to be a good boy and stick to his job, and a letter will follow or shall I wire? Of course, he has no job, except with the W.P.A., to which he has attached himself by fictions and frauds with which all good Southern darkies with itching feet are familiar. I hope the government supports him as long and as loyally as I did, because if it doesn't, I must. I must because Ford is my fate, my Old Man of the Sea, who tells me of Martin and admonishing cooters and angels that do the loop-the-loop, my only tie with Pan and the Satyrs and all earth creatures who smile sunshine and ask no questions and understand.

I wish my parting with him could have been happier or that I could forget it. He had abandoned his truck in a traffic jam and forfeited his job, one that I had procured for him with much difficulty and some misrepresentation. Then he had got looping drunk and last, against all precedent and propriety, he had come to see me; it was late at night when he arrived, stumbling and weeping. He threw himself across the couch and sobbed without speaking. I could not get him up or out, and he wouldn't explain his grief. At last he quieted down and, his face smeared with tears, managed to gasp:

"You cain't do no good, Mr. Will. It don't make no difference how hard I tries or how good I bees, I ain't never gonner be nuthin' but jest Fode."

I wish I had never heard him say that. There are some truths that facing does not help. Something had brought home to Ford the tragedy of himself and of his race in an alien world. Had he been in South Africa or Morocco or Harlem or Detroit, his pitiful cry would have been equally true, equally hopeless and unanswerable. What can we do, any of us, how can we help? Let the man who has the answer cry it from the house-tops in a hundred languages. But there will be no crier in the night, and it is night for all the Fords of the world and for us who love them.

CHAPTER XXIII

A Note on Racial Relations

A superabundance of sympathy has always been expended on the Negro, neither undeservedly nor helpfully, but no sympathy whatever, so far as I am aware, has ever been expended on the white man living among Negroes. Yet he, too, is worthy not only of sympathy but of pity, and for many reasons. To live habitually as a superior among inferiors, be the superiority intellectual or economic, is a temptation to dishonesty and hubris, inevitably deteriorating. To live among a people whom, because of their needs, one must in common decency protect and defend is a sore burden in a world where one's own troubles are about all any life can shoulder. To live in the pretense that whites and blacks share a single, identical culture and way of life is not only hypocritical but illusory and obfuscating. And, last, to live among a people deceptively but deeply alien and unknowable guarantees heart-aches, unjust expectations, undeserved condemnations. Yet such living is the fate of the white man in the South. He deserves all the sympathy and patience he doesn't get. Poor as his results have been, they are better than any wise realist could have anticipated.

A NOTE ON RACIAL RELATIONS

It is true in the South that whites and blacks live side by side, exchange affection liberally, and believe they have an innate and miraculous understanding of one another. But the sober fact is we understand one another not at all. Just about the time our proximity appears most harmonious something happens—a crime of violence, perhaps a case of voodooism—and to our astonishment we sense a barrier between. To make it more bewildering the barrier is of glass; you can't see it, you only strike it.

The incomprehension is wider than the usual distance between practitioners of the security and of the survival virtues. Apparently there is something peculiarly Negroid in the Negro's attitude toward, and aptitude for, crimes of violence. He seems to have resisted, except on the surface, our ethics and to have rejected our standards. Murder, thieving, lying, violence—I sometimes suspect the Negro doesn't regard these as crimes or sins, or even as regrettable occurrences. He commits them casually, with no apparent feeling of guilt. White men similarly delinquent become soiled or embittered or brutalized. Negroes are as charming after as before a crime. Committing criminal acts, they seem never to be criminals.

The gentle, devoted creature who is your baby's nurse can carve her boy-friend from ear to ear at midnight and by seven a.m. will be changing the baby's diaper while she sings "Hear the Lambs a-calling," or indulges in a brand of baby-talk obviously regarded as highly communicative and extremely amusing. All white families expend a large amount of time, money, and emotion in preventing the criminals they employ from receiving their legal deserts. They feel that the murderers and thieves in their service are not evil and have not been made more unfit for society by their delinquencies.

Prosecuting attorneys, judges, and police officers are

eternally at their wits' end trying to deal justly with crimes committed by simple and affectionate people whose criminal acts do not seem to convert them into criminal characters. To punish them as you would a white man appears not only unjust but immoral. Consequently, for a stabbing or a shooting a white man will be charged with assault with intent to kill (a felony), but a Negro with simple assault (a misdemeanor). Those convicted and sentenced to a few weeks in the city jail are often turned loose at night, so they may enjoy the pleasures of domesticity. The injunction to return next morning in time for breakfast is always obeyed.

I asked a learned gentleman from Yale, who was psychoanalyzing the whole Negro population of a neighboring town in three months, for some explanation of the Negro's propensity to crimes of violence. The oracle spoke: "I should say, tentatively you understand, that the frustrated hatred of the Negro for the white man, because of the frustration, is transferred to his own kind for fulfillment." It sounded like Uncle George's "They bite in the mouth."

I submitted the problem to Ford: "Ford, why do colored folks fight, shoot, stab, and kill one another so much?"

Ford giggled: "Well, s'pose a woman comes home and finds her man in bed with another woman—she's sho goin' to slap him in the face with the lamp, ain't she?"

This seemed to me only an argument for rural electrification, so I urged Ford to proceed.

"Well, s'pose some nigger crooks you in a crap game—you sho ain't goin' to let him get away with that and with your thin dime too, is you?"

I demurred and Ford went further:

"To tell the truth, most scrappin' and cuttin' and sech comes from checkin'."

"What in the world is checking?"

"Well, a bunch of boys starts off jest talkin', then they starts kiddin', jest for fun, you know, and then they starts checkin'. That's kiddin' what's rough. Everybody gets kinder riled and biggety. Then some fool nigger puts you in the dozen."

Ford stopped as if the problem had been completely elucidated.

"What's putting you in the dozen?"

"That's sho nuff bad talk."

"Like what?"

"Well," said Ford, modest and hesitant, "that's talkin' about your mommer."

"What do they say?"

Ford was scandalized by the request.

"I couldn't tell you that, Mr. Will, it wouldn't be nice."

Explaining that my inquiry was solely in the interest of science, Ford divulged sheepishly:

"Somebody says: 'Well, your mommer hists her tail like a alley cat.' Then the shootin' begins."

It would require a fat volume to record all the crimes which were committed on my plantation during the nine years I managed it—the thieving of corn and gasoline, of gear and supplies, of hay and merchandise, the making and selling of whisky, the drunkenness and gambling, the adultery and bigamy, the cuttings, lambastings, and shootings. That volume I shall never write, but I can't help believing that some short mention of a few of the casual incidents which within that same period have befallen the transitory dark members of my own ménage might help the earnest outlander to understand, if not to alter, the moral climate in which the well-meaning, puzzled, exasperated Southern white man, day in and day out, pursues his foggy way in his dealings with the Southern Negro.

The last time I saw Mims I asked him how he and his

wife were getting along. He poked out his mouth: "Pretty good, pretty good, I reckon. Cose, I always goes up the front steps whistlin'."

I praised his cheerfulness.

"That ain't it, Mr. Will. I want to give anybody what's in the house and don't belong there time to git out the back way. You know I never did like no rookus."

And then there was Nick's contretemps which came near being serious. He gravely told me about it. Nick had dignity, besides a certain astuteness.

"I knew that woman was married and her husband was servin' time up in Leavenworth. I told her when he got out he could have her back. So we was runnin' the café, doin' very good, and I was treatin' her right. We slept there too, in a little room, and kept the café open all night. It was hard work, but we'd kept at it four years and was doin' good. Well, here last week, in walks that husband of hers from Leavenworth. Cose, it was all right 'cause I had told her it would be all right. They went on to bed and I kept on workin'. I was tired and she couldn't help me none that night. 'Bout four o'clock out they come from the bedroom. I didn't fire but two shots, Mr. Will, but I got 'em both."

Nick paused reflectively and gave me a quick intimate glance. "I forgot to say, cose he made a motion-like in his bosom before I shot."

Nick had destroyed the evidence and in court bore down hard on that "motion-like." When the charge against him had been dismissed he thanked me for a message I'd sent him, but said he hadn't needed no lawyer. He hadn't. That astuteness of his coupled with the excellence of his aim made one unnecessary.

Ernest was a truly devoted creature and loved Mother, but when after ten years in our service I discovered his thefts, he merely observed: "Well, to tell you the truth, Mr. Will, I just love money too much."

Of course drunkenness and running off with automobiles and smashing them up cannot be assigned to the category of crimes. When, however, Lige (the gardener) at high noon on Sunday, against my vigorous instructions, in a Dionysiac frenzy, drove my new car to the top of the levee and turned somersaults down the other side, I was unduly fretted. I lay in bed next morning preparing a speech designed to annihilate him, but while I was putting on the last scarifying touches, Lige glided in with a folded trunk strap, came to the bedside, and presented it to me. "Whup me," was his sole remark, and mine was about as brief: "Get out! Get out!" We have never referred to automobiles since.

Jim was different. He was the most efficient and intelligent servant I ever had in the house; besides he had book-learning and read the Bible assiduously. When I first saw him he was being borne into my office with a cracked skull and trembling as if with palsy. He wanted me to sue the sheriff. He had been in jail on a charge which he convinced me had been trumped up and, while there, had been struck over the head, accidentally or maliciously, with a billet of wood by the jailer. Thoroughly indignant, I procured a doctor and filed suit against the sheriff. The sheriff was furious, stormed, threatened, and became my bitter enemy. I recovered a few hundred dollars for Jim and, considering it inadequate, gave it to him without deducting a fee. But the whole sheriff's office was so venomously hostile to me and to the Negro that I feared he might be attacked and hid him for three weeks on the plantation. Then, to keep him near me for safety, I gave him a job as house-boy and a room on the yard.

Within a few months Jim had stolen all the personal

trinkets on the premises, everything from German field glasses to rings and studs. The colored population was familiar with the whole story. Jim is now a dapper and popular preacher in good standing.

Thinking over these incidents, so close to me and so usual, I wonder and fear. Is the inner life of the Negro utterly different from ours? Has he never accepted our standard of ethics? I remember too those fragments of another world on which I have stumbled, hints of a traditional lore alien to us and unfathomable by us.

I remember the sick Negro in the clinic at Leland, which I visited on an inspection trip during the flood. The doctors explained to me their dilemma: the Negro said he had been hoodooed by a witch-doctor and was going to die on the following Friday. Physically he was perfectly sound, they had made every kind of examination and test—but he was fading away before their eyes. I suggested getting the witch-doctor and forcing him to remove the spell. He had disappeared into the flood. I looked at the Negro. He was quiet, lying on his cot and gazing at the ceiling. I spoke to him. He heard and understood, but was not interested. His eyes were smoldering with terror. On Friday he died.

I asked Jim if he believed in hoodoo. He said, of course not, but he knew of a curious thing that had happened a little while before just three blocks down Percy Street. The sister of a friend of his was low sick; she got thinner and thinner, till you could see her bones. The white doctor couldn't do nothing, so her brother got up the money and sent to New Orleans for the big hoodoo doctor. He came to her bedside, leaned over her, said some strange words, and announced she had swallowed a frog. The frog jumped out of her mouth. The hoodoo doctor went away and the girl began to recover. She gained flesh and strength, then once more she went into a decline and became nothing but skin and bones and eyes. The hoodoo doctor returned. He leaned over her and said: "You've swallowed a cooter. I can't do nothing 'bout cooters." In a few days she was dead.

The county prosecuting attorney (incidentally he had been the Cyclops of the Klan) asked me what to do in a pending criminal case. A woman had cut her husband to shreds with a long knife the Negroes call a crab-apple switch. He was recovering. She acknowledged the occurrence, but pleaded in defense that he had placed a spell on her by means of a cunjer-bag. The bag, still in his possession, contained a piece of her red flannel drawers and a hank of her hair. Its effect was to rob her of connubial allure—in her words, "it stole her nature." She pleaded justification and I thought clearly she was justified. After many consultations with the distracted justice of the peace, on our recommendation the charge against her was dismissed. In the crowded court-room we expected an emotional scene of gratitude. Instead, the woman burst into tears. She lamented that it didn't make no difference to her if she was out of jail, seeing as how she didn't have her nature back. This seemed reasonable and we asked what we could do about it. We were advised that if we could git that cunjer-bag, she could sew the piece of red flannel "back where it come from" and all would be well. We told the husband he'd be immediately chucked into jail if he didn't fetch that bag instanter. He disappeared, while we waited in the court-room. In an incredibly short time he was back with it. The judge solemnly presented the bag to the woman. Everybody was happy. The couple left arm in arm, showing signs of resurgent nature.

How is it possible for the white man to communicate with people of this sort, people whom imagination kills and fantasy makes impotent, who thieve like children and murder ungrudgingly as small boys fight?

Appreciating as I do the Negro's excellences—his charm, his humor, his patience, his exquisite sensibilities, his kindness to his own poor, his devotion and sweetness to all children, black and white, his poetry of feeling and expression, his unique tactual medieval faith, his songs more filled with humility and heart-break than Schubert's or Brahms's—I want with all my heart to help him. But helping him is well-nigh impossible because of one tragic characteristic. No Negro trusts unreservedly any white man—that is understandable enough, though exceedingly unfortunate—but, still more unfortunate, no Negro trusts unreservedly any Negro. That too is understandable, because his leaders betray him, either from their childish ambition to appear "big shots" or from their willingness to exploit his simplicity. So the Negro has cut himself off from any leadership, and leadership is desperately needed by him. He turns not to the rare but magnificent leaders of his own race, but to his country preachers, uneducated, immoral, and avaricious. Trusting no one, without moral stamina, without discipline, without standards, the Negro gropes blindly through an alien white man's world, intricate in the extreme, and gleaming with attractive shoddiness.

The whole atmosphere of America is such as to mislead and endanger the Negro. The sickening adulation paid to Negro athletes and artists, not because of their great abilities but because they are Negroes; rumors of what the Negro does in Paris, in Moscow, in the Northern cities; the promises and bribes of demagogic politicians interested not in his welfare but in his vote; the Negro press's hatred of the white man, its demand for social equality, its bitterness, its untrustworthiness—all these combine to create about the young Southern Negro an atmosphere as dangerous as it is febrile and unwholesome. The work of white sentimentalists is equally perilous. When personal relations with the Negro are too familiar, they are misinterpreted by him. He reasons, plausibly, that if you are willing to dine with him, you are willing and probably anxious to sleep with him. With the genius of the poor for misinterpreting the motives of the rich, added to the Negro's own special genius for suspicion and mistrust, it should require little except common sense to deduce what the efforts of white sentimentalists may lead to. The noblest of them, such as Mrs. Roosevelt, accomplish their insidious evil quite unsuspectingly and with the highest motives. It will never occur to them that the results, however pitiful or savage, will have been of their making.

It is said that race relations in the South are improving because lynching has declined to the vanishing-point and outbursts of violence against the Negro are almost unknown. It should be noted, however, that the improvement, if improvement there is, is due solely to the white man. It should be further noted that the Negro is losing his most valuable weapon of defense—his good manners. When a Negro now speaks of a "man" he means a Negro; when he speaks of a "fellow" he means a white man; when he speaks of a "lady" he means a Negress; when he speaks of a "woman" he means a white woman. Such manners are not only bad, they are not safe, and the frame of mind that breeds them is not safe. Covert insolence is not safe for anybody, anywhere, at any time.

The Negro, not having assimilated the white man's ethics, giving only lip service to the white man's morality, must for his own peace and security accept whole-heartedly the white man's mores and taboos. In the South the one sacred taboo, assumed to be Southern, but actually and universally Anglo-Saxon, is the untouchability of white women by Negro men. It is academic to argue the wisdom or justice of this taboo. Wise or unwise, just or unjust, it is the cornerstone of friendly relations, of interracial peace. In the past it has been not the eleventh but the first commandment. Even to question it means the shattering of race relations into hideous and bloody ruin. But I fear it is coming to be questioned.

It is not difficult to reason why the young Negro is beginning to question this taboo their forefathers accepted so whole-heartedly and unthinkingly. Every black buck in the South today has gone or will go to Chicago, where it is not only possible but inexpensive to sleep with a white whore. Likewise, there are Negro bell-boys in Southern hotels frequented by white whores. But there is a further and more humiliating reason. In former generations, when the taboo was unquestioned, Southern women felt a corresponding obligation so to conduct themselves that any breach of the taboo was unthinkable. Those were the times when Southern white women were either ladies or loose. Today white women drink in public places, become drunk in public places, and public places are filled with scandalized and grossly human Negro waiters. Cars at night park on the sides of roads, and Negroes, like everyone else, deduce what the couple inside is doing. Whenever there's a moral failure on the part of the Southern white, there's a corresponding moral failure on the part of the Southern Negro.

Influenced by bitter half-castes, the young Negro argues that there is no justice in the white man's woman being untouchable to the Negro man, while the Negro woman is not untouchable to the white man. On the surface this seems an unanswerable argument, but it is not even sincere. The whites make outcasts of their white women who have violated the taboo, sometimes punishing them as grossly as they punish the offending Negro. Never are they accepted into even the lowest stratum of white society. But when a Negro girl sleeps with a white man, not only is she not ostracized by the Negroes, she becomes an object of increased allure to Negro youths. Unconsciously and pitifully they pay tribute to the white man by finding desirable his cast-off baggage. The Negro's resentment toward the practice springs from jealousy and from his imitation of the white man's fury when his own women are touched. Though they are sincerely bitter, theirs is only a pseudo-indignation. The Negroes themselves could stop the practice, if they truly resented it, by treating their offending girls as the white man treats his. The Negro's incapacity for moral indignation is one of his most terrifying characteristics. His moral flabbiness is his charm and his undoing.

It is not pleasant to make these bald and bitter statements. I make them because they are true and because I am afraid for the Negro. Only the truth can help him, and that can help him little unless he helps himself.

I have received visits from so many people whose sole reason for wishing to see me was their interest in the Negro problem that I am forced to conclude I am regarded in some quarters as an authority on the problem or as a typical Southerner who happens to be articulate. I am certainly no authority, and I doubt that I am entirely typical. I claim only to be one of that vast number of men of good will who try, with indifferent success, to see wisely and to act justly. As such, I would say to the Negro: before demanding to be a white man socially and politically, learn to be a white man morally and intellectually—and to the white man: the black man is our brother, a younger brother, not adult, not disciplined, but tragic, pitiful, and lovable; act as his brother and be patient.

CHAPTER XXIV

For the Younger Generation

My favorite cousin, LeRoy Percy, died two months before Mother's death, and his brave and beautiful wife, Mattie Sue Phinizy, two years after Father's. Their three boys, Walker, LeRoy, and Phinizy, came to live with me and I adopted them as my sons. Walker was fourteen, LeRoy thirteen, and little Phin nine. Suddenly my household was filled with youth, and suddenly I found myself, unprepared, with the responsibility of directing young lives in a world that was changing and that seemed to me on the threshold of chaos.

Even physically what had seemed adequate and fitting for me seemed primitive, even barbarous, to this generation. I had learned to read—indeed, had done my most absorbed reading—by oil lamps whose wicks forever got lop-sided and smoked. My drinking-water had come from the cistern in the back gallery and sometimes it suffered attacks of wiggle-tails. During mosquito time there were no screens, but we got along under a smudge of insect powder and slapped. If we were hot, we stayed hot and never missed electric fans or air-conditioning. If we were chilly, we ran out and got another scuttle of coal and pulled up closer to the fire. When the unloved, once-a-week ritual rolled round, I didn't turn on the hot and cold water, but quaked on the edge of a tin bathtub six inches deep which brought goose-bumps to the side away from the fireplace. At nature's beck I rushed out in the back yard and sat amid the unpleasant fumes of lime on a splintery seat that could be dismally cold and drafty.

Such early experiences make one apathetic to modern philanthropy which avows that the poor are being brutally treated unless somebody provides for them at somebody's expense electric lights, screens, running water, and modern plumbing. How out of step I find myself when I can't help regarding these things as delightful luxuries one must earn and not as basic necessities of the good life one may demand!

I was equally at sea when I considered how and where the boys should be educated. In my day education had been a disagreeable discipline by which one acquired, if susceptible, strength of soul and delight of mind. Now education is regarded as an easy but expensive aid to crashing society or procuring a better job.

Mother, ably backed by Aunt Nana, used to correct my manners, issue ukases on conduct, render innumerable decisions without written or oral opinions, and it would have been safer to jump in the river than question them openly. Now, I am admonished, a child's personality is as fragile as precious and if you try anything stronger on him than sweet reasonableness you will warp his psyche, foster complexes, and probably end up with a paranoiac or a Jack the Ripper on your hands.

I don't know how I'd have managed if the boys had not saved me the trouble by deciding to be good and infinitely considerate.

The house swarmed with young people. For me it was

delightful, but I knew a reciprocal duty rested on me to direct them toward the good life in so far as I had discovered it. But what good life that I had ever glimpsed was suitable and effective for this world where these children must earn a living and fashion their own happiness? The old Southern way of life in which I had been reared existed no more and its values were ignored or derided. Negroes used to be servants, now they were problems; manners used to be a branch of morals, now they were merely bad; poverty used to be worn with style and dignity, now it was a stigma of failure; politics used to be the study of men proud and jealous of America's honor, now it was a game played by self-seekers which no man need bother his head about; where there had been an accepted pattern of living, there was no pattern whatsoever.

I had no desire to send these youngsters of mine into life as defenseless as if they wore knights' armor and had memorized the code of chivalry. But what could I teach them other than what I myself had learned? True, it was not the South alone that had been killed, but its ideals and its kind of people the world over. The bottom rail was on top, not only in Mississippi, but from Los Angeles to New York, from London to Moscow. In different quarters the effects were dissimilar, but the cause was always the same. In Russia, Germany, and Italy Demos, having slain its aristocrats and intellectuals and realizing its own incompetence to guide or protect itself, had submitted to tyrants who laughed at the security virtues and practiced the most vile of the survival virtues with gangster cynicism. In the democracies Demos had been so busy providing itself with leisure and luxury it had forgotten that hardihood and discipline are not ornaments but weapons. Everywhere the security virtues appeared as weaknesses and the survival virtues as strength and foresight.

Should I therefore teach deceit, dishonor, ruthlessness, bestial force to the children in order that they survive? Better that they perish. It is sophistry to speak of two sets of virtues, there is but one: virtue is an end in itself; the survival virtues are means, not ends. Honor and honesty, compassion and truth are good even if they kill you, for they alone give life its dignity and worth. Yet probably England and France and all the good and the noble and the true of all the world will die and obscenity will triumph. Probably those that practiced virtue will be destroyed, but it is better for men to die than to call evil good, and virtue itself will never die.

We of my generation have lost one line of fortifications after another, the old South, the old ideals, the old strengths. We are now watching the followers of Jesus and Buddha and Socrates being driven from the face of the earth. But there's time ahead, thousands of years: there is but one good life and men yearn for it and will again practice it, though of my contemporaries only the stars will see. Love and compassion, beauty and innocence will return. It is better to have breathed them an instant than to have supported iniquity a millennium. Perhaps only flames can rouse man from his apathy to his destiny.

There is left to each of us, no matter how far defeat pierces, the unassailable wintry kingdom of Marcus Aurelius, which some more gently call the Kingdom of Heaven. However it be called, it is not outside, but within, and when all is lost, it stands fast. To this remaining fastness I knew I should help the children find their way. Yet, knowing how purblind a guide I was, I sent them to the churches. It seemed to matter little what sect they sought for guidance: they and their young friends returned confused, resentful, and distressed. Desperately and as a last resort they came to me with the old ultimate problem which time out of mind has vexed the children of men. None of us, I suppose, has found truth, but we can attain honesty, and that at least the young may demand of us.

One night as Father and I sat talking in the library I remarked flippantly that I couldn't understand the common fear of ghosts, adding I'd like to talk to one. Father was silent and then said in a low, curiously vibrant voice: "I'd crawl across the Sahara on my knees to meet a ghost." He wasn't given to exaggeration. Much later, as he lay dying, he roused after a night of coma and startled me by observing thoughtfully: "I nearly crossed over. You know what I've been thinking? All the while I've been pitying the thousands who have been sent across, terrified by the lies of priests in all the ages. There's nothing to fear."

Those quiet passionate words of his come back to me when I talk to the youth of today and observe their bewilderment, their craving, in a world without faith, among a people without gods. There's plenty of lip service to gods today and fear, but no easy unshakable faith. I think of what is being offered to our young people in their need by the churches, and my heart is filled with anger and sorrow. I asked a clergyman recently why it was that so many prominent church-goers were crooks in business and hypocrites in private life. He replied: "They have been born again." This clarified nothing for me and I told him as much. He explained sadly: "When they are born again, they are certain of salvation, and when you are certain of salvation you may do what you like." But I urged, horrified: "People don't really believe that!" "Hundreds of thousands of them," he rejoined, obviously as grieved as I. "The ethics of Jesus do not interest them when their rebirth guarantees them salvation."

Thus the Negroes believe! Religion to them is an emotional experience, orgiastic or mystic according to temperament, but not related to morals; so their ministers may steal and commit adultery without fear and without inconsistency. As I think of what that implies and of how much it explains, my memory fills with the ghosts of dead phrases—salvation, washed in the blood of the Lamb, He descended into hell, the resurrection of the body, born of the Virgin Mary. They are not the sort of ghosts I care to meet.

Where lies the virtue in attempting to persuade honest young minds to entertain such outworn rubbish? And what have such tenets to do with religion? How nearly impossible the churches have made it for such minds, earnestly seeking the truth, to join a church or even to remain religious! Not science but the Christian sects are causing the death of religion. The pitiful part of it is that it is as true now as it ever was that without faith the people perish, and they are perishing before our eyes. As object of faith Hitler has offered Race, Stalin the State, America Success, which is Mammon. These youths of ours know none of them is worthy, they know too they are sick, but when they turn for cure to the churches, the prescription handed them is written in the language of Hippocrates. These youngsters crave community of aspiration and purpose, they fear to be alone and outcast. A church forgetting its devitalized patter and meaningless incantations could tell them simply there is no unity except the unity of brotherhood, no brotherhood without a common father. Philosophical conceptions—the Trinity, the atonement, the fall, the redemption—cannot save this generation, for they speak a beautiful dead language, when what we need is live words, tender with meaning and assurance. Without them the young drift through the world, aimless, unemployed, with no certainties in their heart to give them anchorage or peace.

However young our old age is to us, to youth it is very

old, a thing depersonalized, spent of passion, by mere duration barnacled with knowledge if not with wisdom; so the young speak aloud to us their troubled queries as they spoke them centuries ago to the riddled rock of the embarrassed Sphinx. In some such fashion I've heard my share of the searching and seeking of young folk today, a brave breed, more honest though no more wise than the youth of my day. It is a sober thing when they come to you so lost and ask the way. I am always afraid for them and afraid of myself. But out of my own darkness, having first placed in their hands the Gospels and the *Meditations* of Marcus Aurelius, I try to point out to them the pale streak I see which may be a trail:

The Gospels were written by simple men who earnestly and with a miraculous eloquence tried to report events which they themselves had never witnessed but of which they had been told. Even what these writers of hearsay set down we have never seen in the words they used, but only in later Greek translations. Consequently the narratives of the four Evangelists as we read them are full of misunderstandings and contradictions and inaccuracies—as every lawyer knows any human testimony aiming at truth is sure to be—yet they throw more light than darkness on the heart-shaking story they tell. They are pitifully human and misleading, but drenched in a supernal light and their contagion changed the dreaming world.

The self-communings of the Emperor, though often cold to clamminess, convince a man he never need be less than tight-lipped, courteous, and proud, though all is pain. It is saving to rest our eyes on nobility, severe and unalloyed, such as a god might pattern after, and in these books, the Gospels and the *Meditations,* we find such nobility like strength turned beauty, a nobility the mere certitude of which makes rational the frantic hope there never was a woman great with child but she had listened to ecstatic Gabriel.

We often forget how pitifully unendowed we are. All we can know is through the tidings brought us by our five inaccurate senses. Others, perhaps, here or elsewhere, may be more suitably equipped with six or a hundred, but we have only five and they rusty and defective. We cannot hear the rushing spheres of our own universe though they must make a sound like trains loaded with thunder. We cannot hear the chirps and squeaks of the insect world which fragile insect ears hear plainly. We cannot see color at night as the owl can, or the rays that dart through space on mysterious errands, or even the germ that kills us. We cannot smell what a dog or Helen Keller or an eagle smells. Our diminished sense of taste has become a mere organ of luxury. Though we can feel the touch of another's hand, we cannot feel the dust on our own lips. Only the faintest wavering glimmer of the shouting light of creation penetrates our dark diminutive cell. Yet our whole knowing must be got through this crude outmoded equipment. No wonder our modes of thought are only three-dimensional!

Mathematicians and philosophers assure us that there's a fourth dimension which, if our faculties could master it, would unfurl to us widths of new knowledge. And if there is a fourth, surely there must be a fifth, and why could there not be a tenth, a hundredth?

But, circumscribed and blunted as we are, we men have always sought a god, a mind at work, a Master Schemer. Through all the centuries we have cried out: "These blue and starred heavens with all their intricate beauty and with man riding the darkness like a god, how come they here? If no god coaxed them out of nothingness, how then were they born, how did they grow and shape themselves, why are they here? And why, why, why are we here?" And finding no quick answer to this, the eldest and most pitiful of all our queries, time out of mind we have complained of the sorry scheme of things, confident it is sorry, dubious it is scheme. But is not our complaint a child's cry of pain rather than an adult's effort of mind? Must not the qualities of the Master Schemer's mind be either subhuman or human or superhuman? Good men in all the ages, materialists and atheists, have averred, bitterly or sadly, it was subhuman, it was no-mind, it was merely matter moiling, and the curve of their argument has always run thus:

In the beginning was the Atom. No one knew how it got there or what it was made of. Perhaps the void flinched. Later some changed its nature a little by calling it an electron, and others irritably dubbed it a particle of electricity. Whatever its name and nature, one day the Atom met up with another atom (antecedents unknown). So, like people, they got together in all that nothingness, and other atoms were the result. Atoms are blessed with a gaudy fecundity, so in no time they were all over the place. They like to agglomerate in outposts and sizable hunks. Heat developed somehow, though they didn't have a Prometheus, and that helped. They passed laws and stuck to them, and became enormously ingenious, forming colonies and sending out pioneers and settlements. At last they formed nations and called them by fancy names—liquids, gases, solids, metals, elements, and the like. They kept on building and gathering and bumping into one another because there was nothing else to do and they had so much room. They even formed into stars and suns and strange rays and marched to an ordered music, though none knew why. But all the time there were just atoms, nothing but atoms, clustering together like hornets or bees. It seems odd, but once, far down in an obscure corner, one tiny cluster, riding a larger cluster, spoke, and it said: "In la sua voluntade e' nostra pace," and another cried out ecstatically: "Heilige Licht," and another said very softly: "Father, forgive them, for they know not what they do." So that is the way the world began and kept on. It would take less than a one-dimensional mind to believe that was the way.

Because that cannot have been the way, because the Master Mind cannot be subhuman, must it be like our own, so defective, so unlighted, so unsteady and afraid? We know that thinking like ours could not have created even this paltry world of ours, yet we know equally that the injustice and horror of the world would not be tolerated by any good three-dimensional mind. We complain of the sorry scheme of things because against all reason and all evidence we assume the Schemer's mind to be dimensioned like our own. We forget that the Master Schemer, worthy of our loyalty and able to conceive and make what our poor faculties perceive, must be possessed of faculties so far beyond our own that the pattern of their functioning, if explained, could not make sense to us. The only god we would be willing to adore must have a god's mind, not a man's, and the hundredth-dimensional mind of a god we could no more comprehend than a beetle could comprehend our own. To the mind that could dream and shape our beaconed universe, what is injustice to us may be unfathomable tenderness, and our horror only loveliness misunderstood. If we but knew, all we ask is that what we see and live in be not chance-built and accident-directed. Our fear is to be participants in unplanned chaos. The rest doesn't matter. We need not assail the sorry scheme—the chaos we see is a hundredth-dimensional plan glimpsed by three-dimensional perceptions.

If the theory of naked matter re-creating itself witlessly be unbelievable and the God-Mind that plans and directs be to us unknowable and incomprehensible, where then may the young neophyte turn for certitude and easing of his loneliness? Where all other young neophytes have turned in the long processional of man's aspiring. Some day we may find we possess new senses with which to perceive, some day we may develop further dimensions in our thinking process: there are intimations of undiscovered powers and aptitudes in our ephemeral bodies—visions and levitations, prophecies and cures, telepathy and communications. But through the equipment we now possess, these five poor senses of ours, we can see daily what no atom built and no dust bred: it is given man to behold beauty and to worship nobility. He is shaken when he sees these two, but not because he feels them alien. Only when he is in their presence does the air taste native and the place seem home. These only are reality to his profoundest self; he needs no proof of them and no explanation. They are, he is, and over him there passes the shudder of a recognition. These recognitions are brief moments, but moments we may live by for our brief years. Who gave us these perceptions gave too, no doubt, the heavens' laws and conjured up creation. I think if one would sit in the Greek theater above Taormina with the wine-dark sea below and Ætna against the sunset, and if there he would meditate on Jesus and the Emperor, he would be assured a god had made earth and man. And this is all we need to know.

But we trouble our hearts with foolish doubts and unwise questionings—the fear of death, the hope of survival, forgiveness, heaven, hell. Rewards and punishments hereafter? What bribes we ask for our perfunctory righteousness! The oak spreads its arms in the sun, puts out leaves and tassels, and, if the season wills, scatters down acorns. But it does not querulously demand to know where fall its seeds or whether they will root and grow to saplings. There should be no question of reward: to function is the task assigned. To seek outlet for our emotions, our intellect, our spiritual cravings, to blossom and fruit with our whole nature, to keep its unity and proportion, of such is our occupation.

As to our pathetic plea for personal survival with all the quirks and foibles that alone make personality identifiable—there is nothing to fret about here. We survive or we are annihilated, and all our anguish cannot undo our fate one way or the other. But we may assuage our vanity by listening to the Buddha's thought. Our dread and torment in this life we lead are its apartness, its eternal isolation. We try to rid us of ourselves by love, by prayers, by vice, by the Lethe of activity, and we never wholly succeed. Above all things we desire to be united and absorbed. Must we insist that our besetting anguish go with us past the grave? To become part of the creating essence and of all things created by it, in this alone might be found fulfillment, peace, ecstasy. At the intensest peak of our emotions—lying on the bosom we love, or lost in a sunset, or bereft by music—being then most ourselves, we dissolve and become part of the strength and radiance and pathos of creation. When most ourselves, we are most not ourselves and lose our tragic isolation in the whole. To be a drop of water, trembling alone forever, lacks something of the peace and grandeur of being one lost drop in the immortal undivided ocean.

Death, Heaven or Hell, Rewards or Punishments, Extinction or Survival, these are epic troubles for the epic Mind. Our cares are fitted to our powers. Our concern is here, and with the day so overcast and short, there's quite enough to do.

So I counsel the poor children. But I long for the seer or saint who sees what I surmise—and he will come, even if he must walk through ruins.

CHAPTER XXV

A Bit of Diary

George and Janet sometimes ask me what I do with my time down in the deep South, now that I've stopped practicing law and LeRoy is managing the plantation. I can never remember. To satisfy my own curiosity I've jotted down the doings of my last week-end. I never heard of anything more inconsequential and daft.

THURSDAY

9.30 a.m. – Ancient sharp-eyed Negress appears in back yard, announces belligerently she has been waiting three hours for me, adds she used to farm on Trail Lake, made ten crops, raised six head of chillun and nursed all white babies from Arcola to Darlove. I ask her to get to the point. She says the point is fifty cents. I see the point.

10 a.m. – Meeting of executive committee of Delta Council. Shall the council endorse a bill now pending before Congress to levee the Yazoo River? Oscar Bledsoe argues it is economically unsound. I suspect it is unsound engineering. Billy Wynn says under all the circumstances our

endorsement is expedient. Long digression on what's intellectually honest and what's expedient. But Will Whitington wants it, so it must be right. All agree, with misgivings. Committee joins Levee Board. Everybody makes a speech. We endorse bill, gingerly, comforting ourselves it won't pass anyhow.

Noon – Rotary Club luncheon. Shall Rotary Club join other service clubs in urging city council to build a hundred-thousand-dollar swimming-pool with W.P.A. funds? Everybody thinks pool fine for underprivileged; nobody wants to increase taxes. Will Francis observes Wage and Hour Law bestows leisure on those unaccustomed to it—would they swim or continue to shoot craps? I mention bread and circuses. Everybody uncomfortable. Action deferred.

1.15 p.m. – An hour of dictation to Mitchell: letters to Lindley about his arthritis, to a gentleman from Tulsa who inquires if I have published "a volume of verse," to the twentieth lady asking permission to set *Overtones* to music, to the Children's Home saying they are mistaken, I am not on their directorate, to a nursery asking about spring planting of camellias and the habits of *Ilex rotundifolia,* to the university saying I will not make a speech on poetry or interracial relations, or the rise of the moron, or anything whatsoever, but I will be present to hiss Dave Cohn's oration.

2:30 p.m. – Pop-eyed youth, hitherto unknown to me, calls to say he must drop out of high school unless I give him financial assistance. It develops under cross-examination he has two grown brothers and lives with his widowed mother. I ask if he dropped out what would be his fate.

Answer: he would have to go to work. I inquire why not. Purposes of education explored with considerable incoherence. I decide he's the kind that would never get educated if he divided the rest of his life between Oxford and the Sorbonne. We part, youth observing he wants to be something better than a ditch-digger, I asking what's better. No conclusion reached.

3 p.m. – Try to nap. Boo [my Persian cat] jumps on my stomach. Wake in vile humor.

3.30 p.m. – A lady I can't identify enters to report that she has just discovered her husband is a drunkard and an alley cat. I brace myself to the melancholy disclosure and ask what I can do about it. Discussion follows on sobriety, fidelity, men, women, fate. No conclusions reached. She says she feels better, thanks me, and withdraws.

4.15 p.m. – I start hunting Lige. Decide he must be in his room asleep. As I approach his door to haul him out, hear unmistakably feminine titters. So outraged, forget why I started hunting him. Try to calm myself by considering it is an old custom–Malvolio on a day-bed with Olivia.

4.45 p.m. – Talk over troubles of Federal Art Center with Leon Koury. Is art compatible with continence and sobriety? Apparently not. But if you were a lady along in years and on W.P.A. wouldn't you fall for something too, almost anything? Leon has no right to have so much sense with so few years and no experience: he's just a genius.

5.30 p.m. – Toddy with Tom and Roy just in from plantation. Discuss price of alfalfa meal.

6.30 p.m. – Bob and Sammy arrive, unannounced, from New Orleans.

6.30 to 9.30 p.m. – Conversation. Subjects: fate of Finland, freight rates in the South, what cures gapes in baby chicks, the diet and discipline of babies, that scene in *Gone with the Wind* where Scarlett's in bed and smiling, politics (national, international, state, and municipal).

10 p.m. – I read *Time.* Turn on radio, turn off radio. Start to glance through Housman's *Collected Poems*, but in interval have lost reading glasses.

10.30 p.m. – Knock at door. Negro friend in tears. Displays lacerated arm which he says wife has bitten from shoulder to elbow in a fit of unwarranted exasperation. Question submitted: shall he kill her or call the law? I give him a dollar and advise him to spend night away from home.

11 p.m. – Go to bed. Phone. Negro friend after receiving dollar and advice went home, gave wife terrific beating, threw neighborhood into uproar, and is now in jail. Will I go his bond? I will.

Midnight – Phone. Same Negro on being released again went home and visited even more memorable chastisement on his consort. Again in jail. Will I bail him out? I will not.

2 a.m. – Long-distance. Detroit calling collect. Ford, of course. I refuse call. Hear Ford observing to operator being as how I near 'bout raised him it sho looks like I'd be willing to talk to him.

2 to 6 a.m. – Can't sleep. Take dose of somnos. Wonder if Ford is in jail and for what.

FRIDAY

Sick in bed. Electric pad on back of neck.

SATURDAY

8 a.m. – David wakes me with best breakfast in world–grapefruit, coffee, grits, and bacon–and the newspaper. Absorbing Popeye, Mickey Mouse, the Gumps, a sex murder, M. Daladier's fall, and Walter Lippmann, when Lige pops his head in door and announces them skrubs has came.

9.30 a.m. – Moping around the stricken long-leafed evergreens. Wizened gentleman appears without warning, announces he's read in *Good Housekeeping* I'm a gardener, and as he is a gardener on his way home to Ohio from warmer climes, thought he'd drop in and chat with me. He chatted: don't I disbud my peonies? Nice tulips, but haven't I any Clara Butts? His father taught Clara Butts to sing. How old do I think he is? No, no, no! He's sixty-five. It's gardening has kept him young: his wife can hardly believe it herself. What is my specialty? He specializes in Madonna lilies. He'll send me a photo of himself with his prize specimen. He leaves me, clammy with apprehension. Good God! At sixty-five shall I be specializing in Madonna lilies and thinking I look young?

10.30 a.m. – Edmund Taylor calls for me to go on our rounds collecting for the Boy Scouts (or is it the Y or the Red Cross, this time?). What a creature! A Methodist and a successful businessman compounded of pure goodness! Pity he isn't a Catholic, so he could be martyred, canonized, and leave behind a legend of quaint miracles.

Noon — Gentleman from Oklahoma wants to buy oil rights on Trail Lake. I don't want an oil well. He guarantees well on plantation at his expense. I refuse permit unless he guarantees not to strike oil. He leaves hastily, figuring I'm insane.

1.30 p.m. — Will Francis rehearses speech on Great Ironists he is to deliver at Ladies' Night of Moorehead Rotary Club. Splendid speech and they'll love it, though they won't understand a word.

2.30 p.m. — Young lady simpers into library, whinnies at ancestors on wall and Epstein's Dave Cohn on mantel. Interview. Excuse: she's "doing" my poetry for her thesis. Archly imperturbable, asks impertinent questions. I inquire if she has read my poems. She has not, but expects to. I burst out, look her over, see there's no use.

3.30 p.m. — Young man calls to see me about his wife's insides. Appears she is practically hollow. Doctors did thorough job snipping off anything in the way. She's recovered from operation but is losing her mind. Injections of some sort, one a week for three months, alone can restore her. The shots cost $13.00 each; he makes $12.00 a week.

4.30 p.m. — As I hover over Bermuda grass praying for energy, old lady peers through garden gate appraisingly and venomously, a real gardener's look. Obviously poor and hard-working. I ask her in. She walks slowly and observantly, insulting me every step. She sniffs: "Horse! Should have been cow." None of my flowers floriferous as hers. I conclude she hasn't a house, much less a garden. On leaving, after standing me down my prize Mrs. Krelages are paper-whites, she proves her case by musing wearily:

"I don't know what I'd do without a garden. I just couldn't stand it."

5.30 p.m. – Whipped down. Julep with Tom and Roy. Helps.

7.30 p.m. – One of Levee Board engineers wants to come out and discuss Morganza spillway. Can't take it. Too tired. To bed.

SUNDAY

8.30 a.m. – Over breakfast study *Delta Democrat Times* and approve Donald's editorial handling of situation we had discussed. Ask David to send in Lige. Lige can't be found.

9 a.m. – Gervys turns up with his colored movie camera to take garden pictures.

9.30 a.m. – Tommy reports new hardening room in his and Crit's ice-cream plant is completed.

10 a.m. – Police telephone Lige is in jail after a night of wassail.

10.30 a.m. – Rufus drops by from mass to say his and Marion's sinuses were miraculously cured by Florida's sunshine.

11 a.m. – Roy and Tom stop painting their fishing-boat in back yard and perch on foot of my bed for Coca-Cola and conversation.

11.30 a.m. — Adah joins us and reports on all and sundry. I remember I've forgotten to ask Aunts to dinner. Send David with conciliatory messages.

Noon — School of fish-faced strangers ask if they may walk through garden. Are joined by another similar school who don't ask. They streak through, looking as if they were inspecting a morgue, and vanish without audible gratitude.

12.30 a.m. — Head of state Federal Art Projects rushes in to wonder which of us would be more unpopular before the city council when the needs of the project must be presented.

1 p.m. — Dinner. Aunts present, 83 and 74, respectively. Their appetites and zest appalling. We marvel.

2 p.m. — I turn on radio for Philharmonic. Curse static. Roy and Sarah flee to golf-links. Aunts ignore static and indulge in a little free-for-all on some topic not related to music.

4 p.m. — Tom, Marie, and children take me for a drive in country. Discuss whooping-cough and public-school system.

5 p.m. — Negro I never laid eyes on says he's Baptist preacher and asks donation for church. Ingratiatingly observes cullud couldn't do nothing without the help of their white friends. I ask how many Baptist churches there are in town already. He doesn't know. I do—fifty-three Baptist, eighteen Methodist, one Episcopal, one Catholic, and a scattering of Sanctified, Holy Rollers, and Latter Day

Saints. I ask why another church is needed. Replies vaguely, concerning sisters who weren't satisfied and wanted to secede from Mount Horeb. Diatribe from me on the Negro's needs—hospitals, playgrounds, clinics, etc.—for which the Negro never raises one penny, while disreputable Negro preachers incessantly milk their congregations for funds to build an unneeded church and keep most of the money in their own pockets. He listens politely, murmurs assent, and beats hasty retreat. All true, but I feel like a miser.

7 p.m. – Memphis chap on verge of nervous collapse drives up, recounts latest symptoms, and asks advice. Give same advice I gave Sunday before last. He feels better and agrees to follow advice, as he agreed Sunday before last. He will be back Sunday after next for same interchange.

8 p.m. – Listen to Marian Anderson on Ford Sunday Evening Hour.

9 p.m. – One of police force drops in to discuss best method of handling dangerous breach of mores which is not breach of law. We agree on a course illegal but wise as it will keep the peace.

10 p.m. – Telephone. I refuse to answer.

10.15 p.m. – Regret I did not answer. It might not have been Ford.

10.30 p.m. – Hear someone outside whistling Tschaikovsky's Andante from the Fifth Symphony. Step out on gallery and see colored delivery-boy on bicycle, feet on handlebars. His rendition loud, inaccurate, and soulful.

10.32 p.m. – Put Boo out. See Orion.

11 p.m. – Crawl into bed, thankful for a beauty-rest.

There is no logical ending to an autobiography, once you've had the effrontery to start the thing, this side of the last gasp. Facts keep on happening and the more of them you set down, the less progress you seem to make toward a likeness. This bit of diary, if continued indefinitely, would not help my guardian angel to recognize me if he met me coming down the middle of the big road. Evidently what doesn't happen is all-important, rather than what does. To catch the likeness of this queer creature with whom I have lived always and for whom I have developed a sort of grumpy affection, I suspect I'll have to ease up on him unbeknownst–say when he is sitting in the garden idly, bemused, not even noticing the wasps on the fat peony buds. It's getting too late for facts anyway and they have a way these days of looking like the Gorgon's head seen without the mirror Perseus used. The garden's the place.

CHAPTER XXVI

Jackdaw in the Garden

Adah and Charlotte and Tom are real gardeners, dirt gardeners, of Mr. Bass's breed. They love the feel of the earth on their naked hands. They attain an intolerable serenity and conceit when because of their ministrations (plus the processes of heaven and luck, which they ignore) a tendril or a tiny green sail or a clenched rosy fist thrusts up where before there was unadorned ground. Tom in April always has the air of the Lord God after He did it in seven days. Adah plants seeds on the sly, not telling you what or where and in burning summer when you haven't so much as a lank strand in any bed you are infuriated to discover her yard strutting with color (though part of it *is* salvia). Charlotte can grow Oriental poppies and gentians, which sets her apart and makes her insufferable. I know my garden's prettier than theirs and gets itself photographed by the *National Geographic* and written about by Julian Meade, but it doesn't fool me. It's mostly for show, it's a substitute for things preferred but denied, and its superiority springs not from greener fingers but from a fatter pocketbook. Demeter would linger in theirs, not mine. I'd probably catch that Roman hussy, Flora, on my premises.

Yet gardening has taught me much, mostly about human nature. If you happen to flush me, trowel in hand, over a patch of coco grass, be not deceived: my mind is not on gardening, but on people.

For years I was distressed by the incessant and diversified troubles of a client of mine: she was always in crisis. One day sprinkling the azaleas with aluminum sulphate, the revelation broke over me. Both the plant and the lady required acid soil—they would perish in sweet soil! She needed tragedy and couldn't thrive without it. Ever since the discovery I have taken acid-loving people calmly.

It took years of battle with root-rot to teach me that it does not ravage with equal devastation every variey of iris. The older purer strains seem immune to it, its greatest toll is from the ranks of the hybrids, in which we have learned to fear Mesopotamican blood. But when we cross human beings we give no thought to the racial compatibility of the bloods fused and neglect to observe whether the human hybrids we produce are unhappily subject to rot of one kind or another. In gardening we have learned that death is the best cure for many diseases.

I am always trying to coddle into remaining with me flowers which want to be farther north, such as lilacs, or farther south, such as Indica azaleas. They will exist if I take enough pains with them, but they are not happy and the meagerness of their bloom betrays their incurable nostalgia. The heart too has its climate, without which it is a mere pumping-station.

In roses we demand now the sunset colors of Talisman or the dawn colors of Dainty Bess, and to hold them with us spend our time fighting black spot and mildew. But Aunt Nana has Malmaisons and Maman Cochets, which Père planted fifty years ago and which she has never sprayed or fertilized. They are just roses, not too beautiful, not like sunset or dawn, but heavy with attar, and they don't need coddling: they are so glad of life they fight for it. After all, strength is one of the primary colors.

But the major moral afforded by a garden comes from watching the fight for sunlight waged by those unhappy things rooted against their will in shade. None of them will flower, but by desperate devices, tragic substitutes, some of them will live. They thrust emaciated feelers, gangling and scant of leaf, toward a spot of light. To escape the deeper shadow they twist themselves into ungainliness. Branches die so that the remnant whole may survive. They are bleached as by a sickroom. They seem to have lost not only their beauty but their dignity in straining for the golden warmth that is their source of life. Standing at the post-office corner I recognize my poor sunless plants in the passers-by, sickly, out of shape, ugly with strain, who still search for a sunlight vital to their needs and never found, or found and lost.

However, even these bits of wisdom I pick up from gardening, as a chicken gathers grit for its craw, are not for me the chief reward of a garden. It's a closed and quiet place, the best sort of Ivory Tower, and you can sit in a corner spattered with sunlight and wonder—that's its real function. It's a starting-point for thoughts and backward looks and questionings. It fades easily into other landscapes that seasons do not change. You sit there and think of the trip you have made, fifty-five years of trip, and you wonder what it means and what it totals up to.

Having gone on for half a century, you find to your surprise you have passed the crest and are going down the shady side of the mountain. It is pleasant country and not sad, though tinged with autumn and life in the air deceptively. Down the long easy slope there are no trees, but wideness everywhere and tall seeded grasses that glisten and tremble. To the right great shafts of low sunlight lie benign and quiet, reaching down and down to the tender blue smudge that must be the sea. But in front, near, though down a way, is the cypress grove to which you know you are going. Purple-shadowed, tall, and very still, you see it, but not by looking squarely. You are not afraid to look, but you are not hankering to be there yet, not quite yet. It will not fade out like the sea and the sunlight, no need to hurry. So I rest quietly and at peace on a low bench by the way. I imagine it to be a bench like the one Tom made me for a corner of the garden from a single slab of Sewanee sandstone. Behind his, the real one, are the Cape jessamines he loves, ailing always though heavy bloomers, and in front are the weeping willow and the silver flowering peaches, eager things and, for all their fragility, stout believers in the resurrection. Here is a chance to remember back and count up.

Half a century is a long time, specially in a world as lovely as ours, as starred with brave and pitiful people with honey at their hearts and on their lips. No use remembering the ugly and the evil, they were never very real anyway and nothing came of them. Evil is for the sunny side, to test the strength of the climbers, I suppose. It is easier to remember the good. So I'll think of Tom in the hot summer evenings watering his roses and dousing the screaming children as they tip up behind him, or of Adah serving a cold drink, as Mother used to do, to the golfers as they stop by for more than a julep's refreshment on their way home; or of Rufus hurrying into his soft-ball suit after the hard day and calling out nonsense to his little one. Trifles and little happenings seem dear when you recall you will not be seeing them always.

I know if by chance I joined these twilight doings of my friends my welcome would be unfeigned and tender. Yet I know if I did not join them, if I never joined them, nothing would cease or change. For the place I have won here and there, early and late, though a good place and a proud one, was never first place in any life, and what was mine to possess utterly and sovereignly, without counterclaim, was only the jackdaw pickings of my curious and secret heart. When your heart's a kleptomaniac for bits of color and scraps of god-in-man, its life hoardings make a pile glinting indeed, but of no worth save to the miserly fanatic heart. Now is the time, now when the air is still and the light is going, to spread my treasure out.

The things you like to remember often happen so quickly and simply you are not certain afterwards that they happened at all. It may be in a garden, a simple home garden without landscaping, and you are walking slowly with one you love and understand (as understanding goes between us mortals), one who is self-contained and inarticulate. You pause together and look a long time at an early spring flower, probably a white narcissus with wonder on it, as if the risen Lord had just stepped there, and you hear your companion say: "And some people say there is no God." Looking up quickly, you catch the tail end of a smile, as absorbed and guileless as Adam's when his lids first opened and he beheld Eden, dappled and fresh in the early sunlight. Of course you observe it is time to begin spraying, but actually you are swinging a censer and repeating: "Laus Deo," while the voice goes on: "Let's try Bordeaux mixture this time."

I gaze down the long slope with its grass that bends and shivers and the memories, my very own, drift through me like dim music, like that appeasing heart-broken theme of the *Pathétique* or Gluck's glimpse of the Elysian fields or the unbearable peace and tears of the Good Friday Spell or Bach's *Komm', süsser Tod,* only the music is blurred, with the anguish gone. It has all been good and worth the tears. I see it as a dream I long to hold, but not to relive. I hear voices unbelievably soft (whose are they, was it in Rio or Barcelona or the islands? No matter) that murmur: Don't go, don't leave me, I love you," and I smile, knowing I will hear them no more and grateful for their music. I watch from my balcony the torches of the Capri fishing-boats far down, sprinkling the deep sea with their stars, serene under the unpausing divine constellations. I pace the south portico of the Parthenon in the morning light across the panels of shadow and glimpse between the luminous columns the misty blue of Salamis, Ægina tremendous in the glare, and the rose and violet peaks behind Sparta and Corinth. I see Ætna bathed in sunset, the purple sea at its feet. I walk the square of Chartres wanting to enter for a last sight of the Tree of Jesse with its miraculous blue, like God's very own, but I can't go in because I still can't decide whether the north or the south spire is the more beautiful. I tell Timi to paddle from under the hibiscus trees into the middle of the bay, so I may hear and see the Pacific break itself to thunder and snowy seethings on the Papatoi reef, while the mountains watch, and the million palms. The incredible loveliness of our star! And how well we men have done by it, having added to its beauty when the gods who fashioned it could not!

And now I recall, for the mere delight of recalling, scenes that somehow I can never forget, my very own, bits of my treasure:

I remember the satyr on the slopes of Parnassus. The road that traverses those slopes is upland all the way. Above it to the left hang the gray and golden cliffs, below it to the right on the broken mountainside stumble the ancient silver olive trees that grope their way to touch far down the river that has died. Beyond the river-bed a treeless range of peaks joins hands to shut the world out and the Corinthian gulf. Here is a high lost world of its own, austere and primitive, antique and changeless. The silver python of the road, sunning itself on the ledge beneath the cliffs, serves the rough folk of these crumbling times as it served Homer's. The crystal air pours down and pools between the mountains and the cliffs as if caught in a warped and golden bowl. It is like no other air of earth, of autumn purity and life, even when fired with summer, and clothing the planets and their kin with legendary brightness. Were I disengaged spirit, I would haunt there, as I often have in these uneasy trappings of mortality.

When I met the satyr it was past sunset time and I had walked into the splendor. I passed the sacred rubble of the temples, wan in the colorless shadow, and watched the eagles homing to their aeries. By the roadside beneath the Castalian spring women were lifting from the vervain and wild heliotrope the wash where they had spread it out to dry, and other women on their donkeys were returning from the vineyards, children and lambs and kids in their wake and their wooden saddles heaped fore and aft with bundles of furze and babies. Their laughter and hale banter were merely tinklings in the deepening silence. Beyond them, where the road skirted a great rock, I paused on the edge above the olive slopes and looked into the depth of air beneath. It was a limpid evening, the whole broad quarter of the lower sky washed with rose tourmaline and witch's green and lemon, and the vast zenith, silver-blue, flawed with a single star. The obsessed cuckoo had desisted, and deep in the lower olives by the river the first nightingales stammered their faint cold music. Then the moon, winning her mountain climb, floated loose into the heavens, a full moon vast and rosy, with a bruise of purple in the sky around her. Facing the steep I had not heard the patter of climbing hoofs, but suddenly up from the shadows at my feet bounded a prodigious he-goat, with sacrificial spread of twisted horns, long mocking beard, and appraising disillusioned eyes of gold; and behind him a brown boy. He was hardly half as tall as the goat-herd's crook he carried. His shock of straight black hair had never felt a comb. Sandals were on his feet and thongs crisscrossed from his ankles to his knees. His goat-herd's short skirt and nondescript tunic were dirt-colored. From the tight-pulled strand of leather that served for belt glared a conspicuous knife. Over one shoulder was slung a coarse striped haversack to hold his lunch. We were both completely startled. He stared at me as though I were a mortal and I said: "Kala mera." It was all the Greek, modern or classic, I knew, but it wasn't appropriate, for it meant "Good morning." He replied in his language. I observed that the moon was full and his herd, which by this time was pouring into the road, was magnificent. He replied lengthily in his language, and I nodded. He asked to see my watch. He shook it and put it to his ear, but of course did not look at the time. We stood together and watched the moon rise and did not feel like speaking. He returned my watch, crinkled his eyes at me, and stepped to the huge ram. I thought he was leaving. But instead he dropped his crook, held his empty musette bag before him, and shook it. From his throat, not from his mouth, issued animal sounds, half cluck, half guttural bleat, he swayed and bent, and raised one knee. The Pan-faced monster opposite rose to his hind legs, tossed his great horns from side to side, and bellowed. They danced together. The full moon and I saw them dance together. They stopped when the nervous herd started moving on its way. From across the road he frowned on me searchingly a long minute and then, deciding perhaps I really believed in him, he ran across the road and took my hand. So toward the Shining Rocks that Phœbus thrust asunder we walked in silence, hand in hand. But when the great shadow of Agamemnon's plane tree covered us, looking up sideways, he smiled once—but it was like a gale of laughter—and was gone. And the night seemed suddenly bleak.

I remember the sheer Anatolian headland where it reared from the gaudy sea into the blinding sunlight. It was high noon and the sea and the sun were laughing. We climbed to the clump of pine trees on the crest. Among the scented needles in the thin unsteady shade we lay with our lunch on the ground and gazed as from a tower's top across the outspread splendor. The sapphire water shook and glistened, the shallows thrust their fronds of pale green, and farther out a splotch of purple showed where some white-stoled cloud paused absently. We seemed suspended magically at some mid-level, sapphire sky above, sapphire water beneath, and brightness everywhere. In front, very distant, barely scrawled on the horizon, rose the minarets and domes of Constantinople and to the left, palest pink and lavender in the ecstatic light, the bare mountains of Brusa. Except that it was live with rushing air and rustling water it would have seemed a fortunate bright dream. We lay on the ground in the penciled shadow, each in his own burnished reverie. . . . At first we were not sure our ears were hearing; it might be music from some inner isle or some old trick of Pan's. It seemed a voice singing. Without interchange, still unconvinced, we listened separately and heard indeed a human voice that sang. The song rose to us, strong and rude and happy, a Turkish song with the strange Turkish cadences and unexpected intervals. We scrambled to our knees and peered down over the edge. A young man, white and naked, with a mop of gold hair, was swimming beneath us, and as he swam he sang. Oblivious of us, enraptured and alone, brimming with some hale antique happiness not ours to know, he clove the flashing water and sang into the sun. At last the dazzle hid him from us, but still we heard his voice.

I remember the forecastle of the ship that carried us to Rio, where after their watches the crew came up to rest and breathe the night. About the equator the seas are lonely, with no passing ships to hail and no sight of land for unending weeks. The very stars have changed and those we knew lose themselves in our wake like phosphorus. Our ship receded from reality, became a tiny world abandoned to itself, and in the tropic night, despite the appeasing pathos of the moon, it seemed a lonely world, forgotten and adrift, pursuing some mysterious course that might not count a port. Our crew had come together by mere chance, haphazardly, from unrelated shores, Portuguese, Samoan, Finnish, American, Greek, and could speak, but could not communicate. Some of them were old men with sharp or dreamy eyes and some were youngsters, desperate and ensorcelled. Looking down in the semi-night of the mounting moon across the forecastle, I watched them moving like somnambulists, the wind whipping their hair, the moonlight turning their bodies slender and unsubstantial, daubing their cheek-bones and shoulders, the arch of their chests or their buttocks with pallor, and a stillness was on them. They came on deck from the hatches in a sudden glory of light as a door swung open and closed, and for an instant the yellow shaft outlined them, before dimness resumed. They came in all manner of garbs, in work clothes or stripped to the waist; mostly they came alone and kept to themselves. There was always a width of moonlight between them. Some sat on the coils of rope or the winches and smoked. The sparks from their pipes flared wildly across the deck like a midget galaxy rushing to extinction. The wind was too loud for talking or singing, but a few tried one and the other half-heartedly, and the wind took the words and the song. They moved like men who were drugged, slowly and vaguely. Before going below again, each of them walked to the rail and leaned there, staring out into the empty ocean. Leaning there on the rail, waist-deep in moonlight, they gazed a long silent time, as if quite alone, and with their lips parted. Perhaps they were thinking each one of different things, of wives or mothers, of sweethearts or children, of women and liquor, or perhaps they were thinking each one of the same thing. The look on their faces was the same as they gazed beyond the moon's small miracle to the enclosing dimness. The patience of loneliness and the tranquillity of unescapable pain were on their faces like grave beauty. I thought of a lost chart and an unknown port, and I too looked to sea.

Then a great clang shattered the darkness, for the young watch at the bow had crashed the hour from his bell. He cupped his hands, turned to the bridge, and shouted, in a voice piercingly young and full of hope: "The lights are bright, sir!"

I remember the city of Babel on Manhattan when the lights come on in the early winter evening. We leaned from the topmost tower of all the world and gazed on the pride of man, the work of his hands, the miracle of fire and steel that he had fashioned. Like gods we looked down on the apogee of beauty, the race's masterpiece. The solemn buildings, housing imperishable light, soared from the stone earth high and higher till they were standing, massive and at ease, in the bird-lanes of the immaculate air—man's revelation of bulk become passionate, solidity ethereal, and mass a thing of flight. Singly or grouped in brotherhoods, they stood in awful silence, with an air of waiting, and between their ribs their million windows shone. Far as the eye could reach the incredible dark forms stood waiting in the night, silent and breathing, from base to summit beautiful with their own inner light. Above the torment of the dreadful world they brooded, and the ocean sound of its incessant strivings rose like a sea-shell's aimless hum.

Yet the great builders of this unbearable beauty were invisible. We peered into the chasms they had made and saw long files of metal beetles trekking a bare yard when the chains of rubies turned to emeralds. And then we spied the lesser insects on the bottom. We watched their tiny scurryings, their nervous sorties and returns, their feverish small haste, and their bewildered pauses. Unwillingly and rueful to the core, we recognized the poor creating gods of all this majesty. A voice at my side was murmuring to itself: "This is the most touching thing I ever saw." And I was thinking, if Satan, standing where we stood, had offered, not the whole world, but this desperate city in all its piteousness, no Son of God could have had the heart to refuse it.

These memories of mine, these tinsel hoardings, lose nothing of their luster in this time of doom. A tarnish has fallen over the bright world; dishonor and corruption triumph; my own strong people are turned lotus-eaters; defeat is here again, the last, the most abhorrent. But the autumn air is tinged with gold, the spotted sun sleeps in the garden, and the only treasure that's exempt from tarnish is what the jackdaw gathers.

CHAPTER XXVII

Home

One of the pleasantest places near the home town is the cemetery. It lies along a curve of Rattlesnake Bayou. Across its front used to run the old dirt road to the river-landing down which the raiding Yankees would dash on their forays inland while Holt and the remaining elders of the countryside would snipe them from the bushes. Now the road is of concrete and its unexpected curve often sends motorists in their cups or out of their wits headlong into the well-dredged bayou, which on drainage maps is now called Dredge Ditch No. 4 D. Across the bayou toward the east have grown up new enterprises of which we are proud, a florist's, a nursery, the golf-links, and an exclusive addition full of very old beautiful trees and very new beautiful residences. The cemetery itself was designed during carriage days, with cedar-bordered roads running in parallel semi-circles and too narrow for automobiles. In spite of the neighboring highway with its strident motor-cars it is a quiet spot, eternally green, and from any grave you may look westerly across open fields to the levee and feel the river beyond, deep in its plumy willows. This home of the dead is, quaintly enough, the home of hundreds of mocking-birds, which, mistaking all time for eternal spring, sing the year round. I have heard them append arpeggios and cadenzas to pitiful unreassuring funeral sermons and rain liquid hope while the priest was muttering *in pulverem reverteris.*

Our lot is toward the back and raised a little, as someone hated to think of the river's overflow covering the graves. In the middle of it, backed by a semicircular thicket of ever-greens, stands Malvina Hoffman's bronze figure of a brooding knight, sunshine flowing from his body as indicated in low relief on the stone stele behind, and the river at his feet. The one word "Patriot" beneath the statue and Matthew Arnold's "Last Word" on the reverse side of the stele show those who loved him that Father lies near by.

I come here not infrequently because it is restful and comforting. I am with my own people. With them around me I can seem to read the finished manuscripts of their lives, forever unchangeable, and beautiful in the dim way manuscripts have. Here sleep Mother and Father, Mur and Fafar, Mère and Père, the small brother who should be representing and perpetuating the name, Uncle George in one corner, his fishing done, in another under a stone marked "Gentleman" Fafar's brother LeRoy beside Fafar's elder daughter, whose death, caused, he thought, by a quack doctor he himself had chosen, so grieved him he ended his own life. Aunt Fanny is here too, no opiates needed now for her long ills, and close to her her husband, Dr. Walker Percy, who, united and gathered to his own, finds no further need to oppose secession. The latest-comer and the loveliest, Mattie Sue, sleeps to the front, her morning-glory air all gone, but the valor not yet faded from her heart. They are all here, and I am glad there's room to spare. It would be indeed a chilly world without this refuge with its feel of home.

I wish a few others out there, under the cedars, could be in this plot of ours. Miss Carrie's bird-body must by now be a mere pinch of dust and would take no space. Father Koestenbrock, far from his native city and his fathers, might feel less lonely here. Here Judge Griffin might dream of a truer ending for his *Ruin Robed.* And I should like to bring from that far corner where the poor sleep well one brown-eyed lad who sleeps alone there, for he had loved me and gaspingly had told me so while death was choking him and he knew it was death.

I am told that in Arab countries strangers volunteer to carry the coffin of a deceased, and in our cities strangers are hired for this chore. But with us friends are asked to bear their friends to the open grave for the last rites. Far as these white stones reach are graves now closed to which I have carried my friends—poor and well-to-do, obscure and prominent, good and bad, men and women, young and old, Jew and Christian, believer and agnostic. Sometimes with the coffin handle in my grip, staggering heavily toward that angular gash in the curving earth, I forget which one it is this time who is preceding me and wonder absently who will be left to do me a like service. A little while and the living town, this tiny world of mine, will all be here, tucked under the same dark blanket, cosily together. Another little while and the last of us, those I loved and those I disapproved, will be sharing oblivion, for no one will remember any of us. The famous do not share our cedars and our mockingbirds. This is private ground for the lovable obscure. Even Father, who warmed and led and lighted our people—no one will remember him, his name and deeds will be forgotten soon, in another spring, or ten, or a hundred, what matter? Strangers will come and, striving briefly, will join us in our dark, and our mockingbirds, unrecollecting, will sing for them with equal rapture.

While people are still alive we judge them as good or bad, condemn them as failures or praise them as successes, love them or despise them. Only when they are dead do we see them, not with charity, but with understanding. Alive they are remote, even hostile; dead, they join our circle and you see the family likeness. As I loiter among our graves reading the names on the headstones, names that when they identified live men I sometimes hated or scorned as enemies of me and mine and all that we held good, I find myself smiling. How unreal and accidental seem their defects! I know their stories: this one was a whore and this a thief, here lies the town hypocrite and there one who should have died before he was born. I know their stories, but not their hearts. With a little shifting of qualities, with a setting more to their needs, with merely more luck, this woman could have borne children who would have been proud of her, and this thief might have become the father of the poor. Now death has made them only home-folks and I like the sound of their familiar names. They lie there under the grass in the evening light so helplessly, my townsmen, a tiny outpost of the lost tribe of our star. Understanding breaks over my heart and I know that the wickedness and the failures of men are nothing and their valor and pathos and effort everything. Circumscribed and unendowed, ailing in body, derided and beguiled, how well they have done! They have sipped happiness and gulped pain, they have sought God and never found Him, they have found love and never kept him—yet they kept on, they never gave up, they rarely complained. Among these handfuls of misguided dust I am proud to be a man and assuaged for my own defects. I muse on this one small life that it is all I have to show for, the sum of it, the wrong turnings, the weakness of will, the feebleness of spirit, one tiny life with darkness before and after, and it at best a riddle and a wonder. One by one I count the failures—at law undistinguished, at teaching unprepared, at soldiering average, at citizenship unimportant, at love second-best, at poetry forgotten before remembered—and I acknowledge the deficit. I am not proud, but I am not ashamed. What have defeats and failures to do with the good life? But closer lacks, more troubling doubts assail me. Of all the people I have loved, wisely and unwisely, deeply and passingly, I have loved no one so much as myself. Of all the hours of happiness granted me, none has been so keen and holy as a few unpredictable moments alone. I have never walked with God, but I had rather walk with Him through hell than with my heart's elect through heaven. Of the good life I have learned what it is not and I have loved a few who lived it end to end. I have seen the goodness of men and the beauty of things. I have no regrets. I am not contrite. I am grateful.

Here among the graves in the twilight I see one thing only, but I see that thing clear. I see the long wall of a rampart sombre with sunset, a dusty road at its base. On the tower of the rampart stand the glorious high gods, Death and the rest, insolent and watching. Below on the road stream the tribes of men, tired, bent, hurt, and stumbling, and each man alone. As one comes beneath the tower, the High God descends and faces the wayfarer. He speaks three slow words: "Who are you?" The pilgrim I know should be able to straighten his shoulders, to stand his tallest, and to answer defiantly: "I am your son."

A NOTE ON THE TYPE

The text of this book is set in Caledonia, a new Linotype face designed by W. A. Dwiggins. Caledonia belongs to the family of printing types called "modern face" by printers—a term used to mark the change in style of type-letters that occurred about 1800. Caledonia is in the general neighborhood of Scotch Modern in design, but is more freely drawn than that letter.

The book was composed, printed, and bound by H. Wolff, New York. The binding is based on designs by W. A. Dwiggins.